Novkov, *Constituting Workers, Protecting Women*

Errata

Page

141, line 19:   For "An evenly divided" read "A split"

175, line 12:   For "While the Court did not invalidate Oregon's statute, it was evenly divided and could not articulate any binding response to these arguments, which thus remained in play for some time to come." read "The Court's upholding of Oregon's statute sent an unclear message, since the justices did not directly confront earlier precedents in their brief opinion."

245, line 10:   For "achieving a tie vote" read "achieving victory"

Constituting Workers, Protecting Women

Constituting Workers, Protecting Women

Gender, Law, and Labor in the Progressive Era and New Deal Years

Julie Novkov

Ann Arbor

THE UNIVERSITY OF MICHIGAN PRESS

2004   2003   2002   2001   4   3   2   1

A CIP catalog record for this book is available from the British Library.

Library of Congress Cataloging-in-Publication Data

Novkov, Julie, 1966–
    Constituting workers, protecting women : gender, law, and labor in the progressive era and New Deal years / Julie Novkov.
        p.   cm.
    Includes bibliographical references and index.
    ISBN 0-472-11198-1 (cloth : acid-free paper)
    1. Women—Employment—Law and legislation—United States—History.   2. Labor laws and legislation—United States—History.
    I. Title.
    KF3555 .N68   2001
    344.7301—dc21   00-012900

For my most constructive critic, best friend,
and loving partner, Joel D. Bloom

Contents

Tables

Acknowledgments

A first book is not, for most people, a solo effort. I have been quite fortunate to have the generous and unstinting support of many individuals since beginning this project as a graduate student at the University of Michigan. Without the help of many of these people and institutions, this book would not exist.

Thanks go to the Gerald R. Ford Fellowship Foundation, which generously funded much of my preliminary research in graduate school. A New Faculty Award from the University of Oregon coupled with a Junior Professorship Development Award enabled me to spend much of the summer of 1997 working on the manuscript.

During my time at Michigan, I relied heavily on the critical insights and support of the members of the Michigan Public Law Reading Group, in particular Paula Denney, Steve Dow, George Lovell, and Joan Sitomer. The members of my dissertation committee, Kim Scheppele, Mark Brandon, Don Herzog, Jackie Stevens, and Sonya Rose, provided me with thoughtful and helpful criticism. Kim Lane Scheppele's early enthusiasm and stalwart support carried me through graduate school, and neither the dissertation nor the book would ever have been completed without Mark Brandon's assistance.

Upon arriving at Oregon, I found a department that was dedicated to helping junior faculty members to succeed. Many of my colleagues from fields and methodological approaches far different from mine were encouraging and supportive. Deborah Baumgold and Ron Mitchell were always available with sage and pragmatic advice, and Deborah was a wonderfully protective chair for a new faculty member. Amy Ash helped me through some frustrating and difficult times. Irene Diamond encouraged me to expand my vision. In Gerry Berk I found a mentor and friend who enabled me to find my critical voice. His support, insight, and willingness to read problematic drafts went far beyond the bounds of duty and probably sanity. If every junior faculty member were fortunate enough to have a colleague like Gerry, our profession would be a happier and more productive one.

I also had substantial assistance from friends and colleagues outside of Oregon. Barry Friedman generously read the entire manuscript and provided invaluable feedback. Chuck Myers helped me to frame the project more effectively. Judy Baer, Ron Kahn, Howard Gillman, Jim Foster, Lief Carter, and Eileen McDonagh provided encouragement and feedback at various critical stages of the project. The 1998 APSA short course on courts and institutionalism and the 1999 APSA short course on gender, political representation, and civic identity were both quite helpful. The book was also substantially improved through the critical feedback I received at annual meetings of the Law and Society Association, the American Political Science Association, and the Western Political Science Association.

Finally, my family helped me immensely by never losing faith in me, even when I came close to losing faith in myself. My father, Ray Novkov, was always optimistic and supportive. My mother, Diane Novkov, and my aunt, Kristi Derry, inspired me: whenever I think of working women, I think of them. Joel Bloom suffered endless conversations about legal and constitutional doctrine and was always a helpful sounding board for ideas. And Asher Novkov-Bloom helped out in his own special way by being an unbelievably easygoing and delightful baby, keeping his mother grounded and helping her to maintain her sense of humor during the process of turning the dissertation into a book.

Chapter 1

Rethinking the Constitutional Crisis of the 1930s: The Forgotten Doctrinal Roots of the Modern Welfare State

In many scholars' views, the modern American welfare state, with its myriad protections for workers and citizens, was born on March 29, 1937. On that date, the U.S. Supreme Court announced its ruling in *West Coast Hotel v. Parrish,* a case that later courts would interpret to eliminate the constitutional barriers to the states' efforts to establish minimum wages for workers, the Fair Labor Standards Act, and a host of other measures taken by the states and the federal government to improve the working and living conditions of citizens. In most constitutional historians' interpretations, the government had a new ability to regulate the workplace arising from a fundamental shift in constitutional principles brought about by the political turmoil of conflicts between the New Deal's supporters and detractors.

The rulings of the federal and state courts in the post-1937 period stand in marked contrast to the courts' activities in the earlier years. The regulatory impulse giving rise to major federal intervention in the labor market was not simply an artifact of the New Deal or the Great Depression. Rather, reformers had been pushing for more regulation for decades, most notably during the Progressive Era. Political activism promoting an interventionist state emerged in the immediate wake of the rise of large industry in the latter half of the nineteenth century, and this activism was initially successful in achieving legislative victories in the states. The problem, crystallized in the Supreme Court's 1905 ruling in *Lochner v. New York,* was that the U.S. courts on both state and federal levels were largely unwilling to sanction the expansion of the state's power that would support such efforts. Instead, many judges actively worked against such reforms, striking down measure after measure that sought to regulate the hours, wages, and working conditions of American laborers.

The New Deal, in most scholarly interpretations, brought this conflict to a head. Congress and the president found themselves at loggerheads with the Supreme Court as Congress attempted to put into effect legislation that would ameliorate the effects of the Great Depression and usher in a host of new federal regulations of labor and the economy. In the early 1930s, the Court rebuffed these attempts, leading to a bitter dispute over questions of constitutional interpretation and in particular over the scope of national and state regulatory authority. This battle reached its climax in 1937, when in the view of most commentators the Supreme Court capitulated to the will of Congress and President Roosevelt. At this time, the Court finally agreed to uphold the kinds of regulatory statutes that it had previously invalidated. This moment is significant, claim scholars, because it foretold the establishment of the modern welfare state on the national level. The case in which this shift took place was *West Coast Hotel Co. v. Parrish.*

Most scholars studying the constitutional roots of the modern welfare state see the ruling in *West Coast Hotel* as a new beginning in constitutional history and as a rejection of a vision of the Constitution that could not function adequately in the modern state. They thus often read the case as having both feet firmly in the future, looking forward to the rise of modern national authority over, and intervention in, the lives of citizens.

This book reinterprets the doctrinal foundations of the modern welfare state by reading *West Coast Hotel* against this familiar grain, understanding it instead as a case with deep roots in the past. Its roots lie in the relationship among gender, political development, and law. By centering the gender of regulated workers in the analysis of the legal battles, we see that the "constitutional revolution" of 1937 consisted of the extension and general application of a standard for judgment that had been meticulously constructed during the second and third decades of the century to apply principally to female workers. Rereading *Lochner* and the doctrinal path to *West Coast Hotel* in light of gender enables a new understanding of the ways that courts constructed labor and laborers in the early twentieth century. Considering gender and political development in light of the doctrinal path to *West Coast Hotel* promotes a rethinking of the debates between and among feminists in the early twentieth century, in particular suggesting that maternalism was both helpful and problematic within and outside of feminism. This analysis will show that the doctrinal pathways established gender-based divisions between laborers that enabled some members of the working class to have statutory protection while others were left unprotected, further contributing to the dilution of class-based interests in politics and law.

The gender of the workers that reformers wished to protect significantly shaped the scope of the ideological alternatives facing the courts and ultimately the nation. Contemporary feminist historians have rightfully focused attention on the ways that Progressive women influenced substantive debates about the meaning of citizenship and other core values. This book will show how a largely middle-class, feminine effort to regulate the labor of working-class women during the early twentieth century shaped the development of the jurisprudence of due process, casting a lengthy historical shadow that still influences constitutional considerations of liberty today.

The Case That Launched a Thousand Law
Review Articles

Between the lean years of 1933 and 1935, a woman named Elsie Lee was fortunate enough to find a job working irregularly as a chambermaid at the Cascadian Hotel in Wenatchee, Washington. She started at an hourly wage of twenty-two cents, which later went up to a quarter (Leuchtenberg 1995, 164). In 1935, the hotel discharged her. She filed a lawsuit against the West Coast Hotel Company, which owned the Cascadian, asking for back pay under a Washington state statute mandating a minimum wage for women. In her suit, she sought the extra money that she would have gotten if the hotel had complied with the twenty-five-year-old Washington law, which set a $14.50 weekly minimum wage for hotel employees (Leuchtenberg 1995, 163–64). At the trial, Elsie, who had married in the meantime and changed her last name to Parrish, testified that the West Coast Hotel Company owed her $216.19 for the years that she had worked for substandard wages. She explained, "I had in mind that I should be paid—should have been paid—the state wage and that it would be paid. I took what they gave me because I needed the work so bad and I figured they would pay what was right" (St. John 1974, 187).

The hotel company defended itself confidently by claiming that this statute violated workers' liberties to make contracts freely with their employers (Roberts and Skeel 1937). The constitutional basis for this argument was the due process clause of the Fourteenth Amendment, which specifically provided that the state could not take away life, liberty, or property without due process of law. First the trial court and then the Washington State Supreme Court ruled in Elsie Parrish's favor, apparently unimpressed by the hotel company's argument. However, the company's attorneys had reason to be optimistic despite losing the case on the state level. After all, the Supreme Court had declared a minimum wage for women unconstitutional in 1923 and had reaffirmed this ruling in 1936 in a case involving female laundry employees' challenge to a statutory minimum wage in New York. Ms. Parrish's case, however, was destined go differently, producing one of the most significant rulings issued by the Supreme Court in the twentieth century.

Politics as Usual: The Post–New Deal Consensus on the Lochner Era

Most observers would agree that early years of the twentieth century saw political and legal negotiation over the relationship between large-scale industrial capitalism and the state. This negotiation took place in every governmental forum, encompassing all three branches of government and involving local, state, and national actors. The wide recognition of the importance of this negotiation has provoked intense scholarly interest in the Progressive and New Deal eras both to enhance understanding of how this negotiation took place and to explain the nature and scope of institutions today. Legal scholars have focused on the judiciary, in particular on the Supreme Court, because the Court was a visible and influential institutional actor. Further, its invalidations of favored progressive measures provoked and continue to provoke controversy about its proper role in a democratic system. The crystallized metaphor for all of these concerns was Lochner, which West Coast Hotel repudiated.

The Supreme Court changed the legal and political terrain irrevocably by ruling in *West Coast Hotel v. Parrish* that state legislatures' actions would no longer be stringently questioned for their infringements of individuals' rights to make labor contracts freely (300 U.S. 379 (1937)). After the ruling in *West Coast Hotel*, the Supreme Court (and therefore all federal courts) suddenly began upholding rather than striking down New Deal legislation, clearing the path for the development and administration of the modern welfare state. This decision thus ushered in a new role for the federal courts and redistributed the balance of power between the courts and legislatures. The courts would no longer use the due process clause as a ground to strike down economic regulations. Scholars have therefore sought to explain the case's meaning in these terms. The Court also set the stage for the Washington state courts to find on remand that plaintiff Elsie Parrish, nearly forgotten in the shadow of these monumental implications, was entitled to her back pay.

The leading interpretations, while quite different from each other, all see *West Coast Hotel* as a watershed moment of change in the history of the Supreme Court and consequently in the history of the nation. Two lines of interpretation are particularly significant: the post–New Deal consensus about the meaning of the *Lochner* era and its demise, and recent historically rooted critiques of this consensus.

The most familiar interpretation of *West Coast Hotel* is a political reading of the case and its significance (Rowe 1999, 231). Prominent New Dealers saw *Lochner* as demonstrating the dangers of excessive judicial power and commitment to a historically superseded formalist conception of contracts (Rowe 1999, 223–31). Their narrative goes as follows: in the early 1930s, the Court had struck down much of the New Deal program endorsed by President Roosevelt and the Democratically controlled Congress. Infuriated by the Court's perceived ability to thwart the popular will, Roosevelt and his advisors devised a plan to nullify the influence of the most conservative justices by adding seats to the Court, effectively bringing its membership up to fifteen. The Court, recognizing the institutional threat that this movement presented, used *West Coast Hotel* as an opportunity to back off from its hard line against New Deal innovations. In a five-to-four decision, the justices accepted a minimum wage statute, in effect ignoring their ruling of only one year earlier in which they had struck down a similar statute based on the 1923 precedent of *Adkins v. Children's Hospital* (261 U.S. 525 (1923)). This "switch in time that saved nine" took the wind out of the sails of the movement to rein in the Court but left the Court a weaker institution for the next several years.

This reading presents the case as the Court's capitulation to the other branches of the federal government, with the justice's acknowledgment that state legislatures and Congress should be permitted to protect workers against greedy or unscrupulous employers. In this understanding, *West Coast Hotel* ushered in a new constitutional era, one in which the courts would be far more accommodating to legislative solutions to social and economic problems. In this interpretation, the case authorized a new understanding of the relationship between the state and its citizens, allowing for a much higher degree of protection for individuals than had ever existed before and thus for the establishment of the national welfare state.

In this view, the change in the Court's reasoning can be attributed to the justices' fear that continued opposition to the Roosevelt administration would lead to crippling limits on the courts and the loss of judicial legitimacy.[1] *Lochner* itself was steeped in political motives, and fears about the loss of institutional authority sparked its demise. Most of those holding this view see the reasoning in the opinions themselves as relatively unimportant; it is the outcome that matters. William Leuchtenberg, while not attributing the outcome in *West Coast Hotel* directly to the existence of the Court-packing plan, still reads the case as the culmination of a political struggle between the courts on the one hand and the president and Congress on the other (Leuchtenberg 1995). Most scholars agree, however, that the Court's abrupt reversal in 1937 brought it back into line with the sentiments of political reformers and the nation at large and that the ruling was designed to accomplish this end (Kens 1995; Conkle 1987; Leuchtenberg 1995).

In this line of interpretation, the *Lochner* era is important as a cautionary tale to the courts about the dangers of thwarting democratic will and institutional authority. While concerns about countermajoritarianism have not always been the direct focus of these scholars, such concerns have maintained the pejorative emphasis on *Lochner* in the period after *Brown v. Board of Education* (Friedman 1998). Studying the *Lochner* era and its end is valuable for these scholars because through

---

1. The best-known version of this argument is probably McCloskey's 1962 examination of economic substantive due process, but a number of other authors have embraced this interpretation from a variety of political standpoints (Conkle 1987; Sunstein 1987; Kens 1995).

understanding the political process behind *Lochner* and its reversal, one can understand the political limits on constitutional jurisprudence.

Recent Reassessments of the Lochner Era and the New Deal Court

Recently, a group of scholars has initiated the process of rethinking *Lochner* and its meaning with the hope of presenting a more nuanced and historicized analysis of the era and its relationship to the present in light of *West Coast Hotel*'s volte face. Constitutional theorists Bruce Ackerman, Cass Sunstein, and Robert Post, and political historians Howard Gillman, Barry Cushman, and others, have questioned the simple political explanation that the *Lochner* era was about judges' reaching illegitimate outcomes on the basis of reliance on their outmoded conservative conceptions of the proper relationship between capital and labor. In its place these authors have substituted deeper inquiries about the shape of the doctrinal path between *Lochner* and *West Coast Hotel* and the relationship between this path and mutable jurisprudential concepts such as police power, liberty, and contract. These revisionists have moved beyond the question of what *Lochner* meant, focusing instead on the historical and jurisprudential developments that *Lochner* and its antecedents set into motion and the political implications of these developments (Rowe 1999, 223–24).

Bruce Ackerman reads *West Coast Hotel* as a deep shift in constitutional philosophy. While he argues that the case was not a definitive turning point but rather "an uncertain herald of revolutionary reform," he nonetheless claims that it marked a profound shift in the constitutional baseline (Ackerman 1998, 366). In Ackerman's view, this shift in constitutional reasoning was part of a larger political process initiated outside of the judiciary by the New Deal (312–33). He finds the roots of the modern welfare state in the New Deal's vision of an activist national government and the confrontation that the New Deal provoked between the president and the Court (359). In Ackerman's view, rather than seeking to protect its institutional authority against a hostile presidential administration and Congress, the Court was acknowledging a deep shift in the political structure of the republic (Ackerman 1991). At this point, the Court recognized that the American people, in a moment of deep political involvement and higher lawmaking activity, had authorized a structural change in the nature of constitutional governance. Ackerman argues that the decision in *West Coast Hotel* marked the Court's acknowledgment of the establishment of a Third Republic. The founding established the first set of constitutional principles, the Reconstruction Amendments initiated of a second set of principles, and the crisis over the New Deal forged a new agreement about the role of the national government in the daily lives of citizens. He thus seeks to show that *West Coast Hotel*'s significance was its new synthesis of values and its rejection of the reasoning established and embraced by courts in the Middle Republic (Ackerman 1991). His reading sees the case and subsequent New Deal rulings as a synthesis of the principles of the First and Third Republics, the goal of which was to articulate a new meaning for the Fourteenth Amendment in which property was no longer the central focus (Ackerman 1991, 103–4). Thus, even more than other authors, Ackerman reads the case as the start of a new era and as a repudiation of earlier trends.

Like Ackerman, Cass Sunstein identifies a deep change in constitutional structure in the ruling in *West Coast Hotel*. Sunstein argues that the decision emphasized the Court's embrace of a new baseline in which workers were entitled to some protection from the state, but like the authors mentioned above, he also reads the ruling as a political choice by the Court (Sunstein 1987). He does not embrace Ackerman's interpretation of the struggles over the New Deal as heralding a fundamental change in the governing structure, though he does find these struggles to be historically significant. While *Lochner* had political elements, the Court was attempting to distinguish in a principled way between illegitimate naked preferences on the one hand and neutral legislation for the public good on the other, an effort that the justices abandoned in *West Coast Hotel* (Sunstein 1993, 41).

For Robert Post, the *Lochner* era signified the Court's efforts to maintain the concept of economic autonomy as having a fundamental connection to selfhood, a connection that began to collapse during World War I's massive disruptions of economy and society (Post 1998). The Taft Court struggled to separate ordinary economic activity from activity subject to managerial supervision, but ultimately failed to do so in a way that had internal coherence (Post 1998, 1528–29). For him, the significance of the *Lochner* era is its demonstration that constitutional meaning must always overlay national social and economic experience, and when the mismatch between meaning and experience grows too great, constitutional meaning must give way (Post 1998, 1545).

As *Lochner* revisionism has recently become a significant strand in constitutional theory, the comfortable consensus about the Supreme Court's motivations and actions has collapsed. In revising the post–New Deal consensus, these constitutional theorists have suggested that the *Lochner* era was transitional, a necessary period of adjustment between the upheavals of the Civil War and the national crisis of the Great Depression. While these views all differ, they reject the idea that the justices were simply imposing a dead economic vision on the nation, suggesting instead that the *Lochner* era marked the Supreme Court's efforts to harmonize an existing analytical framework with swiftly changing economic and social realities.

Recent historical work has also challenged the post–New Deal consensus. As with recent constitutional theory, the constitutional historians do not agree about the fundamental meaning of the *Lochner* era and its demise, but they do agree that the doctrinal pathways that the Supreme Court created were meaningful primarily in their grappling with problems of political and economic development. They also reject a purely political interpretation of both the *Lochner* era and *West Coast Hotel*'s repudiation of it.

Howard Gillman is probably the most significant exemplar of the historical school. For Gillman, the problem of *Lochner* rested upon the courts' well-established reliance on the principle of state neutrality and their aversion for class legislation, doctrinal conceptions with deep roots in nineteenth-century jurisprudence. In the nineteenth century, courts determined that so-called class legislation was an anathema because it benefited only a segment of society rather than the whole, the courts making no distinctions among the classes that might be benefited. The power of this overarching doctrinal framework was strong enough to enable the courts to maintain it through the early twentieth century with only marginal adjustments until the collapse of the distinction between "partial" and "public purpose" laws in the crucible of the New Deal. With ideological roots going back to the framing, the commitment to neutrality on the part of the state locked the courts into an increasingly problematic stance with respect to the emergence of large-scale capitalism. Denial of the legitimacy of class legislation left no room for protection of groups rendered newly vulnerable in a large-capital economy and thus allowed for little amelioration of capitalism's worst effects.

In Barry Cushman's analysis, the key moment in constitutional development was the Court's ruling in *Nebbia v. New York* in 1934,

which upheld New York's regulation of prices for milk. He claims that
this ruling marked the abandonment of laissez-faire constitutionalism
and the loss of the older divisions between public and private, under-
mining the courts' theoretical bases for invalidating protective measures (Cushman 1994, 84–105). For him, the failure of early New Deal
legislation in the courts was a result of two factors. First was poor drafting on the part of the members of Congress and their aides who wrote
the early statutes of the New Deal, and second was the inept defense
that the Justice Department mounted when these laws faced constitutional challenge (Cushman 1994). In supporting his interpretation,
Cushman shows that the Court had reached its decision in *West Coast
Hotel* before the announcement of the Court-packing plan and that the
Court had no reason to perceive President Roosevelt as a serious threat
to its institutional role. Nonetheless, Cushman sees the case as a watershed moment in constitutional history, largely because it marked the
moment at which more carefully drafted statutes that received more
strategic presentations in the courtroom began to succeed.

Historians who view *West Coast Hotel* as a significant break with
past jurisprudence often identify *Lochner* and its progeny as the source
of the problem. The most useful understandings of *Lochner* for my purposes are those that see the case as a response to industrialization and
the growing battles between capital and labor, since, as I shall demonstrate, the problematic place of women in the new industrial order significantly affected the development of the doctrine. For historians such
as John Semonche, the Supreme Court's decision in *Lochner* marked the
difficulty American law had in dealing with emerging large corporations, and the era of economic substantive due process marked the
courts' struggles to assimilate large corporations into an existing legal
framework (Semonche 1978). Morton Horwitz sees *Lochner* as the
Court's way to use abstract values such as freedom of contract to
impose concrete burdens on disempowered workers (Horwitz 1993).
William Forbath argues that the ruling played an important role in
blocking the rise of a radical labor movement in the United States (Forbath 1991). Likewise, Charles McCurdy interprets the case as providing
a disingenuous separation between employment contracts and other
types of contracts (McCurdy 1984). Other authors[2] have studied the

---

2. Muhammed Kenyatta interprets it as establishing a new separation between private and public law (Kenyatta 1987). Balkin reads *Lochner* as a conceptualist adventure;
he argues that the courts in this period maintained allegiance to abstract concepts in the
face of contrary empirical data (Balkin 1986).

doctrinal elements of the Supreme Court's ruling, as well as the parties and groups involved in the litigation.[3]

Recent interpreters of *Lochner* have done well in explaining the case's roots in the labor politics of the early twentieth century rather than simply reading the opinion as an indefensible commitment to wooden doctrine. In these interpretations, the case reflects the struggles between newly organized labor, as labor interests sought to exercise their muscle legislatively, and corporate interests, which had a good deal of control over the courts. These readings, however, imply a complete discontinuity between *Lochner* and *West Coast Hotel* and do not acknowledge the extent to which the intersection of women's history and labor history relevant to the outcome in *Lochner* still played a role in driving the reasoning in *West Coast Hotel*. This relationship only becomes clear when feminist investigations of women's labor history are incorporated into the analysis. These interpretations thus recognize that the struggle of the 1930s was about the issues at stake in *Lochner*, but they do not fully acknowledge the extent to which the Supreme Court's 1937 solution to the problem was likewise linked to jurisprudential trends that they would identify as *Lochner*'s progeny.

Centering Gender as a Means of Rethinking West Coast Hotel

Both the traditional and revisionist interpretations of *West Coast Hotel* and *Lochner* portray *West Coast Hotel* as a complete repudiation of the principles at stake in *Lochner*, focus on judges and on Supreme Court justices in particular, and fail to recognize the role of gender in both cases. The authors discussed above see the two cases as largely discontinuous and antithetical. All argue that in order to understand the tension between the cases, one must focus primarily on the dynamics of the Supreme Court and its relationship to the other branches of the national government. In these interpretations, the justices of the Supreme Court appear to be the primary shapers of doctrine, though they may at times respond to political pressures or to the existence of a constitutional moment in Ackerman's sense.

---

3. Both Kens and Bewig focus on the facts of the case, developing deeper understandings of the parties and their backgrounds. Kens (1995) explores the beliefs and backgrounds of the principal actors in the case, demonstrating their lack of faith in the economic system. Bewig (1994) explains the role that the journeyman bakers' association played in the case, developing his contention that the bakers used rhetoric that emphasized community values rather than individual freedoms.

While the modern scholar can never know the motivation behind the Court's change of heart, this book will show that the shift in reasoning was not simply a political, jurisprudential, or even an ethical choice, nor was it simply a response to better statutory drafting and maneuvering on the part of Roosevelt and the New Deal Congress. While these elements probably had an impact on the outcome in *West Coast Hotel*, they cannot come close to explaining the opinion's historical context and reasoning. Contrary to the above explanations, the earthquake of 1937 was heralded by prior tectonic shifts.

The analysis to come will show that, rather than being an entirely new constitutional moment, *West Coast Hotel* represented the logical extension of a line of development that had started before the turn of the century. Investigating the case's historical roots reveals that it was as much a backward-looking decision as it was a new beginning. The key element in *West Coast Hotel* was not the conflict between legislative and judicial authority. It was not the repudiation of challenges to progressive legislation by conservative judicial actors who were clinging to an outmoded philosophy of substantive due process, a term that was not even in widespread use until the 1950s.[4] It was not even the tension between the Supreme Court and the other branches of the federal government.

Rather, the reasoning in the case reflected the Court's complicated resolution of a debate over women's roles as laborers. Read in this way, the case represented a general extension of standards that had evolved to analyze the place of women in the workplace. The innovation of the case was its extension of a female standard to all workers, but even this development had been foreshadowed by earlier rulings in the state high courts. Rather than asking about the political, social, or ethical incentives for the Court to reverse itself, we must inquire into the development of the framework that the Court articulated in *West Coast Hotel* and explore the process through which the Court was finally convinced to extend this framework beyond its initial application to female

---

4. Substantive due process is the idea that legislative acts should be subject to judicial review to determine whether they interfere with a protected concrete liberty, such as the liberty to make contracts or the modern liberty to choose abortion or to enjoy privacy. In this legal concept, these liberties are located in the due process clauses of the Fifth and Fourteenth Amendments of the Constitution or in a state constitution's due process clause. The phrase first appeared in the Supreme Court Reporter in Justice Black's dissent in *Shaughnessy v. Mezei*, 345 U.S. 206 (1953).

workers alone. This analysis reveals that much of the doctrinal frame-work for the modern interventionist state arose through battles over female workers' proper relationships with the state.

A gendered reading of the shift in constitutional interpretation that grounded the modern state changes the way that we understand the meaning of *West Coast Hotel* and its roots in earlier jurisprudence. The case still stands as a landmark in constitutional history, but questions about its meaning must incorporate an analysis of gender. Thinking of *West Coast Hotel* as the beginning of a new line of doctrine, or path of legal reasoning produced by judicial opinions, pushes questions about meaning into the future, promoting interpretations of it as a moment of change. Thinking of it as a culminating stage in a line of doctrinal development, rather than as a beginning only, promotes questions about the meaning of the framework that it adopts and extends from female workers to all workers. This book will explain how the framework emerged in the early twentieth century and how it came to supplant the generalized but implicitly male framework that had prevailed in earlier cases. Further, this focus on *West Coast Hotel*'s forgotten roots forces a reevaluation of the legal regulation of women's work and the impact of these regulations and challenges to them in the state and federal courts.

Gender, History, and Doctrine

West Coast Hotel has consistently been read as standing for the proposition that the federal courts will no longer strike down laws for their failure to accommodate a substantive liberty in ordinary circumstances.[5] This book will present and defend an alternative reading: the ruling in *West Coast Hotel* made two changes that were rooted in earlier arguments and decisions. First, it marked the embrace of a standard for judging employment legislation initially developed with respect to female workers. Second, it suggested that this standard would now

---

5. Immediately after the ruling, as I discuss in chapter 6, judges often interpreted the case as prohibiting any exercise of substantive due process for any purpose. By 1965, however, some Supreme Court justices had come to the conclusion that the Constitution did protect some substantive liberty interests under the Fourteenth Amendment (*Griswold v. Connecticut*, 381 U.S. 479 (1965)). In the current era, a majority of justices accept the doctrine of substantive due process in limited circumstances (see, e.g., *Planned Parenthood of SE Pennsylvania v. Casey*, 505 U.S. 883 (1992)).

apply to male workers as well, a suggestion that later courts followed. This originally gendered standard balanced the limited impact that a protective statute has on workers' liberty interests against a more substantial state interest in protecting the health of the workers. The process of balancing led to rulings in favor of allowing states and Congress to exercise their police powers to ameliorate conditions that threatened workers' health and welfare, broadly interpreted.

This is how we can understand the case's backward-looking aspects. The case does mark a moment of change, but a moment of change that is rooted in history, not simply in a forward-looking coronation of the welfare state. In this reading, *West Coast Hotel* emerges not as a case in conflict with earlier jurisprudence, but rather as an opinion in dialogue with cases such as *Lochner, Muller v. Oregon,* and *Adkins v. Children's Hospital.*[6] While it allowed for the expansion of state and national authority in a way that permitted the development of the modern welfare state, it did so by picking up and extending old doctrine, not by prospectively authorizing a major constitutional change.

This shift in emphasis and interpretation depends upon reading the case through the lens of a complex history with multiple actors. In order to understand *West Coast Hotel* and its implications for the modern state, we must seek its roots in the past through a return to a time that I shall call the *period of negotiation.* The period of negotiation was the time when the courts addressed attempts within and outside of the legal community to balance and channel the tensions and conflicts inherent in the rise of a modern industrial economy and a modern regulatory state. This period began shortly after the Fourteenth Amendment became part of the U.S. Constitution, and my analysis will begin with the 1873 case *Bradwell v. Illinois,* which was announced the day after the *Slaughter-House Cases.*[7] It ended, as already suggested, in 1937 with the Supreme Court's decision in *West Coast Hotel Co. v. Parrish.*

---

6. In *Muller,* the Court upheld a ten-hour-per-day limit on the working hours of female laundry employees (208 U.S. 416 (1908)). The Court struck down a congressionally set minimum wage for women in the District of Columbia in *Adkins.*

7. The *Slaughter-House Cases* are (in)famous as the Supreme Court's first substantial interpretation of the Reconstruction Amendments; in this case, the Court in effect gutted the Fourteenth Amendment's privileges or immunities clause (83 U.S. 36 (1873)). *Bradwell* involved an Illinois woman's challenge to the Illinois state bar's refusal to admit her to the practice of law. Bradwell sued under the Fourteenth Amendment, but the Court denied her claim (83 U.S. 130 (1873)).

Nodes of Conflict and Constitutional Change

The preceding account suggests that history is important for more than gaining understanding about the past and that constitutional history should not solely be the preoccupation of those seeking evidence about original intentions. Barry Friedman suggests that constitutional interpretation is inherently rooted in history, since history suggests ways to reconcile deep commitments with modern preferences (Friedman 1998a, 77). History itself, though, is created, not discovered. The construction of a historical narrative is necessarily a partial, interpretive, and selective enterprise, privileging some voices and institutions and silencing others.

Writers of constitutional history have typically looked to the actions of judges to understand development. Whether they have attributed judges' actions to simple preferences about policy, to adherence to competing principles, to institutional pressures, or to some combination of these factors, judges and their institutional context have largely been at the center of the analysis. Judicial decisions, whether one considers raw outcomes or the language of the opinions, thus form the most significant body of data for research on the courts.

Recent work by Charles Epp in particular but also by such scholars as Ronald Kahn and Keith Whittington has initiated the difficult task of reweaving constitutional narratives to incorporate the significant impact of other actors. Epp's cross-national study of the generation of an agenda for protecting civil rights incorporates a compelling narrative about the influence of pressure groups, activist lawyers, and governmental actors in shaping the production of legal doctrine. Expanding the scope of analysis beyond judicial opinions brings into focus the impact of the legal community on the production of doctrine while simultaneously raising consciousness about the porous nature of that community and its ability to constrain judicial action (Brigham 1999, 25). Such an analysis is particularly helpful in addressing the shifts in the legal system's institutional means for producing doctrine at the beginning of the twentieth century in response to a growing commitment to legal realism within the legal community.

This analysis starts from the standpoint that, while the courts are political institutions, discourse and interpretation also largely drive them. In order for an interpretive approach to function adequately in addressing the courts, it must take into account both the ways that policy outcomes and processes affect each other and the central role and nature of legal discourse as the process through which legal concepts develop and change (Suchman and Edelman 1996, 903). Addressing both of these elements provides an explanation of the contingency inherent in legal processes and locates the points in the system at which agency exists. Such an analysis also requires a focus both on a broader conception of the legal community and on moments of conflict rather than on moments of consensus.

An understanding of constitutional decision making that is simultaneously interpretive and institutional suggests an alternative to the interpretive historian's usual focus on the individual judicial decision and its content as the center of the analysis. Rather than thinking about constitutional decisions as chapters in a chain novel as Ronald Dworkin does or as acts that kill off narrative alternatives as Robert Cover does, we should focus on the contested narrative space in which these decisions take place. These spaces are nodes of conflict, or moments in the development of doctrine during which the various groups of actors who have access to the legal community struggle among themselves and with each other to establish their interpretations of a particular legal concept or phrase as the dominant norm. While the process for identifying and studying nodes of conflict shall be sketched briefly here, the true utility of this approach will only become clear through its implementation.

Ronald Kahn, Howard Gillman, and others have shown that institutionalized relationships provide the framework through which the law develops discursively. The approach of studying nodes of conflict emphasizes the structural positions of three types of actors: judges, attorneys, and interested lay activists. Since the dawn of the Progressive Era, each of these actors has had a specific role in the legal system requiring them to interact with and respond to the other actors. The formalized framework through which these interactions take place structures the nature of legal conflict and promotes focus on particular contested constructions at certain historical moments. These contested constructions serve to crystallize disputes, providing interest groups and social movements with conceptual hooks on which they can hang their substantive agendas even as judges seek to make these constructions coherent and cohesive (Bussiere 1999, 157).

Charles Epp has developed this point, showing that constitutional litigation does not occur in a conceptual or structural vacuum. Rather, he argues, it depends upon the existence of a support structure for legal mobilization that includes lawyers, organizations, funding, and sometimes governmental commitments (Epp 1999, 256). Intensive focus on a particular area such as civil rights will not occur if judges are hostile to it, but such interest also will not develop unless the topic is litigated extensively (Epp 1999, 278). His research has shown that the Supreme Court's agenda developed in response to changes in the support structure for legal mobilization; changes in the support structure have largely driven major developments in the Court's agenda (Epp 1999, 277).

The interaction between support structures for mobilization and the Supreme Court's agenda is a legacy of the Progressive Era, which saw the formation of major rights-advocacy organizations that were willing and able to use the courts to advance their agendas (Epp 1999, 277). Epp's main examples are the American Civil Liberties Union and the National Association for the Advancement of Colored People; other organizations undoubtedly saw the successes that these and other progressive organizations were able to achieve and modeled their legal strategies on these examples (277). Epp also identifies the rise of law schools as a significant factor since law schools exposed budding lawyers to legal realist approaches, encouraging them to develop and rely on social scientific evidence to bolster their legal arguments (277). As these changes took place, legal conflicts moved away from disputes among legal technicians over formal legal categories and toward broader-based disagreements about such deeply contextualized concepts as due process. Furthermore, the range of participants with institutional roles in the legal process expanded dramatically.

Building on this approach, the analysis to follow will present the legal system as a complex discursive field. Rather than moving together toward a triumphant confirmation of a particular doctrinal development, judges' opinions reflect the inherently conflicted nature of the enterprise of constitutional interpretation. Near the turn of the century, judges under the influence of other actors within the legal system (lawyers and academics) and lay activists with a stake in the outcomes of cases began to produce through their opinions a varied landscape composed of doctrinal fissures and ruptures. Interpretation is in this view an inherently multivocal and conflict-laden enterprise, as judges struggle to define the conceptual frameworks in which they are operating. Most scholars see these conflicts readily when they take place between judges voting with a majority and those dissenting in a panel, but this phenomenon highlights only a small fraction of the conflict that drives doctrinal development. Other conflicts occur between state judges and federal judges. Still others occur across geographic boundaries. Some even occur within a single opinion written by a single judge, as contemporaneous interpreters develop alternative readings.

The opinions function to crystallize and ultimately to institutionalize the nature of the conflicts, which have some of their roots outside of the judicial arena. The tensions that arise in opinions both reflect and transform broader interpretive debates taking place among lawyers and lay activists. Because the opinions generate the beginning and end of the process of interpretation, focusing on the way that they present these conflicts enables the analyst to see how the debates, conflicts, multiple voices, and different options prevalent among attorneys and lay activists have influenced this complex process. The opinions provide the most focused and coherent picture of the conflicts, presenting them in their essential form.

How is doctrine actually produced? Institutionalized relationships and processes operate to transform ideas into doctrine and ultimately in some cases into nodes of conflict. Ideas, expressed from every possible perspective and for every possible reason, enter into the legal system through the narrow gateway of briefs. Lawyers' briefs filter and select the possible lines of argument to allow only those that will be permissible and coherent to the courts. Finally judges determine which arguments are valid and which are not, disagreeing with each others' outcomes and reasoning along the way. The lines of influence also flow in the opposite direction. Judges must react to issues that raise public concern, and only issues that generate intensive debates among laypeople can create large nodes of conflict. Attorneys react to the decisions of the courts, framing their arguments to address the most recent rulings and to appropriate them for their purposes. The interested lay public reacts to judicial decisions, framing changes in policy or in their practices to take into account the effect of a ruling upon their interests. The entire process is mediated through legal concepts that develop through the efforts of the legal community as it is driven by concrete interests often outside of it. The opinions that judges write provide a durable record of this process as certain subjects and conceptualizations of problems come to dominate their interpretive field.

The lay public provides the first layer of constitutional interpretation by raising the issues subject to constitutional litigation. It is from the public, of course, that the issues subject to constitutional litigation come. On the other end of the process, they also react to decisions by the courts, incorporating the courts' rulings in their day-to-day operations or working to develop new ways to resist the courts' intervention into their concerns. Attorneys serve as the gatekeepers of the legal system by translating lay interests into legal language (Fish 1995, 21). They can also facilitate organizations' desires to expand the scope of conflict, however, by offering resources to overcome cost barriers and by forming networks to share information and strategies (Epp 1999, 261). Judges are at the center of this dynamic process, and their opinions provide evidence for how it occurs. Like lawyers, judges in the new realist world of the early twentieth century saw their institutional roles change somewhat. They faced the new task of evaluating large quantities of social scientific evidence and placing this evidence in its proper legal context. More importantly, they had to deal with the heightened reactivity of a system that encouraged sustained participation in the production of legal concepts not only from the bar but from lay advocates as well (Epp 1999, 265).

While judges have the authority to change the arguments substantially from the form in which the attorneys have presented them, a court's opinion will usually bear the mark of the briefs. As the courts accept certain kinds of legal language and reject others, they subtly or dramatically change the legal categories into which attorneys must fit their next rounds of legal arguments. Judges negotiate legal categories not only with the attorneys in the cases they decide, but also in relation to their colleagues' work on the bench. Their agendas are shaped principally by the conflicts they have with other judges in deciding how to address the information they receive from lawyers and lay activists.

So far, none of this is particularly remarkable. No constitutional theorist would deny that attorneys and the public play some role in setting the agenda of the courts. What the study of nodes of conflict demonstrates, though, is that the individual judges writing opinions not only do not completely control the subject matter and framing of the cases that reach them, they also do not exert complete control over the development of doctrinal pathways in constitutional law. This development takes place through the conflicts among judges over the proper ways to frame the legal and empirical arguments that attorneys and lay activists bring to the courts.

The production of meaning takes place in two stages. First, an idea must be expressed in legal language that the community recognizes as legal language in the context of the particular issue and the particular historical moment during which it is expressed. Second, the community must validate the expression of the idea by using the expression in future discussions. Through this process, the community legitimates the legal expression of an idea and enables it to become a subject of factual debate. As with other communities, the legal community itself produces meaning not through the pronouncements of any individual member, even if that member is a Supreme Court justice, but rather through community practices and responses that frame a particular discursive moment's significance. The upshot of this understanding is that considering nodes of conflict diminishes reliance on the concept of the judge as one who says what the law is and focuses rather on the judge's function as a participant in the process of identifying and shaping particular nodes.

Nodes of conflict present a point at which the public, attorneys, and the courts are all in communication. Attorneys read decisions by the courts and identify points of ambiguity. They then focus on these areas in their briefs, working up legal arguments around them and disagreeing about their significance. Public interest organizations also read decisions issued by the courts and find the issues on which their worldview could be integrated into the law. Finally, the courts, presented with briefs and often with large amounts of evidence around each node, have to decide whether to incorporate some of this reasoning in their decisions or to continue to leave the node as a site for further argument and interpretation. In the process of doing so, judges often disagree with each other about the role that the nodes are to play in their rulings. Their opinions provide evidence of both the existence and development of these nodes.

An important factor to note in this process is that none of these actors—not the courts, the lawyers, or the public interest groups—are in complete control. The public interest groups expend resources and research the nodes, but they do not select them. The lawyers interpret them and translate them into legal language, but they shape them through reference to decisions by the courts rather than creating them out of whole cloth. The courts may in a few cases intentionally leave a particular area ambiguous, but more frequently the initial process of creating a node is probably dependent upon the attorneys. No decision can make everything completely clear, and not even the Supreme Court can settle every issue in a particular case in one opinion. Some things must be overlooked, brushed aside, or glossed over—and these things have the potential to become nodes of conflict.

The development of a node of conflict depends upon the social context in which the particular legal ambiguity exists. Legal rulings are masses of ambiguity; obviously not every question left unanswered by the courts will be successfully developed into a node of conflict. Lay activists push their agendas, and when they cannot get satisfaction in the legislative or executive arena, often turn to the courts for help; they are willing to use almost any strategy to achieve the desired substantive result. Lawyers frequently seek to create ambiguity in order to generate arguments, and judges rely on these ambiguities to frame their decisions in ways that seek to convince other members of the legal community that their understanding is correct. The social context frames the kinds of disagreements that give rise to legal struggles, as does the political climate of the time. Nodes of conflict require three factors: the creation and acceptance by the legal community of an ambiguity in the law, a contested social issue, and the development of a connection between the ambiguity and the social issue.

The production of an active node of conflict requires a synergistic relationship among the judges who are considering particular issues; judges must also receive input from the lay public, attorneys, and judges. Few ambiguities in legal language lead to the development of full-fledged nodes, and with proper intervention by interested members of the legal community, nodes may develop around points that do not seem at first to be particularly ambiguous. Language that can easily be transformed into a node of conflict may lie dormant for a short or long period of time, waiting to be addressed. If enough public interest exists in a particular topic and if this interest gives rise to litigation, attorneys will intensively seek to find or create areas of ambiguity in the law within which they can frame their legal arguments. Judges will then have to address these arguments in decisions and, unless they work to resolve the interlocking questions of law and fact completely, will often give more substance and nuance to the developing node. As a particular node becomes hotly contested in one jurisdiction, laypersons or attorneys in other jurisdictions may notice it and bring it to their legal turf. Additionally, judges citing cases from other jurisdictions may inadvertently import a node of conflict into their own jurisdictions by quoting language that identifies a particular contested area in the law. After a major case in which such language is cited, judges can expect to find additional litigation around that language and how it will apply in different circumstances within the legal and political arenas in their jurisdictions.

This description implies that not every interpretable ambiguity in legal language develops into an active node. No judge or attorney may ever construct a particular ambiguity in the law in a way that gives rise to substantial conflict. Even if an attorney identifies an ambiguity, the court considering the argument the attorney develops may not invest as much significance in the ambiguity as the attorney does. There may never be enough public interest in a particular issue to engender the intensive research necessary to identify and develop a potential node. Likewise, nodes may develop in unexpected contexts from language that initially seemed peripheral to the main point of an argument or decision.

A full-fledged node will be one that sparks debate and conflict nationwide in both state and federal courts. A single attorney's attempt to claim that legal ambiguity exists and a single judge's acceptance of this argument does not guarantee that a node of conflict will develop. Other attorneys and laypersons must recognize the node as having potential for their causes and employ it in their arguments. Judges must then continue to allow the node to exist by not moving to close it off immediately in independent decisions nationwide. The most highly contested nodes are those in which no simple resolution can be reached and judges suggest different resolutions for individual cases arising within the node. This process results in a legal system that is contingent yet simultaneously rooted in historical context; this view of the legal system emphasizes the important institutionalist insight that policies influence politics and vice versa in a continuing feedback loop (Skocpol 1992, 57–60).

Rethinking the Basis for the Constitutionality of the Modern Welfare State

Many scholars of the Populist and Progressive eras have addressed the deep tensions in the economy, society, and legal system over work and workers that marked the transition to a full-scale capitalist economy. Recently, feminists have drawn attention to women both as actors in the debates over workers' roles and as workers themselves. Ground-breaking work by social historians Alice Kessler-Harris, Sybil Lip-schultz, Theda Skocpol, and others has shown that concern over women's work was a significant factor in the struggle for regulation. These scholars and others such as Wendy Mink and Linda Gordon have noted the role of maternalism as a grounding justification for regulation, debating over its usefulness to promote feminine and feminist interests for working women.

Taken as a whole, this scholarship suggests that much of the ferment over protective legislation, and thus much of the debate over the proper scope of the regulatory state, involved the protection of women. In keeping with the study of nodes of conflict, legal history is best sought by looking for the points of debate, dissension, and disjuncture. In light of feminist historians' identification of deep tensions over the regulation of women's work and the significance of maternalism in U.S. politics and culture, the gendered nature of labor regulations in the late nineteenth and early twentieth centuries warrants a closer examination.

In the United States, the late nineteenth and early twentieth centuries witnessed a jurisprudential struggle over the meaning of liberty and over the way it would balance against the public interest. During the latter years of the nineteenth century, many state legislatures began to pass laws that sought to limit for the public good the terms and conditions of individual employment contracts; these laws then came under legal attack. The new Fourteenth Amendment and its state analogues quickly became interpretive sites, open invitations for attorneys to seek to exempt their clients from regulations enacted on the state level under the theory that such regulations interfered with their clients' liberties. The courts, both state and federal, frequently supported challenges to protective legislation under the due process clause's protection for liberty and property. The key question for both state and federal courts during this period was how to balance the liberty guaranteed by state and federal constitutions against the state's interest in exercising its police power on the behalf of its citizens. Courts and attorneys debated this question in its most pointed form with respect to protective labor legislation, or laws that changed the terms and conditions of labor ostensibly in the interest of protecting employees. From the very beginning of the debate, gender played a major role in shaping the contours of this debate.

The book focuses principally on cases that addressed the question of whether a particular statutory protection of an employee violated the due process clause of the Fourteenth Amendment or a parallel guarantee contained in the state constitution. *West Coast Hotel Co. v. Parrish* was such a case, and the line of doctrine with which it was in dialogue was composed of these cases. As the previous discussion suggested, thinkers have understood the ruling in *West Coast Hotel* as addressing tensions between the courts and the legislature, over the scope of national and state authority to regulate citizens' lives, and over the scope and nature of substantive due process. While the case had implications for all of these tensions, its reasoning centered principally on the substantive question of the legitimacy of minimum wages for female workers.

The issue of liberty versus the state's public authority to regulate is a broad way of thinking about the deep constitutional question of the New Deal era, but courts rarely tackle questions in broad, vague, conceptual forms. Rather, they focus on narrower questions about particular doctrinal problems that cast light on the broader issues through analogy. In the late nineteenth and early twentieth centuries, the U.S. courts struggled with the broad puzzle of liberty and the state's authority in the context of a meticulous consideration of facts about workers and their liberties under a particularized and substantive reading of the due process clause. The broad puzzle could have (and did) come up in other factual and doctrinal areas, but the consideration of it that led developmentally to *West Coast Hotel* took place in the context of questions about the constitutional legitimacy of protecting workers by statute. We must seek the historical roots of *West Coast Hotel* and thus of the broader developments that the case heralded in this more limited doctrinal question.

Three central tensions underlie the jurisprudential history of *West Coast Hotel;* an exploration of the roots and development of these tensions will comprise the substance of this book. The *first* is between liberty and the state's public interest legitimately exercised through police power. The *second* is between regulating men's work and regulating women's work. The *third,* related closely to the first two, is between regulating the work that is done and regulating the workers performing it. The tension that has interested most legal scholars is the first, but the argument will demonstrate that one cannot understand the development of the relationship between liberty and police power in isolation. One must simultaneously consider the ways that the two other tensions drove the development of jurisprudence in the area of protective labor legislation. The development of this historical story will show how judicial considerations of gendered regulations of work formed the basis for the constitutional legitimation of the broadly based interventions of the modern state in *West Coast Hotel*, ensuring that gender rather than class would be the analytical category that would drive the legal development of regulation.

The historical record supports another important modification of current thinking about this period in American constitutional history. The evolution of substantive due process as a constitutional doctrine was not driven solely by the Supreme Court's decisions or even by judicial decision making generally. Rather, attorneys and interested laypersons also played significant roles in determining the development of substantive guarantees of liberty during the period of negotiation. Likewise, rulings in the state high courts often had as great an impact as those issued by the Supreme Court, particularly in the early years. Attention to these factors brings into focus much more clearly the nature of both liberty and police power in their intimate and problematic connections to gender.

Throughout this work, the role of liberty is not a static concept but is in question at each moment. The book will demonstrate throughout how liberty was connected to the individuals who held the guarantee of due process and how judges understood individuals' capacities to exercise liberty. This enhanced understanding of the role of liberty influences these interpretations of the reasoning and outcomes in cases involving such claims by focusing attention on the shifts and discontinuities in the doctrine. As the book demonstrates, these shifts and discontinuities centered around gender.

Stages in the Period of Negotiation

Figure 1 details the frequencies of cases involving challenges to protective labor legislation during the period of negotiation. The top curve indicates the frequency of all such cases, showing how the question emerged in the 1870s, peaked before 1920, and gradually tailed off in the 1930s. The two other curves demonstrate an interesting feature of these cases. The curve labeled "general" gives the frequency of cases that addressed statutes that did not mention gender (including gender-

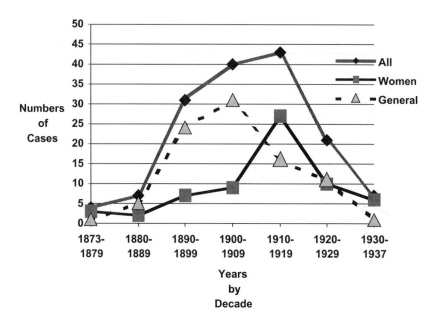

Fig. 1.   Frequency of cases between 1873 and 1937

neutral statutes regulating children's work). Most of these statutes limited work in specific occupations such as mining, and most of these statutes applied primarily to male workers. The curve labeled "women" gives the frequency of cases involving statutes that applied specifically to female workers. As the graph suggests, the cases involving women's legislation gradually came to play a more significant role in the development of doctrine, coming to dominate the legal landscape after about 1910.

The numbers of cases in each area do not tell the whole story, however. Upon considering the way that doctrine emerged in this area, we see that the cases fall into four rough historical categories. The early period, that of generalized balancing between liberty and police power, began in the 1870s and ran through the mid-1890s; it was characterized by the legal community's debates over what liberty meant under the Fourteenth Amendment and parallel state provisions and over how traditional conceptions of police power were to fit into the newly emerging constitutional framework. During these years, opponents of regulation challenged statutes concerning both women's and men's work, but the courts did not consider these statutes in specifically gendered terms. The second period, a time of specific balancing between workers' liberties and the state's authority to regulate, began in the mid-1890s and ran through 1910; it encompassed several moments of transition and uncertainty. In the early years of this period, the legal community continued to work through the difficult task of balancing liberty interests against police power. At the same time, judges and lawyers began to articulate a separate analysis for cases involving women's protective labor legislation, applying the principles developed to address general legislation in somewhat different ways.

Toward the end of the first decade of the twentieth century, the center of the debate shifted. The next period, marked by the legal community's adoption of laborer-centered analysis, began in 1911 and ended in 1923 on the eve of *Adkins v. Children's Hospital* (in which the Supreme Court invalidated a minimum wage for women in the District of Columbia). It encompassed the time when the legal community focused principally on questions about women's protective labor legislation. By the end of this period, cases involving women's legislation had become the central points in the debate over the role that due process was to play in a modern industrial society. The final period, a time of gendered rebalancing of the tension between freedom and regulation, began with the Court's decision in *Adkins* and ran through its reconsideration of this ruling in *West Coast Hotel*. It saw an intensive conflict over women's minimum wages. Through this conflict, the principles that would guide later courts were developed and refined, to be fully articulated in *West Coast Hotel* in 1937.

Centering gender reframes how we understand the sweep of doctrinal history. This book will show that the courts' struggles over economic substantive due process were not simply debates over the authority of state legislatures to intervene in private labor contracts for the public interest. As time went on, the debate over protective labor legislation gradually developed into a debate over the nature of the relationship between female workers and the state. The legal community thus shifted from analyzing the type of labor involved to focusing on the laborers. In the later years, lawyers and judges discussing women's protective labor legislation made both gender-specific and general arguments that had differing implications for general protective labor legislation. Through this debate, the courts fashioned principles and policies that would ultimately apply to all workers.

This study of the cases will show that as gender became more significant as a category of analysis, it in effect pushed property out of the debate over workers' rights and shifted the terms of the debate from an analysis of work to a discussion of the extent to which workers needed protection. The ruling in *West Coast Hotel* was the culmination of this process; the conclusion will explore the implications of this insight.

Examining this historical period and this particular set of issues shifts understandings of the central questions about the constitutional basis of the modern welfare state. Most scholars have asked questions that assume that the Great Depression and the New Deal opened the door for the shift in reasoning. In contrast, this book will address the following three questions: (1) What impact did the judges' articulated understandings of gender roles have on decisions regarding women's place in the wage labor system? (2) How did social understandings of gender influence the judges' understandings of gender through the legal process? (3) How did substantive due process relate to the judges' perceptions of what rights women possessed and the ability of women to exercise these rights? The book will analyze these questions together by developing a contextualized understanding of constitutional interpretation and the relationship among courts, attorneys, and laypersons. These groups' changing understandings of individuals' capacities to exercise liberty strongly influenced the ways that the Fourteenth Amendment protects individuals. Further, beliefs about gender differences shaped the ways that judges framed individuals' possession of the capacity to exercise liberty. The finding that the state had a legitimate public interest in women as reproducers was also a powerful means for maintaining control over women's sexuality and procreative capacities. All of these questions underlie the ruling in *West Coast Hotel*, and all continue to have present-day relevance.

Finally, the courts incorporated social understandings of gender into their reasoning, an issue of perennial relevance. Investigating the means through which social understandings influenced courts' opinions grounds the historical aspects of this project more comprehensively than limiting the research to reported opinions by judges would enable. Historical interpretive work emphasizes the importance of developing, understanding, and using theory within a historical context. Doing so shows that the revolution of the 1930s was a revolution in the ancient, not the modern, sense of the word: it was a reworking and reclaiming of an established tradition.

The Doctrinal Record

In order to understand the development of doctrine, a comprehensive review of the cases decided during these years is necessary. The best-known cases of the era were litigated in the Supreme Court, but such cases as *Munn v. Illinois, Lochner,* and *West Coast Hotel* were adjudicated in the context of a lengthy national negotiation over issues of gender, public versus private, and liberty and police power. Like most rulings of the Supreme Court, the leading cases of the period of negotiation drew from developments in the lower federal courts and the state courts.

The basis for the analysis to follow is a review of all reported decisions of state and federal courts regarding the legal regulation of employees in the workplace from the late nineteenth century (starting in 1873) and going through the Court's decision in *West Coast Hotel* in 1937. These reported decisions are significant not only for their outcomes but also for their reasoning, which was available for reformers, attorneys, and judges to ponder in their later considerations of the issues. The approximately two hundred cases encompassed challenges to almost all of the protective measures passed in the states and by Congress during these years. The legislation thus challenged included setting maximum hours for labor or minimum wages, controlling conditions in certain kinds of work, protecting members of labor unions in various ways, and protecting some classes of laborers (often by occupation).

Between 1873 and 1937, the U.S. courts issued opinions in 45 cases on the federal level and 106 cases on the state level. When the entire group of opinions is taken together, 94 of them support protective legislation under the state and/or federal constitutions, while 57 strike down such legislation (62 percent and 38 percent, respectively). Separating the cases into one group that involves protective legislation generally and another group that involves only protective legislation for women reveals a stark difference. While courts considering general protective labor legislation upheld it about half the time, they upheld such statutes limited to women almost 80 percent of the time. General legislation was written in gender-neutral terms but largely applied to occupations that were dominated by male laborers, such as mining.

As contemporary observers complained, the federal courts certainly struck down much protective labor legislation; critics of *Lochner* pointed to many other examples of what they believed to be inappropriate judicial behavior. During these years, the federal courts invalidated protective laws on the state and federal level in 40 percent of the cases for which they reported opinions. As in the complete group of cases, though, the same judges were much more willing to allow legislation aimed at women to prevail. The courts struck down general protective labor legislation slightly less than half the time, but only did so in a third of the cases involving women's labor legislation.

Much less scholarly attention has focused upon the role of the state courts than upon the federal courts in determining the fate of protective legislation.[8] As it turns out, they were also active participants in the

TABLE 1.   Decisions in All Cases Involving Protective Labor Legislation, 1873–1937

	Upheld Protective Legislation	Struck Down Protective Legislation	Total
All cases	94 (62%)	57 (38%)	151
General cases	46 (51%)	44 (49%)	90
Cases involving women	48 (79%)	13 (21%)	61

TABLE 2.   Decisions in Federal Cases Involving Protective Labor Legislation, 1873–1937

	Upheld Protective Legislation	Struck Down Protective Legislation	Total
All cases	27 (60%)	18 (40%)	45
General cases	14 (54%)	12 (46%)	26
Cases involving women	13 (67%)	6 (33%)	19

TABLE 3.   Decisions in States Cases Involving Protective Labor Legislation, 1873–1937

	Upheld Protective Legislation	Struck Down Protective Legislation	Total
All cases	67 (63%)	39 (37%)	106
General cases	32 (50%)	32 (50%)	64
Cases involving women	35 (83%)	7 (17%)	42

8. Urofsky's examination of state court rulings during the Progressive Era is a notable exception (Urofsky 1983).

process of judicial intervention into progressive legislation, invalidating laws in their reported opinions at levels almost identical to those of the federal courts. They struck down over 37 percent of the legislation they considered in reported opinions. At the state level, though, the difference gender makes is evident. State courts were much more willing to uphold such legislation. Courts struck down about half the general statutes but struck down only 17 percent of the statutes for women.

Another area in which courts were willing to uphold protective legislation was such legislation directed at minors. Despite the Supreme Court's unwillingness to permit the implementation of a national statute barring child labor, many state statutes limiting or prohibiting such work survived constitutional challenge. On the state level, 11 of the 106 cases addressed child labor provisions. When these cases are excluded from the analysis, the gap between legislation involving women and general legislation broadens. Here, the rate of striking down protective legislative enactments not related specifically to women reaches 60 percent.

Thus, across the board courts tended to treat protective labor legislation much more favorably when they were considering statutes that addressed women's situation in the labor marketplace. This difference is made even starker by excluding legislation protecting children, which had certain parallels to women's protective labor legislation that justify excluding these cases from the analysis.

The numbers of cases hint that gender played a significant role in shaping the development of doctrine, but cannot show what this role was. The substantive chapters of the book present close textual analyses of the cases, the briefs, and the social debate over protective labor legislation. Throughout, the historical record shows how earlier arguments influenced and shaped the scope of possibilities at later points in the doctrinal story.

TABLE 4.   Decisions in State Cases, Excluding Cases Dealing with Children, Involving Protective Labor Legislation, 1873–1937

	Upheld Protective Legislation	Struck Down Protective Legislation	Total
All cases	56 (59%)	39 (41%)	95
General cases	22 (41%)	32 (60%)	54
Cases involving women	34 (83%)	7 (17%)	41

Outline of the Book

As suggested above, the period of negotiation over the fate of protective labor legislation under the due process clause falls into four temporal segments. The emergence and articulation of certain nodes of conflict characterize each segment. We cannot determine precisely when a particular node emerges as a full-fledged node and when it has been sufficiently resolved by the legal community to no longer warrant description as a node. Nonetheless, the major nodes of conflict regarding protective labor legislation are fairly distinct in their appearance, development, and disappearance in the activities of judges and attorneys. Further, two major cases, *Adkins v. Children's Hospital* and *West Coast Hotel v. Parrish,* provided clear starting and ending points for particular nodes due to their impact on significant outstanding legal questions.

During the first segment of the period of negotiation, which ran from about 1873 through roughly 1897, the major nodes of conflict centered around questions of how the new Fourteenth Amendment and parallel state provisions would affect constitutional interpretation. We can think about these years as a time of *generalized balancing* between liberty and police power. The discussion in chapter 2 will detail how the tension between liberty and police power emerged as the central focus of claims grounded in due process, outlining the initiation of the constant conflict that would take place between liberty and police power during the entire period covered by the book. Attorneys initially argued over whether the privileges or immunities clause could be used to guarantee particular substantive rights to all citizens, but the Supreme Court foreclosed this debate in the *Slaughter-House Cases.* The due process clause simultaneously emerged as the basis for far more fruitful nodes; in fact it continues to do so today. In conducting their analyses of due process, the legal community highlighted the fundamental tension between liberty on the one hand and police power on the other. A major source of contention during the period of generalized balancing was the question of to what extent the due process clause could form the basis for substantive guarantees of rights, particularly liberty. A second significant issue was the popularization of the conflict over what constituted a valid public interest warranting the exercise of police power; this conflict would persist throughout the entire period of negotiation. These beginnings of nodes combined as the players in the legal system first began to encounter the perceived conflict between the liberty to make contracts and the new forms of protective labor legislation.

The second segment of the period of negotiation extended from roughly 1898 through 1910. This portion of the period provided the most intensive focus on and debate over general protective labor legislation, and can be thought of as the period of *specific balancing*. Chapter 3 will show the legal community's adoption of two different specific frameworks, one addressing types of labor and the other addressing classes of laborers, to address and adjudicate cases involving general and women's protective measures respectively. In their analyses of general protective labor legislation, attorneys, judges, and the lay public continued to debate fiercely the role that the Fourteenth Amendment and parallel state provisions would play in determining the constitutionality of such laws. In this period, however, they began to focus principally upon the type of labor that the states were seeking to regulate. Also during this portion of the period of negotiation, women's protective labor legislation began to emerge as a significant and separate focus. Here the legal community concentrated on the reach of police power, the role of public health in justifying protective labor legislation, the extent to which women had liberty rights parallel to those of men, and the significance of women's childbearing and child-rearing roles. In their efforts to analyze protective labor legislation for women, the legal community considered women as a class and construed female workers as different from the normative male worker whom general protective labor legislation addressed. The period of specific balancing coincided with intensive feminist activity on behalf of the Nineteenth Amendment.

In the years between 1911 and 1923, women's protective labor legislation became the central area for debate within and beyond the legal community regarding legislative intervention into employees' bargains with their employers. Chapter 4 addresses this period of *laborer-centered analysis* and explains the by-then fully developed framework for adjudicating claims against women's measures and demonstrates the dominance of this framework. In the period of laborer-centered analysis, the courts issued rulings in more cases involving women's legislation than in cases involving general legislation. The central nodes of conflict were the justifications that could be used to show that protective labor legislation for women was legitimate. During these years, the legal community solidified its focus on the worker rather than on the type of work she or he was performing. Also during this time, the modes of analysis developed with regard to women's protective labor legislation began to appear in discussions of general labor legislation. Like the previous period, these years saw a great deal of feminist activism, but toward the end of the period of laborer-centered analysis, major splits among groups of feminists that had previously been developing under the surface came to the fore.

The final years of the period of negotiation, which extended from 1923 through 1937, also featured a concentrated focus on women's protective labor legislation, though many fewer cases were decided. These years, the focus of chapter 5, were the time of *gendered rebalancing* of the tension between liberty on the one hand and the state's authority to regulate on the other. Chapter 5 completes the description of the period of negotiation by outlining the impact on minimum wages of gendered and gender-neutral arguments advanced with differing intentions and shows how these debates culminated in the Supreme Court's ruling in *West Coast Hotel*. Discussions of protective labor legislation centered around its operation for women rather than on facially gender-neutral protective statutes. This period included the worst part of the Great Depression, which raised substantial questions about the extent to which severe economic distress justified a revision of constitutional standards. It ended decisively with the Supreme Court's ruling in *West Coast Hotel v. Parrish*. The central nodes of conflict in cases decided and reported during this part of the period of negotiation were focused intensively on women's protective labor legislation, and in particular on minimum wages. The first node was the continued debate over liberty—did women have fundamentally less liberty than men, and to what extent did the adverse market conditions contribute to a need for protective measures to enhance liberty? The other node centered around the role of women in the workplace, continuing a conversation about the status of justifications for protective labor legislation that had been developed in the years between 1911 and 1923. These justifications fell into three categories: women's maternal and wifely roles, the health risks associated with low pay, and, finally, exploitation by employers in the marketplace. The legal community, along with feminist activists, struggled over whether these justifications were gendered or could rather be expressed in gender-neutral terms. These debates formed the fundamental basis for the reasoning in *West Coast*

Hotel. As this brief description suggests, the gendered rebalancing took place with respect to both male and female workers.

The final chapter rearticulates the theoretical arguments made in the book and explores their significance in broader contexts. It shows that a gendered rereading of the era of economic substantive due process revises scholarly understandings of the doctrine's formative period and the battle over the doctrine in the 1930s. These insights extend beyond the period for which they were developed, and the conclusion explains their implications for broader understandings of liberty, substantive due process, and the relationship between public interest and private freedom.

This analysis thus establishes and defends a new conception of substantive due process that is more sensitive to the role of courts' understandings of individual capacities to exercise liberty and a new conception of the role of cases involving women in the development of the doctrine. The center of the analysis is the relationship among the three tensions identified earlier: allowing liberty versus sanctioning the state's exercise of public interest, regulating men's work versus regulating women's work, and regulating the work that is done versus regulating the workers who perform it. This interpretation of the history casts a new light on the struggles of the 1930s and places *West Coast Hotel* in its appropriate context. The analysis also addresses the (at least!) three-cornered struggle among judges, lawyers, and interested laypersons to define and control areas of constitutional conflict. The conclusion discusses the implications of this approach, with reference to the contribution it makes to constitutional interpretation and development.

This book provides a helpful intervention into ongoing recent debates about the significance and meaning of the courts' role in the New Deal era. The story is one of how change occurs; it exposes the hidden nature of one of the most significant cases in the twentieth century. This interpretation of *West Coast Hotel* and of substantive due process generally suggests that the roots of modern employment law and of modern doctrine on liberty have grown in deeply gendered ground.

Chapter 2

Generalized Balancing: The Early Struggles over Protective Labor Legislation

This chapter analyzes the way that the courts in the United States dealt with protective legislation between 1873, when the Supreme Court decided *Bradwell v. Illinois*,[1] and 1897, the year before the Court decided *Holden v. Hardy*.[2] In this period, the nodes of conflict that were to consume the courts at the turn of the century began to emerge in preliminary form. They were not yet full-fledged nodes of conflict, being confined largely to the legal community, but they did establish a basic framework within which the later battles would take place. The central issue concerning the legal community in these years was the proper interpretation of the new Fourteenth Amendment and its viability as a ground for challenging a wave of statutes protecting workers. The debates took place largely in legal rather than in factual terms. After some initial discussion, the legal community settled upon transporting to the postbellum landscape the preexisting concept of due process as a hedge against the state's authority to initiate protective measures. The fundamental question was then how to balance in general and abstract terms the liberty and property interests inherent in due process against the state's police power.

These years thus witnessed the initiation of the period of negotiation, which centered around two monumental shifts not directly related to gender. The first was the passage of the Fourteenth Amendment with its language of privileges or immunities, due process, and equal protection. The rapid turn to litigation over the amendment's meaning testifies

---

1. In this case, the Court upheld Illinois's refusal to grant Myra Bradwell a license to practice law (*Bradwell v. Illinois*, 83 U.S. 130 (1873)).

2. This case upheld a statute establishing a maximum workday for miners (*Holden v. Hardy*, 169 U.S. 366 (1898)).

to late-nineteenth-century lawyers' recognition of its potential significance in transforming the legal landscape. Whether one wished to preserve the regulatory status quo as far as business was concerned or to overturn it, arguing on the basis of the amendment was necessary and pressing because of the breadth of its language. Nonetheless, the passage of the amendment alone was insufficient to initiate the debate; the tension between liberty and police power had a long history, and the Fifth Amendment, which became part of the Constitution in the 1780s, included some of the same language as the Fourteenth.

The second shift was the rapid postwar development and disruption of the economy and the subsequent drive to regulate the workplace legislatively. The years between 1873 and 1897 were a time of ferment and change for American workers. Mass industrialization simultaneously provided enormous and widespread economic and social benefits and provoked broad-based economic and social misery, and the instability of the economy on the local and national level created both opportunity and deep insecurity. The period opened with a serious economic crisis sparked by bank failures resulting from postwar speculation. The bank failures led ultimately to a depression marked by sustained unemployment among the working classes, both male and female. In the 1870s and 1880s, labor unions struggled to achieve organized bases among workers to combat the worst excesses of industrialism, calling major strikes for cap makers, textile workers, sales clerks, railroad workers, cigarmakers, and many other organized trades.

Social unrest and economic upheaval spurred legislative change. Calls for regulation of industry, while present in the antebellum period, took on a new urgency, and reformers began to contemplate the regulation of private businesses that had no direct or indirect connections to the state. These years saw the emergence of some sentiment in favor of protecting workers through the passage of protective labor legislation. Some of this legislation was driven by the trade unions themselves; Paul Kens provides an analysis of the role of the bakers' union in passing the legislation that formed the basis for the Supreme Court's decision in *Lochner v. New York* (Kens 1995). Other laws, however, were the fruit of middle-class reformers' efforts (Wood 1968; Skocpol 1995). Many of these laws were challenged in the state and federal courts, leading to an emerging legal discussion about how the new Fourteenth Amendment was to function. The social sciences in the United States were also in a period of ferment, with realist and empirical challenges to older frameworks emerging and threatening complacent acceptance of American exceptionalism (Ross 1992). These shifts, however, were not yet having a major impact in the legal field, which largely retained its commitment to formalism until the turn of the century.

These two sea changes, one legal and one socioeconomic, initiated a sustained debate over the legal legitimacy of regulating businesses that would persist until the early 1940s. While litigants and attorneys of the time probably could have predicted that a lengthy debate would take place in the courts, not even the most prescient could have realized in advance how long the debate would take or the contours that would evolve. Certainly, not even the most knowledgeable judges and jurisprudes of the late nineteenth century had any forewarning that the kinds of issues raised in two state court cases in Massachusetts and Illinois involving limitations on women's hours of work would ultimately become the battlefield on which the doctrinal and factual issues central to the modern American economy were to be fought.

The passage of the Fourteenth Amendment and the rise of industrialization initiated a series of largely legal questions that provoked conflict in the years of generalized balancing. While later periods featured both legal and factual disputes, the first fights were largely over the Fourteenth Amendment's meaning and its relationship to the industrial order. Judges sought to develop workable standards and definitions to administer the new amendment and to ensure that the legal and business communities would understand the acceptable parameters for regulation. At the same time, formed legal theorists developed interpretations of older regulatory concepts within the new constitutional framework. As the theory of nodes of conflict suggests, however, these attempts to develop settled answers would ultimately lead to new questions as the emerging definitions would become contentious points for new legal and factual arguments in the coming years.

Modern scholars can understand the period of negotiation in a variety of ways, as chapter 1 suggested. The doctrinal questions, however, centered largely on the tension between two concepts that emerged fully in the 1870s and were subject to deepening refinement and controversy over time. These concepts were the due process clause's protection for substantive rights and the state's regulatory authority. While both concepts were actively present in the legal sys-

tem of the United States prior to the 1870s, after the passage of the Fourteenth Amendment and the emergence of mass industrialization their
significance was enormously enhanced. The legal community quickly
latched on to the tension between these concepts as the key framework
within which the legitimacy of regulation would be debated, and in the
broadest of terms, the debate remained within this framework until the
Supreme Court's ruling in *West Coast Hotel v. Parrish* in 1937.

The debates that took place between the 1870s and 1890s were not
yet full-fledged nodes of conflict. While they engaged the legal community, these debates did not yet evoke the deep connection between
legal arguments and factual analyses on the part of advocates that characterize nodes. Later chapters will show that as time progressed, the
factual responses from legal and lay advocates increasingly influenced
the contours and shifts in litigation, but in the first few decades, the
arguments remained largely within the legal community and took
place in largely legal terms. Why? First, some sort of stable legal
ground had to be established before an effective interplay could
develop between activists and the legal community, and second, the
legal system's commitment to formalism in the late nineteenth century
was only just beginning to erode in the face of the emergence of modern American social science. By the end of the first decade of the twentieth century, the growth and professionalization of the social sciences
in the United States and the legal community's simultaneous and
related turn to scientifically based factual inquiries would spur the
rapid development of full-fledged nodes.

The initial debates were legal questions about how the concept of
due process was to work in relation with the state's authority to regulate. The legal community's members by and large addressed the early
cases by engaging in generalized balancing—weighing fairly abstract
conceptions of liberty and the right to contract against broad formulations of police power. This chapter first addresses a potential node of
conflict that the Supreme Court foreclosed—the Fourteenth Amendment's privileges or immunities clause as a basis for substantive rights.
The legal community then turned to a sustained discussion of the due
process clause and its meaning. This debate had two facets: it highlighted a definitional dispute over liberty as a legal concept within due
process analysis, and it laid the groundwork for the legal connection
between due process and labor regulations. At the same time, the legal
community began its considerations of police power as a counterbal-

ance to the due process clause's guarantee of liberty in the context of labor regulations. The discussion of police power had three major aspects: initial questions about police power as the ability to intervene in issues affecting the public interest and related questions about the meaning of public and private.

These discussions continued a conversation already in progress about due process. James Ely places the roots of the idea that modern due process claims can encompass protection for substantive rights in the antebellum period. He argues that antebellum courts developed the concept of due process by drawing on the central placement of liberty in the matrix of American legal thought traceable to the classic jurisprudence of Coke and Blackstone (Ely 1999). In his view, the rights guaranteed under due process first became a significant counterweight to the state's authority during the Jacksonian period as the courts used the principles of equal rights and disfavor for economic privilege to trammel governmental attempts to impose legislation affecting only part of the community (Ely 1999). Later, influential legal scholars such as Thomas Cooley promoted due process's protection for property as a means of limiting governmental authority in accordance with fundamental values rather than simply as a matter of procedure (Ely 1999, 342–43). The disfavor of class legislation that Progressives excoriated as the hallmark of the *Lochner* era had its roots in these early discussions of due process (Gillman 1993; Ely 1999).

During the postbellum years of generalized balancing, judges following the lead of Thomas Cooley sought to reestablish firm boundaries between public and private, thereby defining what was and was not subject to regulation (McCurdy 1975). These efforts, which judges viewed as ways to close off problematic legal controversies, ultimately had the ironic effect of setting the stage for further legal and factual conflicts in later eras. The guidelines that judges developed in the last few decades of the nineteenth century were useful in highlighting for attorneys the significance of categorizing regulations as merely private or as in the public's interest, but the courts could not give enough content to the categories of public and private to forestall conflict over how regulations were to be classified. This problem would persist well into the twentieth century.

Women's protective labor legislation was not a significant factor in setting the initial terms of the debate. This is not to say, however, that gender was absent or insignificant. On the contrary, members of the legal community clearly and sometimes explicitly based their reasoning on the qualities of male workers and their particular role in the economy and in society. The concept of liberty that emerged in these early years was that of male liberty. A small subset of cases dealt with prohibitions on female workers in establishments serving alcohol, but these cases did not have an impact on the developing stream of jurisprudence address-ing male workers' capacity to make labor contracts. The two cases deal-ing with female labor that were to influence later discussions of women's work, *Commonwealth v. Hamilton Manufacturing* and *People v. Ritchie,* both addressed the issues of substantive rights under due process and police power in the same terms in which other courts dis-cussed these issues with respect to legislation limiting men's work. Attorneys and courts later would recognize the value of differentiating explicitly between women and men; in the early years the ground was not yet stable enough to necessitate such a differentiation.

The Universe of Cases between 1873 and 1897

The courts were just beginning to address questions about how the Fourteenth Amendment was to function with regard to the states dur-ing this period. Only seven cases were reported on the federal level and twenty-seven on the state level. This group of cases is significantly smaller than the next groups; between 1898 and 1910, the courts deliv-ered fifty published decisions in such cases; between 1911 and 1923, forty-nine opinions were issued.

In this small initial group of cases, fifteen supported protective labor legislation under the state and/or federal constitutions, while nineteen invalidated such legislation. Even in this initial phase, sepa-rating the cases into those that involve general protective legislation and legislation aimed specifically at women highlights the difference in the outcomes. As table 5 demonstrates, the statutes specifically involv-ing women fared much better. Many of the statutes struck down in this period involved attempts by states to protect union members; others sought to limit the hours of labor generally or to regulate various aspects of particular industries.

The federal courts rarely considered the constitutionality of pro-tective labor legislation between 1873 and 1897. They upheld four statutes and struck down two, but the major cases to be decided by the

Supreme Court would not be heard until after the turn of the century. The federal courts decided only one case involving women's protective labor legislation during this period, but also heard such landmark cases as *Bradwell v. Illinois* that influenced the later debates over women's protective labor legislation.

The state courts in this period were significantly more active than the federal courts, though not as active as they would be in the coming decades. In the period of generalized balancing, the state courts heard twenty-seven cases and began to develop reasoning addressing the questions that would preoccupy the Supreme Court in the decades to come. The state courts were notably hostile to general protective labor legislation, striking down more than three-quarters of such measures. This pattern foreshadowed the outcome in *Lochner v. New York*.

During these years, the courts developed frameworks through which to evaluate the conflict between protected liberties and police power. They occasionally considered women's protective labor legislation but did not yet focus on the complex inquiries that would be common in the later periods. The ways in which they debated these issues, however, contributed significantly to the development of a legal climate in which women's laws would be analyzed separately; even in

TABLE 5. Decisions in All Cases Involving Protective Labor Legislation, 1873–97

	Upheld Protective Legislation	Struck Down Protective Legislation	Total
All cases	15 (44%)	19 (56%)	34
General cases	8 (32%)	17 (68%)	25
Cases involving women	7 (78%)	2 (22%)	9

TABLE 6. Decisions in State Cases Involving Protective Labor Legislation, 1873–97

	Upheld Protective Legislation	Struck Down Protective Legislation	Total
All cases	10 (37%)	17 (63%)	27
General cases	4 (21%)	15 (79%)	19
Cases involving women	6 (75%)	2 (25%)	8

these early years, members of the legal community had begun to separate statutes involving women's work from laws that protected workers without regard to gender.

Overview of Initial Debates and Litigation in the
Period of Generalized Balancing

The preliminary debates during these early years were more diffuse
than they would be later, focusing on broad interpretive questions
about various constitutional guarantees rather than on specific factual
questions about the applications of these guarantees. These discussions
did not generate full-fledged nodes of conflict for two reasons: first, the
legal community had not yet defined the constitutional questions
sharply enough to initiate a nationwide discussion, and second, legal
realism had only started to emerge on the scene.[3] In these years some
members of the legal community were beginning to back away from
formalism and develop modes of legal reasoning that relied more
directly on facts on the ground, but the transition was still taking place.
By the end of this period, courts were clearly considering the impact of
facts more directly in their production of doctrine, but the real break-
through would not come until the next period. Given this situation,
proregulatory activist groups had started to view the legal system as a
productive locus for the expansion of conflict but were not yet using
the legal system to the extent and in the ways that they would in the
coming years. The initial battles fought in these early cases thus cannot
be understood as full-fledged nodes of conflict.

These early stage-setting discussions largely centered around the
scope of the constitutional protections established by the new Fourteenth Amendment as the legal community struggled to assimilate the
legal and political implications of its text. When attorneys first began to
experiment with the amendment, they did not have the strong associations (positive or negative) with progressive and feminist interests that
would characterize future nodes of conflict. Nonetheless, some elite
actors, such as early female attorneys Myra Bradwell and Belva Lockwood, saw the Fourteenth Amendment's potential as a tool for achiev-

---

3. While critiques of formalism were beginning to percolate through the legal community in the last quarter of the nineteenth century, many scholars note the 1897 publication of Oliver Weldell Holmes's critical essay "The Path of the Law" as a significant
turning point.

ing reform. During these years, some members of the legal community worked to articulate a framework through which judges and lawyers could analyze general protective labor legislation; cases involving protective measures for women remained on the periphery. In establishing this initial framework, the legal community largely balanced liberty and property on the one hand against police power on the other, but did so in a fairly general and abstract sense.

The early years were marked by the categorical battles that would attract the attention of many individuals beyond the legal community in the next several decades. These initial struggles remained focused within the legal community, becoming full-fledged nodes of conflict a few decades later as the lay public began to consider the emerging categories. In this first period, the legal community wrangled over the boundaries of the legal field that would greatly interest reformers, representatives of business interests, and attorneys general throughout the nation after the turn of the century. Thus, the general balancing of these years would invite more specific and factual analyses in the years to come.

Many early tensions inherent in generalized balancing were discussed either in gender-neutral terms or in specifically male-gendered terms. This gender neutrality should not mask the fact that the implicit subject of these discussions was emphatically male. Nonetheless, these discussions set the stage for the shift that was to occur in the early years of the twentieth century as the cases and arguments regarding women's protective labor legislation came to take precedence. A brief summary of the leading cases will help to contextualize the conceptual discussion of due process and police power to follow.

The initial period begins with the Supreme Court's decision in *Bradwell v. Illinois;* these cases arise from the first attempts to use the Fourteenth Amendment as a basis for substantive rights of liberty and equality. The thematic link among the cases of the first period is that they represent the legal community's struggle to frame the legal categories of liberty and police power in a preliminary sense as these concepts related to attempts to regulate labor.

The breadth of the Fourteenth Amendment's language as well as its history invited conflict. Numerous interpretations were advanced after its passage, and varied readings could be supported by alluding either to the Radical Republicans who supported the amendment in Congress or to the more conservative state legislatures that voted to add the amendment to the Constitution. The language of the Fourteenth Amendment clearly repudiated the Supreme Court's divided ruling in *Dred Scott* denying citizenship to African Americans, but its further implications were clouded.

The second sentence of the first section declared, "No State shall make or enforce any law which shall abridge the privileges or immunities of citizens of the United States; nor shall any State deprive any person of life, liberty, or property, without due process of law; nor deny to any person within its jurisdiction the equal protection of the laws." As this sentence made no reference to race, judges and lawyers had to determine whether its historical roots would allow its use only to ameliorate the appalling conditions in which the recently freed slaves lived or rather if it would establish new limits on the states' authority to govern the daily lives of their citizens.

On the federal level, the first attempts to advance broad readings of the Fourteenth Amendment's guarantees used the privileges or immunities clause. The amendment was ratified in 1868, and the first case to address the scope of the privileges or immunities clause reached the Supreme Court five years later. The Court acted decisively in the *Slaughter-House Cases* to close off speculation about the implications of the vaguely worded clauses, focusing particularly on privileges or immunities. The justices held that the privileges or immunities of citizens of the United States were not the same as those belonging to citizens of individual states and that the amendment produced no change in those rights or their protection by the federal government against the states' actions (*Slaughter-House Cases*, 83 U.S. 36 (1873)).

The Supreme Court continued to insist that the privileges or immunities clause would provide no basis for broad claims of substantive rights, and lawyers turned instead to due process and equal protection.[4] In 1877, the Supreme Court again ruled that a state statute did not violate the Fourteenth Amendment, but acknowledged the growing interest in due process. This interest was shortly to contribute to a wave of litigation concerning due process and the appropriate balanc-

---

4. As late as 1905, the Supreme Court had to remind the litigants that the privileges or immunities clause could not be used as a basis for substantive claims of rights. See *Jacobson v. Massachusetts*, 197 U.S. 11 (1905). Equal protection, as mentioned above, was intimately connected to due process reasoning during the *Lochner* years. See Howard Gillman's analysis of courts' uses of the concept of class legislation to strike down protective laws prior to the late 1930s (Gillman 1993). An analysis of equal protection is beyond the scope of this book.

ing of liberty and police power. In *Munn v. Illinois* (89 U.S. 113 (1876)) the Court held that an Illinois statute setting maximum charges for grain storage warehouses and further regulating their activities did not run afoul of the due process clause's protections of liberty and property. The Court did point out, however, that its ruling depended upon the statute's effect of limiting the use of property that had a significant impact upon the public.

In 1885, the Court ruled constitutional a statute regulating the laundry industry by limiting workers' hours of labor in *Barbier v. Connolly* (113 U.S. 27 (1885)). Opponents had challenged the law on due process and equal protection grounds. An 1888 case, *Powell v. Pennsylvania*, did not deal with protective labor legislation but nonetheless addressed police power, equal protection, and due process. In that case, the Court ruled that states could regulate the manufacture of oleomargarine (127 U.S. 678 (1888)). The arguments in this case, as well as the Court's reasoning, provided important early indicators about how the debates were to be structured in future cases.

As discussed below, leading state cases addressing general protective labor legislation mostly focused on regulation of particular industries. The leading case on general protective labor legislation during this period was the ruling by the New York Court of Appeals on a statute designed to prevent the manufacture of cigars in tenements (*In re Jacobs*, 98 N.Y. 98 (1885)). The court struck down the prohibition, and other legal actors seeking justifications for invalidating protective labor legislation quickly adopted its reasoning.

The state cases reflected a diversity of approaches and outcomes with respect to particular issues. The West Virginia Supreme Court ruled in favor of a statute barring payment in scrip to employees of mines in *State v. Peel Splint Co.* (36 W. Va. 802 (1892)), but the Illinois high court struck down a similar regulation in *Frorer v. People* (141 Ill. 171 (1892)). In *Eden v. People* (43 N.E. 1108 (Ill. 1896)), the Illinois Supreme Court struck down a law mandating the closure of barber shops on Sundays, but New York's Court of Appeals upheld such a statute in 1896 (*People v. Havnor*, 149 N.Y. 195 (1896)).

Several cases addressed women's roles as workers and citizens, though not all of them dealt with protective labor legislation. While not dealing with a specific statute, the litigation over Myra Bradwell's desire to practice law in the state of Illinois provides a useful starting point, since it was the first case in which the Supreme Court considered a claim that a state was denying a woman's right to work in the context of the Fourteenth Amendment. Bradwell had challenged her exclusion from the Illinois bar on the basis of her sex, arguing that the state's action violated her rights under the privileges or immunities clause. The Supreme Court, issuing its ruling the day after deciding the *Slaughter-House Cases,* expended little interpretive energy upon the case, simply holding that the practice of law was not a privilege or immunity protected by the Fourteenth Amendment and therefore that the *Slaughter-House Cases* precluded relief (*Bradwell v. Illinois,* 83 U.S. 130 (1873)). Facing similar arguments in Belva Lockwood's suit demanding admission to the Virginia bar, the Court rebuffed her claims summarily in 1894, despite the fact that Lockwood had practiced law in the District of Columbia for several years and was even admitted to the Supreme Court bar (*In re Lockwood,* 154 U.S. 116 (1894)).

While most of the early doctrinal developments regarding interpretations of the due process clause and the role of liberty addressed general protective labor legislation, the first series of cases to question the concrete impact of the Fourteenth Amendment on the framework of the states' regulatory authority involved women. Several states and cities had passed statutes and ordinances prohibiting women who were not the wives or daughters of bar owners from serving alcohol in bars as employees. Bar owners or managers convicted under these statutes and ordinances challenged their convictions under the due process and equal protection clauses, claiming that the rights of the women working under them had been violated by these prohibitions. Such challenges resulted in five reported decisions on the state and federal levels.

The first case concerning a challenge to such a statute under the Fourteenth Amendment took place in Indiana in 1873; the state's prohibition of black servers was struck down but the prohibition against female servers remained intact (*Blair v. Kilpatrick,* 40 Ind. 312 (1873)). The next case occurred in 1881 and involved a San Francisco ordinance preventing women from serving in bars. The California Supreme Court found that the statute violated California's constitution, which provided that individuals could not be prevented from pursuing lawful employment on account of sex (*In re Maguire,* 57 Cal. 604, 609 (1881)). The Board of Supervisors for the City and County of San Francisco, San Francisco's governing body, then amended the ordinance. The California high court upheld the amended law as applied in 1893 in *Ex parte*

Hayes (98 Cal. 555), undercutting *Maguire*. In 1894 its application was again challenged by a theater owner whose license had been denied because he had employed females in the past; the ordinance again passed constitutional muster (*Foster v. Police Commissioners*, 102 Cal. 483, 492 (1894)).

This vigorous debate in California went unremarked upon by courts in other states considering the same issue. In 1884, Ohio's Supreme Court judges claimed simply that the state's broad authority to regulate matters involving liquor implied the lesser power to regulate who was to sell these products (*Bergman v. Cleveland*, 39 Ohio 651, 653 (1884)). The federal district court in Washington, upholding such a limitation on similar grounds in 1897, issued the single federal court ruling on women's protective labor legislation during this period (*In re Considine*, 83 F. 157 (D. Wash. 1897)). Such general reasoning based largely on factors other than gender, paralleling the Supreme Court's reasoning in *Bradwell*, prevailed until the late 1890s, when courts began to consider more fully the moral implications of women's presence in contexts where alcohol was also present.

The divergent outcomes in two state cases in the early period became particularly influential. In 1876, the Massachusetts Supreme Court ruled constitutional a statute prohibiting women from working more than sixty hours per week in a manufacturing establishment. In 1895 in *Ritchie v. People*, the Illinois Supreme Court reached the high-water mark in its hostility toward protective labor legislation, striking down a law limiting women workers to eight hours of labor per day in manufacturing establishments. The Massachusetts case, *Commonwealth v. Hamilton Manufacturing Co.*, was frequently cited by other courts to support upholding protective labor legislation specifically for women, although the reasoning in the case was not, by and large, gender-specific. *Ritchie's* reasoning, however, ultimately provided a helpful basis for the few courts that did decide to strike down protective labor legislation geared toward women.

During these years, attorneys and courts began to sketch the outlines of a doctrinal framework within which they could apply the commands of the Fourteenth Amendment. The development of a workable legal framework was the main achievement of this period. While much of the interpretive activity addressing due process centered around general protective legislation rather than laws protecting women, the discussions nonetheless began to identify the key concepts that would

provide the basis for later legal and factual disputes. As courts and
attorneys argued over the scope of liberty and police power, they
focused principally on the tension between liberty and the public's
interests. Courts responded by balancing these concepts against each
other in generalized and abstract terms. In engaging in this general balancing, they were unintentionally setting up later tensions based on
gender.

Due Process, Its Scope, and Its Key Elements

The antebellum courts had established the usefulness of the rights protected under due process as significant limits on the states' authority to
regulate property broadly conceived. The systematic use of due process
for this purpose, however, received a significant boost with the publication of Thomas Cooley's treatise on constitutional limitations in 1868.

Cooley's analysis was influential among legal scholars of the postbellum generation. Described as "the most influential constitutional
writer of the late nineteenth century," he sought to produce a comprehensive restatement of constitutional law that simultaneously
described doctrinal developments and presented a unified theory of
the proper relationship between state and individual (Ely 1999, 342).
For lawyers and judges grappling with the questions raised by the
Fourteenth Amendment, his *Treatise on the Constitutional Limitations
Which Rest Upon the Legislative Power of the States of the American Union*
was an indispensable source. In this volume and in his other writings,
he distinguished himself as one of the principal authors and proponents of substantive due process (Sklansky 2000, 91). His treatise has
been identified as the most widely read book on American law produced in the late nineteenth century (93).

For Cooley, due process implied more than correct procedure. He
explained that "general rules may sometimes be as obnoxious as special, when in their results they deprive parties of vested rights" (Cooley
1868, 355). While he acknowledged that private rights to property were
subject to legislative interference, he saw the scope for such interference in a relatively narrow light. He asserted that legislative infringements upon property were justifiable only if the purpose were specifically public, claiming that "no reason of general public policy will be
sufficient . . . where they operate upon specific vested rights" (357). He
recognized the state's authority to exercise police power, but noted that

its exercise could not conflict with the rights guaranteed in the Constitution (574). He thus set up the analytical framework of efforts to regulate labor as inherently implicating the tension between the state's authority to regulate under police power and constitutionally guaranteed rights of liberty and property. In combination with his commitment to serious limits on so-called class legislation, this stance placed regulatory efforts in a tenuous position almost from their postbellum inception. His later works in addition to revised versions of the *Treatise* revealed his fears for the continuing viability of private property in the face of class-based disruptions in the 1880s (Sklansky 2000, 95). Later versions of the treatise reiterated and reinforced these conceptions of the proper relationship between protections for liberty and property on the one hand and the state's regulatory power on the other, thus maintaining the analytical framework for general legislation established in 1868 (Cooley 1890, 1903).

Given the existing tendency to use due process as a limit on the state's authority to regulate, it is unsurprising that the main argument made in these and subsequent challenges to protective labor legislation, both general and gender-specific, was that such statutes violated the due process clauses of the federal and often the state constitutions of the states in which they applied. This claim required the use of arguments concerning the relationship among liberty, property, and due process. Initially the principal authors of these arguments were manufacturing interests who used them to shift the locus of conflict from the state legislatures, where they were losing the battle against regulation, to the courts, where they saw opportunities for victory (Epp 1999, 262–63). For the first time in U.S. history, a substantial body of nongovernmental organizations with the capacity to pursue long-term strategic litigation had emerged, but by and large the legal community was still interested in formalistic arguments only. The legal conversation thus centered around the concepts of liberty and property as formal elements of due process. Both because of the formalistic focus of the legal conversation and because statutes specifically limiting women's work were relatively rare except in the context of saloons, gender remained beneath the surface. This analysis will first consider the role of discussions regarding the definition of liberty and then trace briefly the development of the right to contract. Finally, this section will explain how these concepts were used in cases involving women's protective measures before the turn of the century.

Defining Liberty

Early discussions of due process highlighted disagreements over its legal scope. These disputes established the tension between the liberty interests protected by the due process clauses of the federal and state constitutions and the states' authority to regulate in the public's interest. The first debates over due process, while formalistic and somewhat vague, nonetheless identified the nature of the liberty element of due process as a significant factor in these cases. Those seeking to uphold state laws interpreted due process and liberty broadly, while those who opposed protective measures sought to narrow their reach and impact. During this period, these debates did not take place in explicitly gendered terms, though the gender of the bearer of liberty was implicitly male.

The initial debate over the scope of due process was broadly conceived in legal terms. At this early stage, the particular facts under which the cases arose had not yet been coupled with the analysis of due process. Nonetheless, the legal community relied upon liberty as a key factor in understanding due process, linking it to property and labor. Those seeking to strike down state statutes spent much energy analyzing liberty, while those who sought to sustain these laws simply asserted that liberty did not pose a significant limit. Nonetheless, those supporting state statutes had to address the opposing arguments, which led to the rise of liberty-centered analysis despite their efforts. With liberty as the centerpiece, the stage was set for a later gendered division among the cases based on beliefs about the scope of women's liberty and men's liberty.

Even in these early cases, members of the community also saw liberty in an implicitly gendered way. The image of liberty presented in the cases was a classic conception of masculine authority to make contracts and exercise other forms of autonomy. Until the recent passage of married women's property acts in several states, married women had not been able to contract for themselves; unmarried women were largely under the control of their households, primarily their fathers. As Amy Dru Stanley has shown, the authority to contract was fundamentally a question of self-ownership and full citizenship (Stanley 1998). The ability to make contracts was the hallmark of freedom because it implied a relationship between equals. Implicit in this framework was the assumption that the formally equal contracting parties were white and male (Stanley 1998, 59).

In these early years, attorneys and courts seeking to invalidate statutes or policies vigorously pursued broad and abstract definitions of liberty under the Fourteenth Amendment. For instance, attorneys arguing against Pennsylvania's law barring the sale or production of oleomargarine promoted a sweeping interpretation of liberty, claiming that social, civil, political, and personal liberty fell within the Fourteenth Amendment's ambit (Weiss & Gilbert, Watson, and Rodgers 1887, 18). In this analysis, to take away such liberty was to change utterly the form of government by subjecting the individual to illegitimate paternal control (44). The attorneys for the State of Pennsylvania responded to this argument by brushing aside the question of the specific content of liberty rather than engaging in a discussion on these grounds. They claimed that the liberty at stake was more a matter of convenience than of a necessary limit on government (Wintersteen and MacVeagh 1887, 18). In their analysis, the protected liberties under the Fourteenth Amendment did not include commercial accommodations by the state, but this limit was obvious enough for them not to warrant analysis.

This pattern occurred in judicial discussions as well. Judges focused on the nature of liberty itself, not spending much time addressing the implicitly male subject of the guarantee of liberty. Courts on both the federal and state levels disagreed about the significance of definitions; courts that voted to strike down legislation endorsed specific descriptions of broad guarantees of liberty, and those that upheld such legislation did not address the definition of liberty. The debate described above between the attorneys in *Powell v. Pennsylvania* resulted in a victory for regulation with little discussion of liberty's meaning (127 U.S. 678, 686 (1888)). In contrast, in 1896 an Ohio federal district court struck down a law barring contracts signed by railroad employees absolving railroads of any responsibility for personal injuries. In doing so, the court found many different violations of the Fourteenth Amendment, including infringements of the guarantees of both due process and equal protection. In this analysis, the inappropriate law acted to deprive the employees not only of liberty, but also "of the right to exercise the privileges of manhood 'without due process of law'" (*Shaver v. Pennsylvania Co.*, 71 F. 931, 939 (N.D. Ohio 1896)). In this case, the court made explicit the manly nature of contracting for one's labor, a gendered reading left implicit in most other discussions.

The state courts carried the analysis and debate further. By this time, there was a settled understanding that the right to be free of governmental interference was not absolute and depended upon the governing body and the protections it provided for its citizens. Washington's high court explained the relative nature of rights, asserting a startlingly modern conception of liberty as created and bounded by governmental protections (*Ah Lim v. Territory*, 1 Wash. 156, 165 (1890)). The court here described liberty as a natural right but suggested that its contours and limits were dependent on the actions of the state; the protection provided by the government in this view gave substance to the abstract guarantee of liberty (165). This view suggested that the relationship between expressions of natural liberty and the government's capacity to limit such liberty was malleable, a concept that would gain some currency in the future.

The significance of this debate was that liberty became a central focus in the analysis. In these cases, the legal community was struggling to define liberty and its reach in a broad sense, but members of the community were learning the lesson that a successful argument regarding liberty's scope could win a case or firmly ground an opinion. In the later years, arguments regarding the breadth of the due process guarantee would become more specific and factual, leaving behind the more abstract and formalistic arguments, but at bottom, they would continue to center around the question of liberty's scope and operation for protected individuals.

The state courts mostly agreed that liberty included to some degree the freedom to choose one's employment, though women often would not experience an equivalent degree of freedom during this period. The connection between labor and liberty was the engine that would drive the courts' willingness to strike down protective measures for the next five decades. In the early years, the main discussions addressed the nature of the relationship between labor and liberty through the constitutional protection of property in state and federal due process clauses. In doing so, they drew on existing understandings of liberty from the antebellum period as well as the influential formulations in Cooley's treatise, embedding these conceptions of liberty in the grounding interpretive case law of the Fourteenth Amendment.

In 1885, the New York Court of Appeals wrote the words that would form a popular basis for this concept in an opinion striking down a statute barring the production of cigars in tenement buildings. While the broad definition the jurists articulated was not new, their words would be the standard definition for later judges and lawyers. The justices defined liberty as "the right . . . of one to use his faculties in all lawful ways, to live and work where he will, to earn his livelihood in any lawful calling, and to pursue any lawful trade or avocation" (*In re Jacobs*, 107). Under this commercially based definition, unless a law was passed in accordance with the proper exercise of police power, "All laws . . . which limit one in his choice of trade or profession, or confine him to work or live in a specified locality . . . are infringements upon his fundamental rights of liberty" (107). Other courts began to rely on this concept to strike down protective labor legislation as interfering with the liberty of employees and employers to make labor contracts.[5] The definition implied that individuals' choices about work were fundamentally private in their nature and consequences and therefore that any attempt by the state to interfere in these choices was an illegitimate intrusion.

The Supreme Court endorsed this principle in 1877, declaring that employers had the liberty to determine the size of their workforces and that employees and employers were left to their own devices to set the wages and hours of labor (*U.S. v. Martin*, 94 U.S. 400 (1877)). (In this case, the principle supported a congressional statute, since Congress had exercised its authority as an employer to limit the hours of federal employees.) The case's outcome and reasoning relied on the Supreme Court's attempt to clarify the nature of the relationship between employer and employee; the two appeared in the Court's reasoning as abstract equivalent units exercising their bargaining power with each other independent of outside influences. The emphasis here was on the autonomy of employer and employee, regardless of the employer's public status. In this case the presentation of the employer and employee as sharing a relationship insulated from outside pressures resulted in the validation of protection for workers, but the more common result would be invalidation, as the employer would not be the state.

The New York and California courts followed suit in 1888 and 1896 respectively concerning employees, claiming that laborers had the freedom under the Fourteenth Amendment to choose lawful work and pursue it (*People v. Gillson*, 109 N.Y. 389, 398 (1888); *Ex parte Jentzsch*, 112 Cal. 468, 473 (1896)). The California court, striking down a Sunday clo-

---

5. For instance, the Missouri Supreme Court explained in 1892, "Liberty we have seen includes the right to acquire property and that means and includes the right to make and enforce contracts" (*State v. Loomis*, 115 Mo. 307, 319 (1892)).

sure law for barber shops, explained that in the United States, the individual "is treated as a person of responsible judgment, not as a child in his nonage, and is left free to work out his destiny as impulse, education, training, heredity, and environment direct him" (473). This understanding emphasized the individual's private capacity to choose the employment best suited for him and to negotiate for himself the best deal for his labor. It also emphasized the crucial distinction between adult workers and child laborers, which would ground the future successes of reforming interests in convincing the courts to uphold child labor legislation on the state level (Novkov 1997).

The legal community understood labor to be related both to liberty and to property. Thus in 1893 the Illinois Supreme Court, ruling unconstitutional a statute providing for weekly payment to workers in the mining industry, explicitly linked property, labor, and liberty through the right to contract. The justices explained: "The property which each one has in his own labor is the common heritage, and . . . the liberty to enter into contracts by which labor may be employed in such way as the laborer shall deem most beneficial . . . is necessarily included in the constitutional guaranty" (*Braceville Coal Co. v. People*, 147 Ill. 66, 71 (1893)). The court saw labor as something owned by the worker that he or she exchanged for money through the labor market. Labor was thus a form of private property and a commodity about which the employer and employee had the right to bargain freely.[6]

Attorneys debated the scope of property just as they debated liberty's reach under the due process clause. Attorneys seeking to persuade courts to rule in favor of state statutes framed property narrowly (Wintersteen and MacVeagh 1887, 18), while their opponents embraced broad definitions (Goudy 1876, 513). The arguments largely followed the same lines as the discussions of liberty, with those opposing legis-

---

6. American courts' protection of property predated the Fourteenth Amendment in the states. The Fifth Amendment's due process clause simply reiterated a principle that was already firmly fixed in the legal system prior to the adoption of the Constitution. The state courts produced a thorough discussion of property's role during the early period. As early as 1856, the New York Court of Appeals ruled that the prosecution of a Buffalo tavern owner under the state's prohibition law interfered with his property interest and liberty to secure his livelihood (*Wynehamer v. People*, 13 N.Y. 378 (1856)). In 1858, a Vermont court struck down a law that established a specific agent to purchase alcohol for a town as violating due process (*Atkins & Co. v. Town of Randolph*, 31 Vt. 227 (1858)). This attitude was heightened during the period of negotiation with the entrance of the specific textual guarantee of the Fourteenth Amendment's due process clause.

lation engaging in lengthy explanatory efforts, while those who supported state statutes gave this question short shrift.

Courts also worked to address the scope of property, generally agreeing that it went beyond physical objects owned by individuals. This understanding also emphasized that property included one's labor and one's right to dispose of it. Courts relied on this connection with regard to cigar manufacturers (*In re Jacobs*, 105), steelworkers (*Godcharles & Co. v. Wigeman*, 113 Penn. 431, 436 (1886)), miners (*State v. Goodwill*, 33 W. Va. 179, 183 (1889), overturned by *State v. Peel Splint Coal*) unionized workers in manufacturing industries (*State v. Julow*, 129 Mo. 163, 173 (1895)), and barbers (*Eden v. People*, 1109). In all of these cases, the courts held that various protective statutes infringed upon the workers' property rights by depriving them of the opportunity to contract freely with their employers.

Some courts nevertheless recognized limits on property rights. Even the *Jacobs* court, which struck down a New York measure barring cigar manufacturing in tenements, acknowledged that under police power "the use of property may be regulated so as to interfere, to some extent, . . . with [its enjoyment]; and in cases of great emergency. . . , property may be taken or destroyed . . . without . . . due process of law" (*In re Jacobs*, 108). Discussions of the precise limits on the right to hold property would soon dominate analyses of due process as more cases worked their way up through the state courts.

Several courts asserted that the Fourteenth Amendment's guarantees of protection for liberty and property merged in the right to contract, a relationship that would become an intensive node of conflict in the next period. The Illinois high court defined the right to contract as both a liberty and property right in 1892 (*Frorer v. People*, 181). The Ohio high court refined this explanation, claiming that the property aspect of the right to contract was related to the fact that property was acquired and protected through contracts (*Palmer v. Crawford & Tingle*, 55 Ohio 423, 440 (1896)). In many courts' reasoning, because the existence of property relied upon the right to make contracts, the right to make contracts itself was protected under the Fourteenth Amendment even more directly than in the Constitution's admonition that the right to make contracts could not be impaired (*Commonwealth v. Perry*, 155 Mass. 117, 121 (1891)). Since labor was considered a form of property, it was directly linked to the right to make contracts. Thus, as the Illinois Supreme Court ruled more than ten years before *Lochner*, decisions about wages and hours rested within the right to contract, and interferences with this right in the form of statutory protection for workers deprived them of both liberty and property (*Braceville Coal*, 75). These connections would play a large role in the discussions within the legal community after the turn of the century.

The right to contract, though, was not unlimited or unchallenged. The West Virginia Supreme Court acknowledged the legislature's authority to regulate contracts in many ways. "The power of the legislature to declare the nature and effect of contracts, validating some, and invalidating or entirely prohibiting others, has never been questioned" (*State v. Peel Splint Coal*, 822–23). Some judges understood contracts as creations of the state, since only the backing of the state's coercive power made them enforceable; therefore, the state had the authority to control them in order to protect itself or the public.

While the early courts disagreed on many aspects of the right to contract, they did agree that definite limits existed upon the right to contract, limits that related to individuals' impact upon the rest of society. The right to contract had emerged as a private right held by both employers and employees; it could be limited to the extent that its exercise had public consequences. In its early formulation, both the employer and the employee appeared as abstract entities engaging in arm's length bargains with each other. Their actual status and relationship regarding each other was not a central part of the inquiry. The abstract parties to the labor contract were, however, assumed to be formally equal, which meant that they were assumed to be male. In the wake of the abolition of chattel slavery, contract was transformed from a generalized voluntary political submission to a concrete representation of the freedoms enjoyed by citizens of the reforged republic (Stanley 1998, 59). One who exercised liberty of contract was no longer merely a "not slave" but instead was an affirmatively free agent with the masculine authority to control the direction of his life.

Later, a node of conflict would emerge over questions of how the right to contract could be limited, whether the legislatures or the courts were the appropriate arbiters of public interest, and what kinds of facts would warrant regulation. In the early years, however, the legal community worked to understand the nature of the right to contract and its relationship with liberty in the new jurisprudential landscape of the Fourteenth Amendment. Here as with direct considerations of liberty, the right itself took center stage, as the implicitly male subject of the guarantee required little analysis. The legal community learned quickly that successful framings of the right to contract could support their arguments effectively and thus began to focus on this issue. When gendered divisions emerged between the cases after the turn of the century, the right to contract in the context of substantive due process would itself become explicitly gendered.

Cases Involving Women's Protective Labor Legislation

At this point, cases involving legislation pertaining explicitly to women had not yet fully emerged as their own category. For most members of the legal community, the differences between men and women were obvious enough not to require much commentary or analysis. As discussed above, some lawyers tried to argue that women had the same liberty as men to engage in the profession of their choice (Carpenter 1871; Lockwood 1894), but these claims were largely ignored by the Supreme Court. The early era provided two possible models for dealing with women's legislation. The first was considering these cases as separate categories, as many courts appeared to do with the cases involving ordinances preventing women from serving alcohol. This line of reasoning paralleled the logic in the cases involving women's entry into the professions—while men had the right, perhaps even the duty, to make contracts for wages and support themselves through employment, women's work was more properly understood as occurring at the sufferance of the state. The second model was to analyze them within the same framework and using the same terms used to address general protective labor legislation, as the Massachusetts and Illinois courts chose to do.

Arguments regarding liberty played minor roles in such cases as *Maguire, Hayes, Foster, Bergman,* and *Considine,* all of which addressed women's capacity to serve alcohol or work in bars; except for *Maguire,* which focused on California's equal rights amendment, the main discussions in these cases centered around the state's authority to limit through licensing the vice and immoral behavior associated with alcohol *(In re Maguire; Ex parte Hayes; Foster v. Police Commissioners; Bergman v. Cleveland; In re Considine).* While this agenda certainly tied into the beliefs of some women's groups involved in the drive for temperance (Tyrrell 1991), the cases themselves attracted little notice within the legal community or outside of it.

In addition to the cases involving women's capacity to serve alcohol, courts also began to hear the first cases dealing with women's positions in the workplace. Most of the arguments were relatively undeveloped, and as with general legislation, the judges and attorneys spent much of their time arguing about the scope of the due process and equal protection clauses and the impact of the privileges or immunities clause. Few of the early cases included in-depth analyses of women's rights as they compared to those of men, and neither judges nor attorneys had yet begun to question the scope of women's liberty and whether it might differ from that of men.

The two state cases that were to have large impacts immediately, *Commonwealth v. Hamilton Manufacturing* and *Ritchie v. People,* were both notable in their failure to discuss the issues in gendered terms. The *Hamilton Manufacturing* case addressed the claim of Mary Shirley, an employee of the Hamilton Manufacturing Company, a textile factory; Massachusetts had recently enacted a law limiting women's work for manufacturing concerns to ten hours per day and sixty hours per week. Shirley sued, wanting to work longer hours in order to increase her wages. The Massachusetts high court, upholding the limitation, responded to the charge that the statute infringed on workers' due process rights using language that could have come from any of the early cases involving hours limitations. The court wrote that "the law does not limit her right to labor as many hours per day or per week as she may desire; it does not in terms forbid her laboring in any particular business or occupation . . . ; it merely prohibits her being employed continuously in the same service more than a certain number of hours per day or week" (*Commonwealth v. Hamilton Mfg. Co.,* 120 Mass. 383, 384–85 (1876)). The court thus reasoned that the law in question simply limited Shirley's ability to work excessive hours for the Hamilton Manufacturing Company; it did not prevent her from taking another job, and it did not curtail her choice of employment in any substantial way. The court's focus throughout the case was on the law and its compliance with the guarantee of liberty, not on the affected workers. The opinion's author took no particular notice of the fact that the workers Massachusetts sought to protect were exclusively women. The opinion was thus notable more for result (upholding the law in question) than for its reasoning.

Similarly, the Illinois Supreme Court in deciding the *Ritchie* case did not take much notice of the female workers affected by the statute at issue in the case. The Illinois legislature had passed legislation limiting women's work in factories and shops to eight hours per day, but the Illinois high court found that the statute violated both the Illinois and federal constitutions. The court read the right to contract broadly, in keeping with its earlier decisions in such cases as *Frorer* and *Braceville Coal Co.* The reasoning in *Ritchie* was phrased in general terms. The court explained some of the possible limits on the right to make contracts, declaring that this right was "subject to limitations growing out of the duties which the individual owes to society, to the public or to the government" (*Ritchie v. People*, 155 Ill. 98 (1895)). These limits, however, were no more than the general laundry list of public concerns involving the proper use of property and rules regarding property imbued with public significance. The court explicitly denied that gender should make a difference in the outcome or the reasoning of the case. Later attorneys and courts would argue fiercely over the extent to which the right to contract could legitimately be burdened by the public's interest in women's reproductive capacity. At this point, though, these concerns had not yet explicitly emerged. The legal community in the early period did not analyze liberty extensively in cases involving legislation affecting women, instead simply adopting the analyses that were developing with regard to general legislation.

The early cases regarding women were nonetheless significant in their analyses of due process. A small body of cases largely supported the idea that women's employment choices and opportunities could be legitimately limited. The establishment of this rule implied the validity of considering statutes affecting women to be a distinct analytical category, whatever route the differentiation might take. While the analyses in these rulings did not depend explicitly on gender, the fact that the statutes in question addressed women rather than men had an impact on the attorneys and courts involved in the cases, since the outcomes in the cases often favored regulation. It would not take those supporting protective measures long to recognize that such laws could often survive constitutional review in this particular context. The two groups of cases provided alternative models for framing arguments in favor of protecting women. The licensing cases suggested a more limited range for liberty against the background of state-based authority in light of the state's ability to control and manage certain types of workplaces or professions, while the cases involving limits on women's hours hinted through their outcomes that something particular about women themselves grounded the rulings that addressed their liberty of contract.

The Role of Police Power

In the years following the passage of the Fourteenth Amendment, the legal community struggled over the role of police power as a valid counterbalance to protected freedoms. This conception of police power dated from the antebellum era but gained refinement and currency in Cooley's popular treatises on constitutional limitations. Attorneys in several leading cases agreed that states could properly use their police powers to limit liberty and property without running afoul of the due process clause, and they embraced the general formulation that measures properly taken in the public interest constituted appropriate exercises of police power. The disagreements arose from attempts to delineate the boundaries between public and private by identifying the proper scope of public intervention. These debates were significant in that they highlighted two elements of police power as the points on which outcomes would ride: the public or private nature of regulations, and the impact of regulations on public health. The existence of both of these elements as key points of contention contributed to the rise of a separate analysis for women's legislation in later years. This section first discusses the emergence of both of these issues and then shows how they played out in the cases involving women's legislation.

The Nature of Regulations under Police Power

During the period of generalized balancing, attorneys opened a lengthy conversation concerning the limits of public regulation in light of the new constitutional order. In these years, as with due process, the discussion was initially formalistic and somewhat vague, focusing on broad questions regarding the differentiation between regulations that touched some public interest and those that were purely private in their natures. Likewise, the legal community began in these years to sketch the broad outlines of certain categories of regulations that could be considered appropriate exercises of police power. Depending on whether they were defending or attacking protective measures, attorneys and judges then sought to show that the regulations they addressed either fit or did not fit within these categories.

The briefs filed in *Munn v. Illinois* provide good examples of how these arguments were structured. The State of Illinois argued that the law in question was a public measure rather than a limit on the control of private property. The attorney general then claimed that the law could restrict particular uses of property that affected the public interest without running afoul of constitutional protections (Idsall 1876, 633). In *Munn*, the attorneys for Illinois identified the public element in question as the fact that the public had to deal with the operators of grain elevators. Because of this necessity, the state had the authority to regulate prices (among other things) (Idsall 1876, 644). Their formulation sought to legitimize the regulation of any business with which the public (left undefined) had to deal. The Supreme Court largely accepted this principle when it decided *Munn* in favor of the state.

Attorneys opposing regulation pushed for a strong differentiation between public and private and the establishment and maintenance of an unregulated private sphere. In their analyses, the proper exercise of the state's authority extended only to situations that directly affected the general public beyond the relationship between employer and employee, which they viewed as fundamentally private. Later, as gender became an organizing factor in these cases, the relationship between public interest and private liberty in due process analysis would be debated with increasing intensity, but in the early years it was simply another point to address. The attorney for operators of grain elevators in Illinois argued that their business was entirely private and thus should be immune from state legislation (Goudy 1876, 483). Another attorney for an affected grain elevator operator excoriated the legislature's incursions into privacy, claiming that the Illinois statute endangered the entire framework of private rights and property (Jewett 1876a, 554). Their goal was to define all of the operations of businesses not connected to the state as broadly private and thus as protected from intervention by the state. In doing so, they encouraged the courts to tackle the question of where to draw the line between public and private.

As with liberty, those opposing regulations spent much time and effort delineating the precise scope and definition of private rights, while those who sought to uphold regulations brushed aside these claims. By the time of the briefs in *Munn* and subsequent state court rulings, the question of whether a regulation truly addressed the public interest had become a significant point of contention. The attorneys for the grain elevator operators argued along these lines, claiming that their business was no more public than that of a farmer, tailor, or merchant and thus that the state was using its authority illegitimately (Goudy 1876, 520).

Both federal and state courts attempted to develop coherent principles regarding the limits of police power, but this question was destined to remain troublesome for several decades to come. The Supreme Court claimed in *Munn v. Illinois* that the legislature could not intervene into purely private affairs but reserved the state's authority to regulate in the interest of preventing injury to other citizens (89 U.S. 113, 124 (1876)). The Court went on to explain that the regulation in question was aimed at just this interest, constituting a valid limit on what was in effect a public business (124). The statute in question set a maximum price that grain elevator operators could charge for storage; its purpose was to prevent grain prices from rising too high. Because the price of grain had a direct impact on most citizens through its relationship to food prices, regulations that directly affected the price of grain were in the public's interest.

The case provoked a dissent from Justice Field joined by Justice Strong, who claimed that the regulations inappropriately subverted private property by subjecting it to public intervention (*Munn v. Illinois*, 145). They advocated instead a fairly narrow view of police power: "The State in such cases exercises no greater right than an individual may exercise over the use of his own property when leased or loaned to others" (145). The objections of these justices centered around their fear that the standard the Court had established violated the clear division between public and private established in earlier cases addressing other doctrinal areas (McCurdy 1975). These justices hoped to close off extensive litigation over the extent of the public's interest in particular privately owned and operated businesses and feared that the ruling in *Munn* would precipitate more lawsuits to clarify the boundary between public and private. The only justification for broader regulatory authority was in industries in which the companies had allowed regulation as an implicit condition on their capacity to do business, which would bring the relationship between the company and the state within the realm of contract (Kens 1997, 164–66). Their fears that the Court would provoke further litigation were justified.

The *Munn* Court ruled in favor of establishing a legislative price ceiling because it saw the grain business as having a close connection to the public interest. "Property does become clothed with a public interest when used in a manner to make it of public consequence, and affect the community at large. When, therefore, one devotes his property to a use in which the public has an interest, he, in effect, grants to the public an interest in that use, and must submit to be controlled by the public for the common good" (*Munn v. Illinois*, 126). Property, even if private, could be tinged sufficiently with public interest to warrant state regulation.[7] Generally, the federal courts' analysis of police power centered on the nature of the property in question. In doing so, these judges advanced the analysis of public and private, enhancing the attractiveness of such arguments to future litigators. This settled the ground for conflict as the nature of public and private but did not settle the empirical claims regarding public and private. On the contrary, empirical claims about what constituted private employment relationships and public interest would be the center of successor inquiries.

On the state-court level, judges began a lengthy discussion over the role of police power in the new constitutional structure. Like the federal judges, state judges were concerned about the public nature of police regulations, but the courts also crafted different explanations for how police power could be appropriately exercised. In these cases, the first hints of balancing began to emerge. If the advocates for regulation could convince the courts that the law in question had a particularly weighty public purpose, the law might survive constitutional scrutiny.

The legal community disputed precisely what the states could do under police power. The Illinois Supreme Court ruled that police power could be exercised only to prevent individuals from using their liberty or property to put at risk the liberty or property of other individuals (*Frorer v. People*, 185). Courts' most frequent framing of this power was that it could be exercised to protect or promote health,

---

7. In 1896, the Supreme Court upheld a law that prohibited railroads from running on the Sabbath under a similar justification. The majority ruled that Sunday laws provided absolute rest and quiet for the entire populace and thus that the law served an overriding public interest for all citizens (*Hennington v. Georgia*, 163 U.S. 299, 308 (1896)).

peace, morals, and general welfare for the people of a state or munici-
pality.[8] In such instances, police power would override liberty.

Other judges, though, balanced police power less favorably
against the dictates of due process, claiming that it could not overcome
constitutionally guaranteed rights to liberty and property. In New
York, judges cited constitutional rights as significant limiting factors.
The *Jacobs* court claimed that regardless of how broadly one understood police power, its authority could not exceed that of the Constitution; thus police power remained forever subordinate to constitutional
rights (*In re Jacobs*, 108). This disagreement ultimately would lead to a
conflict over whether liberty or police power had central precedence.
At this point, the legal community had not yet confronted or even
framed the ultimate question about the extent to which a state, acting
legitimately in the public interest, could limit liberty interests squarely
within the center of the due process guarantee.

On both the state and federal level, the nature of police power
quickly became a significant focus and area of conflict. The federal
courts largely considered whether particular regulations were public or
private in their nature, and the state courts disagreed over the proper
balance between liberty and police power. On both levels, the judges
engaged in generalized balancing, pitting the abstract legal categories
against each other and assessing their relative weights. Both of these
issues encouraged the development of finer-grained categories for
analysis. Future attorneys would seek to develop analytical categories
that could be generally accepted as public or private and then argue
that particular categories warranted heavier weight on the police
power or liberty side. This development would contribute to the rise of
gendered analyses in the later years.

---

8. This guarantee took similar forms in cases decided in different jurisdictions. The
Supreme Court declared that the police power allowed the states "to prescribe regulations to promote the health, peace, morals, education, and good order of the people, and
to legislate so as to increase the industries of the State, develop its resources, and add to
its wealth and prosperity" (*Barbier v. Connolly*, 31). In 1888, the Court declared that the
police power allowed for the protection of "the public health and the public morals"
(*Powell v. Pennsylvania*, 683), while the Illinois Supreme Court referred to "the comfort,
welfare or safety of society" (*Ritchie v. People*, 110). California relied on "the preservation
of health and the promotion of good morals" (*Ex parte Jentzsch*, 472) to uphold a Sunday
closure law for barbers, while Illinois decided the same issue the opposite way, asking
"How . . . is the health, the comfort, safety, or welfare of society to be injuriously affected
by keeping open a barber shop on Sunday?" (*Eden v. People*, 1110).

The State's Authority to Protect the Public Health

Even opponents of regulation conceded that the state had the authority to exercise its police power to protect the public health. Protection of health would become a central node of conflict as the focus shifted from general legislation to laws aimed at women. Protecting health was a public goal that could enable the state to breach the privacy of the relationship between employer and employee. In the early years, it provided a significant justification for upholding statutes that arguably infringed upon liberties guaranteed by the due process clause. An example was New York's ruling that upheld a law prohibiting barbers from working on Sundays; the court claimed that such laws protected the health of the barbers by forcing them to rest during one day of the week (*People v. Havnor*, 204).

What constituted a health regulation, though, began to be debated sharply, and no consensus on this issue would emerge until much later. The regulation of health as a node of conflict would emerge most fully during the periods between 1911 and 1923 in cases involving women's legislation, but courts laid the groundwork for this disagreement early. While the *Havnor* court was upholding a Sunday regulation for barbers, Illinois's supreme court, which was quite hostile to protective labor legislation during this period, was striking down a limit on hours for miners. The Illinois court explained that protection for mine workers was unnecessary and paternalistic (*Millett v. People*, 117 Ill. 294, 302–3 (1886)). In the court's view, such regulations did not protect the individual miner's safety or property, nor did they have any effect outside of the mining industry, unlike the statute at issue in *Munn v. Illinois* (*Millett v. People*, 302–3). Thus the court ruled that the relationship between limiting the hours of a miner's labor and that miner's safety was not sufficiently close to constitute a valid protection of health (303). This understanding of mine work would not ultimately prevail in the Supreme Court; twelve years later, the justices would uphold a similar protective statute in *Holden v. Hardy*.

Judges often pointed out that a purported police regulation had to have a definite relationship to one of the appropriate categories of police power; public health was the most obvious and accessible category because it was both concrete and flexible. The *Jacobs* court articulated a standard for analysis in ruling that a prohibition on the manufacture of cigars in tenements was not closely enough linked to health to be valid. The court explained, "When a health law is challenged in the courts . . . on the ground that it arbitrarily interferes with personal liberty . . . without due process of law, the courts must be able to see that it has . . . some relation to the public health . . . and that it is appropriate and adapted to that end" (*In re Jacobs,* 115).[9] The same court later extended this reasoning with regard to the invasion of property rights, claiming that such rights could not be circumscribed unless the regulation had a clear relationship to the protection of health (*People v. Gillson,* 404). The Missouri Supreme Court also endorsed this proposition in 1895 (*State v. Julow,* 177). During the next period of more specific balancing, this reasoning would come into conflict with the justifications of those in favor of tipping the scales more heavily toward the legislature's judgments about health risks.

Some members of the legal community thus began to rely on risks to health as a means of intervening in the relationship between employer and employee. The claim that a statute implicated public health was easiest to make if this claim could be extended to individuals outside of the employment relationship. Nonetheless, some attorneys and judges began to claim that even a direct threat to the health of certain employees was of sufficient concern to the public to warrant legislative action. Even in such cases as *Jacobs,* the court left the door open for a legislative claim that public health was directly enough related to the legislative purpose to warrant a finding that the legislation was valid. As claims based on public health thus began to emerge as a means to validate legislation, attorneys supporting protective labor legislation were encouraged to make them more frequently.

The question of health regulations ultimately provided the basis on which analysis of women's statutes split off from analysis of gender-neutral statutes aimed at men's work. In these early cases, little hint of this coming division may be found. Nonetheless, members of the legal community were quick to recognize the power of arguments based in

---

9. This view was endorsed again by the Court of Appeals in 1893 in *People v. Rosenberg,* in which the court claimed, "The legislature, under the police power, may certainly regulate or even prohibit the carrying on of any business in such manner and in such place as to become dangerous or detrimental to the health, morals or good order of the community. But how far it can go in the direction of absolutely prohibiting such business when it is neither alleged nor claimed that in its nature or from the manner in which it is conducted it injuriously affects the community, is quite another question" (*People v. Rosenberg,* 138 N.Y. 410, 415–16 (1893)).

concern for public health, and advocates for protective legislation began to cast their work in these terms. The next period would be marked by the dramatic failure of this tactic with regard to laws regulating male labor and its simultaneous success with laws limiting women's work.

Police Power in Cases Involving Women's Protective Labor Legislation

In this early period, the legal community was beginning to identify the principal areas for disagreement and interpretation with regard to police power and its exercise. Members of the community considered its general scope and its application as it balanced against liberty. For the most part, they envisioned a narrow scope for police power and gradually came to settle on a default position that broad regulation of industry would not be permitted unless special justifications were available. The early cases addressing the appropriate scope for police power in the context of women's protective labor legislation were not influential outside of their particular subject matter and largely followed the general analysis, though with different outcomes.

As discussed above, the main category of cases involving women were challenges to laws prohibiting women from serving alcohol or working in bars. In their analysis of police power, however, these opinions largely addressed the state's capacity to regulate businesses requiring licenses in the interest of morality rather than health. While regulation to preserve health and public safety would become a central focus for interpretive concern after the turn of the century, in these years the cases largely turned on the licensing authority. In most courts' views, the state's capacity to grant licenses gave it the power to limit the activities performed under the auspices of these licenses.

In all five of the cases in which such statutes were upheld, when addressing police power, the courts referred explicitly to the state's capacity to regulate the sale and distribution of alcohol on moral grounds *(Blair v. Kilpatrick,* 40 Ind. 312 (1873); *Ex parte Hayes; Foster v. Police Commissioners,* 492; *Bergman v. Cleveland,* 653; *In re Considine).* Nonetheless, this reasoning was somewhat beside the main point for the courts hearing these cases; while morality was a factor in the state's ability to limit the sale of alcohol through a licensing procedure, morality was not the direct reason for allowing states to limit women's work. All of the challenges were framed more as questions of whether the owners or operators of the bars could be legitimately prevented from having female employees, and the judges found dispositive the fact that the state had the authority to license the sale and distribution of liquor. Since the state could regulate heavily or even prohibit the sale of liquor, the judges writing after *Maguire* found no constitutional bar to the specific regulations enacted by the states and municipalities in question (Indiana in *Blair*, San Francisco in *Hayes* and *Foster*, Cleveland in *Bergman*, and Spokane in *Considine*). As discussed above, the opinion in *Maguire* focused on California's constitutional protection for equal rights for women; this 1881 case did not engage in a full review of police power and its application.

Nonetheless, the early opinions regarding laws affecting women hinted at a trend that was soon to become pronounced, that of allowing regulation when certain vulnerable groups of individuals were involved. A few state courts had taken this path in deciding to uphold regulation of the mining industry based on the risks inherent in mining, but with the women's cases the courts would ultimately focus on the laborers' natural vulnerabilities rather than on the inherent risk of the labor. The early judges did not incorporate extensive analyses of the potential threats to particular workers. In upholding statutes prohibiting women from serving alcohol in bars, state and federal courts ruled that the state's regulatory authority included the power to keep women out of such positions, but did not spend much time considering women's special risks. Likewise, the New York Court of Appeals upheld a statute barring children from performing on stage, claiming simply that when the police power was extended "manifestly to secure, or to tend to the comfort, prosperity, or protection of the community, no constitutional guaranty is violated" (*People v. Ewer*, 141 N.Y. 129, 132 (1894)). (The child performer in *Ewer* was a seven-year-old female ballet dancer, and the appealing party was her mother, who had been convicted of violating the statute.) While both of these cases involved regulations for "special" classes of persons (women and children), the grounds upon which the statutes were upheld did not depend directly upon the state's capacity to ensure special protection for women or children. This distinction would emerge later when gender would become a central focus for debate and controversy.

As mentioned above, *Commonwealth v. Hamilton Manufacturing* was to become a key opinion within and outside of the legal community among those who wished to validate protective labor legislation. What, then, did the Massachusetts high court have to say about police power in 1876? Like its contemporaries, the opinion did not rely on the fact that the workers involved were female in order to justify the regulation in question. Rather, the court framed its reasoning in general terms, claiming that the statute constituted a straightforward exercise of police power for the purpose of preserving health. The statute, by this reasoning, "merely provides that in an employment, which the Legislature has evidently deemed to some extent dangerous to health, no person shall be engaged in labor more than ten hours a day or sixty hours a week" (*Commonwealth v. Hamilton Mfg.*, 384). The court saw nothing problematic in this type of regulation, claiming that it could easily be upheld: "There can be no doubt that such legislation may be maintained either as a health or police regulation, if it were necessary to resort to either of those sources for power. This principle has been so frequently recognized in this Commonwealth that reference to the decisions is unnecessary" (384). The obvious and conclusive nature of this reasoning was belied by the large number of courts that did not find it to be a good reason to allow general protective legislation in their jurisdictions. The *Ritchie* case, which reached the opposite conclusion in Illinois in 1895, dealt with police power even more summarily.

The few cases regarding protective labor legislation for women thus mostly followed the general pattern. Either the courts recognized the legislation regarding women as falling within an exceptional category, like the liquor laws, or their analyses used the same language and reasoning that had applied in other cases involving limitations on hours. While the outcomes were more favorable for protective legislation than in cases addressing nongendered limitations, the legal community by and large did not yet appear to perceive such cases as warranting an independent analysis. Regulations of women's work in bars fell under the general rules regarding states' abilities to govern licensed businesses, a power that the courts readily acknowledged. As far as limitations on the hours of labor were concerned, high courts in both Massachusetts and Illinois saw no need to reason differently about police power simply because the workers involved in the cases happened to be female.

Generalized Balancing and the Framing of the Emerging Conflict

The early part of the period of negotiation established the themes that would loom large in the later decades. Many of the issues that attorneys and courts raised in this period would become full-fledged nodes of conflict in the next several years as disputes over protective labor legislation intensified and lay activists began to join the discussion. The early years saw three important developments that would shape future litigation. First, the due process clause (along with equal protection) became the central focus of Fourteenth Amendment analysis. Second, police power emerged as a significant counterweight to the Fourteenth Amendment's guarantee of liberty, leading judges and attorneys to balance these concepts against each other in generalized and abstract terms. Finally, as the courts began to consider and decide cases involving women within the emergent general framework balancing Fourteenth Amendment rights and police power, they fell into a pattern of upholding such laws for women.

The period of generalized balancing saw the establishment of a set of legal principles that would provide the ground for future conflict. The legal community had settled on the idea that questions about the legitimacy of protective labor legislation were fundamentally about the tension between specific rights of due process for the individual and the government's authority to regulate. Following the existing definitions and uses of the due process, the legal community rooted the Fourteenth Amendment's guarantees in antebellum conceptions of liberty and property and reiterated the conceptual contours of liberty in relation to liberty of contract. Regarding police power, the Supreme Court took the important step of acknowledging that the state could regulate industry as long as it did so in the public interest.

In the first few decades after the Fourteenth Amendment's ratification, legal thinkers struggled to define its significance in reshaping the constitutional framework. This process produced a situation in which the initial battle lines were sketched out over protective labor legislation that primarily affected but did not explicitly aim at men, a battle that would be joined by many state courts and legislatures in the years to come. Courts and attorneys did establish some degree of consensus on some important matters. The privileges or immunities clause was closed off as a ground for the protection of substantive rights under the

Constitution, and the legal community acknowledged that some form of a right to liberty was protected under the Constitution. In contrast, while the due process clause had begun to emerge as a home for substantive rights not specifically enumerated in the text of the Constitution, the scope and nature of these rights were yet to be determined. Courts now faced the question of what substantive rights were guaranteed under these clauses and how far the Constitution went to protect them. They also began to grapple with the framing of the right to contract and its reach.

Many judges and attorneys had sought to settle the boundaries between public and private by interpreting the relationship between employers and employees as fundamentally private and protected from intervention by the state. Other judges and attorneys, however, used the concepts of public health and public interest to justify state intervention in the relationship. Neither perspective, however, was able to establish a coherent and stable dividing line between public and private. Some theorists have framed the problem of what is public as a question of access, inclusiveness, and ultimately full citizenship; in this sense, the difficulty of conceiving of what was *public* makes sense in light of the open tensions over precisely these issues of access and citizenship during the same period (Allen 1988; Green 1999).

This analytical dispute set the stage for the next round of inquiries, which would focus on the precise nature of particular public interventions. Before the turn of the century most members of the legal community appeared to accept the private nature of the relationship between employers and employees, though the licensing cases were an important exception. The link between privacy and freedom of contract was necessary in light of the antebellum conceptions of liberty addressed above, but the new ascendancy of the free-market labor system raised the stakes significantly. Generalized balancing between categories was necessary. The analytical categories themselves had unexamined contents that were in the process of shifting in response to industrialization and the expansion of the regulatory impulse, but in these years, such questions could be temporarily deferred in favor of drawing formalistic lines between private and public, between liberty and police power, and between the due process clause's guaranteed rights and the state's authority to regulate.

Initially, attorneys and judges concentrated much of their analysis of due process on general protective labor legislation aimed toward male workers. In doing so, they considered the extent to which the vital connection among liberty, labor, and property precluded extensive state legislation protecting the employee from striking an exploitative bargain. They implicitly envisioned the holder of the guarantee of liberty as male. The universal subject from traditional liberal philosophy was unquestionably male, and women were not understood as independent individuals in this framework; as a result, the idealized subject in a classical contractual relationship was a male subject (Horton 1999). As the legal community struggled to work through the scope of liberty and its relationship to the right to contract, its members also began to deal with this right's application in cases involving limits on women in the workplace, but they did not address women's divergence from the unspoken standard of the rational wage laborer who was implicitly male.

The early cases addressing the relationship between due process and women's protective labor legislation relied on the same frameworks set up to analyze general protective labor legislation. In these cases, attorneys opposing regulations argued explicitly or implicitly that women had the same liberty rights as men and thus that their ability to make contracts should be treated the same way that men's ability was treated. Those supporting regulations argued that the states had the authority to control licensed industries in the interest of moral issues, outweighing any liberty or property interest individual employers (and secondarily their female employees) had. In these cases, neither the courts nor the attorneys considered carefully the precise scope of women's liberty, nor did they question the extent to which it paralleled that of men.

Police power had also begun to emerge as an important interpretive focus. Before the passage of the Fourteenth Amendment, the extent of its reach had rarely been substantially questioned. Now courts had to determine the extent to which police power was subordinate to constitutional rights. In addressing general legislation, the state courts in particular were hostile to an expansive interpretation of police power, viewing it instead as a limited authority to intervene in particularly compelling circumstances. As with liberty, the legal community imagined an implicitly male worker who would be subject to the states' attempts to limit employment contracts for the public good.

With regard to legislation aiming to protect women, few were interested in the early years in articulating an analysis of police power that acknowledged that women were the subjects of protection. The frameworks for analysis for both general and gendered legislation were the same; only the outcomes really differed. The analyses of both due process generally and police power more specifically referred implicitly to male labor and male laborers, and the legal community used these existing categories to reason about cases involving female labor and female workers. Nonetheless, embedded in the existing system was the belief that while women were not full citizens in their abilities to exercise the rights and privileges of men, they were legitimate objects for the exercise of public policy for the benefit of state and society writ large (Nackenoff 1999). Activists and attorneys would soon begin to recognize the strategic importance of the differences in the outcomes in these cases and link these differences to women's differential citizenship.

The last years of formalism's dominance witnessed the initial discussion of the Fourteenth Amendment largely in terms of abstract legal categories. At the same time, two new phenomena began to have an impact on the nature of legal reasoning: the rise of legal realism and the emergence of a class of litigants who were not connected with the government but engaged in planned litigation to forward their social interests. As interested observers began to notice the unmistakable successes that manufacturing interests were having in the courts, the stage was set for more even-handed battles in the coming years.

In the years around the turn of the century, the discourse concerning protective labor legislation became more sophisticated and more contentious. Now that the legal community had established a role for the Fourteenth Amendment, conflicts arose within and outside of the legal community over the precise shape and scope of that role. In the next decades, this broad framework would produce unexpected complications for the legal system. For the remainder of the 1890s and into the early 1900s, state legislatures would continue to pass and employers to contest protective labor legislation in terms of the conflict between police power and liberty, adding more nuance to the framework. A key development in these battles was about to occur, however. Increasingly, the legal system would come to question the nature of the labor being regulated, a trend established on the Supreme Court level in *Holden v. Hardy* in the late 1890s and confirmed in *Lochner v. New York* in 1905. As the next chapter shows, this development would also have significant implications for women's protective labor legislation, allowing for the initiation of an analytical split between cases involving women and those involving men.

Chapter 3

Specific Balancing: Regulating Labor and Laborers

The years between 1898 and 1910 witnessed significant developments in the battle over protective labor legislation both with regard to general measures and with regard to laws aimed at protecting female workers. The initial debates of the late 1900s now developed into full-scale nodes of conflict with the increased participation and interest of lay activists who promoted protective measures for both men and women. In these years, the cases involving laws regulating women's work emerged as their own category, encouraging the legal community to analyze them separately. This separation mirrored a division between the cases in terms of their outcomes as well; while general legislation was frequently invalidated, laws regulating female workers became firmly established as a class of legislation that could be expected to fare well in the courts even in the face of extreme judicial hostility to Progressive legislative impulses. The legal community, now more sensitized to address the facts in the cases, began to engage in specific balancing between liberty and police power. The legal community calibrated the weights in the balance more carefully by determining the appropriate category for the case in question and by considering the relationship between the factual circumstances of the case and the appropriate balance between private right and public interest based on the type of labor or laborer being regulated.

The initial years of the period of negotiation had set the terms of the debate regarding substantive due process. By the 1890s, the legal community had agreed that, in the context of protective labor legislation, arguments about due process were arguments about the proper balance between liberty and police power. The abstract debates over categories had encouraged the legal community to focus its interpretive energy around liberty on the one hand and police power on the other. The second phase of the period of negotiation began with the Supreme Court's ruling in *Holden v. Hardy* in 1898 and continued through 1910. The main development in these years was that the analysis of cases involving women's protective labor legislation began to diverge from that in the cases involving general legislation as the legal community engaged in specific, rather than generalized, balancing.

With respect to liberty, the early period saw the legal community ultimately agreeing that liberty was freedom from governmental intervention and that liberty included protection for the right to make labor contracts. Furthermore, the legal community had largely agreed to frame the relationship between employer and employee as private, explicitly adopting the laissez-faire model of the employment relationship. These settled questions, however, gave rise to new problems for the next generation of attorneys and judges. What kinds of labor were private and therefore not subject to regulation? What kinds implicated the public interest sufficiently to warrant regulation?

Discussions of police power had also generated some consensus. The legal community largely endorsed police power's antebellum definition as involving the legitimate exercise of the state's authority in the public interest. Public health had been confirmed as a permissible justification for the state's regulatory activities. Some judges sought to establish clear analytical boundaries between public and private but could not do so in a way that would determine the outcome in all cases. Nonetheless, as with liberty, agreement about the exercise of police power ushered in new conflicts. The major question that the legal community (and increasingly individuals outside of it) would address was the empirical determination of what constituted a valid public interest. The need for empirical determinations pushed members of the legal community away from abstract legal categories and toward more specific discussions of how the tensions were to balance against each other.

This period differed from the years of generalized balancing in two significant ways. First, the initial battles over the legal categories were largely resolved. In part this closure occurred because the legal community had settled on the abstract parameters of the categories of liberty and police power, but also the rise of legal realism pushed the debates away from purely formalistic concerns and toward a deeper factual inquiry. Second, additional parties were beginning to influence the development of doctrine. As chapter 2 explained, before the turn of the century, the principal lay actors were business interests who sought to expand the scope of conflict into the judicial arena where they could obtain better results. Now Progressive reformers increasingly began to join the fray through direct participation in litigation as they discovered that the advances they had gained legislatively were often nullified by the courts. Since the manufacturers had largely been battling attorneys general in the early years, they had not initially had to face many opponents who had strong ideological as well as institutional interests in the policies they were defending. All of this began to change after the turn of the century.

The years of specific balancing saw further ferment over industrialization. The wage-labor sector of the market continued to grow; between 1880 and 1900, workers in industry jumped from 30 percent of gainful workers to 37 percent, and by 1920, they composed 44 percent of gainful workers (Dawley 1991, 34). Unions maintained their confrontational stance toward employers, pushing for the eight-hour work day, seniority, standardized wages, and an end to the practice of laying off employees during slack times in individual industries (Dawley 1991, 81–82). Periodic strikes in particular industries continued to disrupt manufacturing throughout these years; the meat-packing plants in Chicago suffered major upheavals in 1904, as did the collar-starching business in Troy (Dawley 1991, 83–85; Foner 1979, 305–7). Union members' political orientations ranged from the mainstream and somewhat conservative positions of trade unions such as bakers' unions (Bewig 1994) to radical socialist forces such as the Industrial Workers of the World (IWW), which actively worked to improve conditions in industries dominated by women, people of color, and immigrants (Foner 1979, 392–412). At the same time, industries such as meat packing and manufacturing began to move to systems of highly divided and mechanized labor, promoting higher levels of efficiency and opening up the possibility for increasing profits through increasing the speed of the machines (Dawley 1991, 81).

The unions' struggles for recognition and reform received assistance from the rising tide of Progressivism. A growing class of social workers began to investigate the American workplace, studying the lives that workers led and seeking to inform the public about their findings (Skocpol 1992, 321–72). Photographers such as Lewis Hine and Jacob Riis documented the lives of working-class immigrants, as reformers such as the Goldmark sisters Pauline and Josephine, Margaret Dreier of Brooklyn, and Ellen Henrotin of Chicago wrote pamphlets and monographs detailing and criticizing the worst abuses of the wage-labor system (Foner 1979, 303–12). Advocates of reform encouraged consumers not to purchase goods produced through sweated labor, and state legislatures began to pass laws that reflected the arguments of elite and middle-class reformers in favor of limits on employers' ability to negotiate and enforce exploitative bargains with their employees (Skocpol 1992, 321–72). Many of these advocates were laypersons, but some were attorneys who could simultaneously promote reform in the political arena and develop legal categories that would advance their causes jurisprudentially.

The rights of women also moved up on the American social agenda. Feminist activism expanded beyond the struggle for the vote, and some individual feminists embraced a broad agenda for reform in the workplace and in relations between women and men (Dawley 1991, 88–90). Many of these reformers promoted protective labor legislation for women, some because they believed that this was the best means to promote such legislation for all workers eventually, and others because they believed that women needed special protection (Dawley 1991, 88–90). One of the most significant reforming organizations was the National Consumers' League, a mostly middle-class group founded in 1899 that sought to improve industrial standards for working people and focused particularly on working women (Skocpol 1992, 189). Florence Kelley, reformer, socialist, and veteran of the settlement house movement, was instrumental in developing the Consumers' League and establishing chapters in several states (Foner 1979, 292). At the same time, local reformers were working to enroll women in trade unions, and in the early 1900s, the National Women's Trade Union League was established to further this process (Foner 1979, 290–99). Many of these individuals and organizations scrutinized litigation concerning protective legislation and became players in shaping the developing legal landscape. Their influence on litigation was a new phenomenon in U.S. legal circles; even though previous organizations of reformers (in particular abolitionists) had sought to influence public policy, they had not launched systematic campaigns in the courts (Epp 1999).

The National Women's Trade Union League at first strongly advocated the unionization of women's work, adopting at its national convention in 1907 a resolution that all workers be organized into trade unions (Foner 1979, 304). After *Muller v. Oregon* provided a dramatic example of how limits on hours could successfully be mandated through legislation, however, some members of the NWTUL urged for a shift in its strategy to engage in an enthusiastic campaign for protective labor legislation. So encouraged was Florence Kelley by this development that she began pushing for legislation even above further labor organization, believing that seeking legislation would be a more efficient and effective strategy (Foner 1979, 304).

In these years the pool of influential actors within the legal arena expanded. In the early period, manufacturing interests were the main nongovernmental players in litigation over protective labor legislation. By 1910, a new group of actors—advocates for reform—had turned to the courts to defend the legislative victories they had achieved. The growth of their participation was the result of several simultaneous, loosely related developments.

First, the legal profession itself had begun to change. Legal realism was beginning to take hold beyond academic circles; its increasing popularity coincided with the continuing professionalization of the social sciences. While individual attorneys had interests in progressive reform before the turn of the century, they were relatively unorganized. The rise and popularization of law schools led to the training of a new generation of lawyers who were well versed in sociological jurisprudence and legal realism and who saw the law as a tool for making policy (Epp 1999, 269).

Second, organizations promoting reform recognized that they would have to counter the manufacturing interests' arguments in the same forum if they were to achieve their goals. All of their successes in persuading state legislatures to pass regulations mandating maximum hours of labor and other restrictions would change nothing as long as manufacturers could persuade the largely conservative bench that such provisions were invalid. The situation was growing increasingly urgent, as state court after state court struck down protective measures. In particular the National Consumers' League stepped in to take the lead, promoting research that would lead to the development of a powerful legal tool: the richly detailed factual brief.

In 1908, the Supreme Court's public endorsement in an opinion of a new kind of legal brief confirmed a radical change in modes of legal argument. The so-called Brandeis brief was the fruit of the rising influence of legal realism; it operated by presenting a concrete mass of empirical data to support its reasoning rather than relying upon conventional arguments from precedent or deductive logic (Ducat 1995, 528). At this point, the lines between activists and attorneys began to blur. The brief, filed under the name of noted Progressive attorney Louis Brandeis, cited detailed information about the risks of overwork to women in order to persuade the Court to uphold a statute limiting female laundry workers to ten hours of labor per day. Josephine Goldmark, Brandeis's largely unacknowledged coauthor of the famous amicus brief in *Muller v. Oregon,* was a member of the National Consumers' League and had been involved in research on the ill effects of excessive labor on both genders (Goldmark 1912). Florence Kelley was also a key figure in assisting with the development of legal arguments in such closely watched cases as *Muller* (Foner 1979, 304).

Coming from the battles of the late nineteenth century, the legal community recognized that the most significant Fourteenth Amendment guarantees were the equal protection clause and the due process clause. These provisions, along with their state parallels, limited the states' ability to intervene in citizens' lives. In the future, a justification for intervention under the police power would have to be present. During the years between 1898 and 1910, the legal community struggled to articulate the nature of the required justifications in specific terms. As the struggle progressed, a split developed between cases addressing general protective labor legislation and legislation limiting women's terms and conditions of labor. As the arguments became more specific and factually rooted, the frameworks established in the initial debates now began to ground a mostly unguided and unintentional separation between the analysis of general legislation and laws regarding women's terms and conditions of labor.

The Universe of Cases between 1898 and 1910

In the years between the Supreme Court's decision in *Holden v. Hardy* and the Court's decision in *Adkins v. Children's Hospital,* the legitimacy of protective labor legislation was a major question for both state and federal courts. This chapter addresses litigation producing reported opinions in the highest courts of the states and the federal courts between 1898 and 1910. In these years, the courts reported ten cases on the federal level and forty state cases that directly addressed protective labor legislation.

In the entire group of opinions, courts tended to uphold protective labor legislation more frequently than they struck it down (64 percent and 36 percent, respectively). Looking at the cases divided by whether they dealt with statutes specifically limiting women's work, however, provides a modified picture. Fifty-nine percent of the general cases upheld protective legislation, as compared to over 80 percent of the cases dealing with protective legislation specifically aimed at women.

The most famous case of this time was undoubtedly *Lochner v. New York;* of the ten cases heard on the federal level, three struck down protective labor legislation using the kind of reasoning made famous (or infamous) by the Court in *Lochner.* As *Lochner* demonstrated and the outcomes of other cases confirm, plenty of controversy still existed with regard to cases involving general legislation. Two of the federal cases— *Muller v. Oregon* and *Cronin v. Adams*—upheld legislation directed at women. The remaining eight cases upheld various general regulations in the workplace.

This period was busy for the state courts. They participated actively in the process of judicial intervention into progressive legislation; often their decisions prefigured those of the federal courts. While not as hostile to protective labor legislation as they had been previously, state courts still struck down over 37 percent of the legislation they considered in reported opinions. As on the federal level, though, the difference gender makes is evident. State courts were much more willing to uphold laws affecting women. Once the nine cases involving explicitly gender-based legislation are placed in their own category, the rate of striking down general protective laws in reported opinions rises to 42 percent. The state courts were particularly amenable to upholding such legislation for women: only two cases resulted in the reversal of a protective measure for women.

TABLE 7. Decisions in All Cases Involving Protective Labor Legislation, 1898–1910

	Upheld Protective Legislation	Struck Down Protective Legislation	Total
All cases	32 (64%)	18 (36%)	50
General cases	23 (59%)	16 (41%)	39
Cases involving women	9 (82%)	2 (18%)	11

As discussed below, the courts were particularly willing to uphold protective labor legislation directed at minors. Eight of the twenty-five state cases that upheld protective legislation between 1898 and 1910 dealt with laws designed to limit children's participation in the workforce. When the cases involving such legislation are excluded on the state level, the difference between courts' attitudes toward general protective legislation and protective legislation for women increases. Here, while the rate of striking down statutes relating to women remains at only 22 percent, the rate of striking down protective legislative enactments not related to women reaches 58 percent.

The courts thus upheld women's protective legislation more frequently than general protective legislation on the whole, at the federal level, and at the state level. When cases involving children are excluded from the analysis, the strongest contrast emerges, with courts being notably hostile to most forms of general protective legislation while strongly supporting such legislation for women. While this record may not suggest an overwhelming ideological opposition to the progressive agenda, it does show that legislative attempts to regulate the terms and conditions of men's labor ran into significant roadblocks in both state and federal courts.[1]

TABLE 8.   Decisions in State Cases Involving Protective Labor Legislation, 1898–1910

	Upheld Protective Legislation	Struck Down Protective Legislation	Total
All cases	25 (62.5%)	15 (37.5%)	40
General cases	18 (58%)	13 (42%)	31
Cases involving women	7 (78%)	2 (22%)	9

1. Phillips argues that the *Lochner*-era courts were not particularly hostile to progressive measures, claiming that the Supreme Court's record reveals that it did not view substantive due process as "a potent weapon against government regulation of social and economic matters" (Phillips 1998, 461). While he properly rejects the simple political explanation that the justices were voting on the basis of their support for capitalist interests, he does not recognize the significance of the categories of regulations that the Court and other courts on the federal and state levels upheld and invalidated. He argues that the Supreme Court justices' rulings can be explained as support for the principle of economic liberty; the analysis to come will show, however, that liberty was a problematic category for judges on both state and federal levels.

Brief Overview of Nodes and Litigation in the
Period of Specific Balancing

The major nodes of conflict during this period arose directly from the emerging battles of the previous decades. The discussions about liberty, property, and police power now grew into full-fledged nodes of conflict, provoking responses in jurisdictions throughout the country both within and outside of the legal community. As the central legal questions became increasingly tightly defined, attention began to shift toward developing and expressing the facts as effectively as possible. This led the legal community to engage in specific, rather than generalized, balancing, weighing the factual content of the legal categories established in the previous period. Attorneys during these years began to work more directly with reformers, using the information reformers had developed to advance their legal arguments.

Attention centered around liberty and its role but in a more concrete fashion. The legal community further articulated the relationship between the due process clause and liberty of contract in a grounded way, analyzing closely the guarantees of liberty and property. The earlier period had confirmed the default normative position that regulation was improper; special justifications relating to the type of work or worker were needed to justify statutory protection. At this point, interpretations of liberty in cases involving women's protective legislation began to diverge from interpretations in cases addressing general legislation. With regard to general protective labor legislation, the legal community focused on liberty and its role, continuing to rely upon a conception of a male subject of the guarantee of liberty. As reformers began to convince courts that protective legislation for women was constitutionally acceptable, the terms of the discussion about liberty in

TABLE 9. Decisions in State Cases, Excluding Cases Dealing with Children, Involving Protective Labor Legislation, 1898–1910

	Upheld Protective Legislation	Struck Down Protective Legislation	Total
All cases	17 (53%)	15 (47%)	32
General cases	10 (43%)	13 (57%)	23
Cases involving women	7 (78%)	2 (22%)	9

cases involving legislation regulating women's work began to shift. This gradually led to a situation in which liberty did not play a central role in such cases. The focus of these cases instead became women's relationship to liberty and labor, leading to an increasing emphasis on police power.

Police power, particularly in its relationship to public interest, also provoked major conflicts during these years, and analyses of its impact on general and female-oriented protective labor legislation began to diverge. With regard to general legislation, the legal community sought to delimit the scope of the state's authority to regulate, focusing on the meaning of health regulations. The touchstone was whether the regulation of a particular industry could validly be said to serve the public's interest. In these battles, the arguments were largely disputes about how the facts of particular cases fit into the legal frameworks developed in the earlier period. In light of the decisions made before the turn of the century, legislatures and attorneys seeking to validate limits knew that they could not prevail without a strong argument regarding police power; increasingly they argued that the statutes they supported addressed a particular kind of labor that was subject to regulation.

In cases involving women, the legal community began to consider the laborer in question more closely than the nature of the labor. Questions about police power quickly became questions about the state's capacity to regulate in favor of morality and in favor of women's reproductive health. Drawing on the outcomes and interpretive frameworks of the earlier cases, reformers worked to develop factual information linking regulation to the goals of the state, and some members of the legal community began to use this information to achieve their goal of legitimating state policies limiting women's work. The maternalist conception of the primacy of women's civic duties of childbearing and child rearing proved powerful as a justification for regulating feminine labor in the interest of the state as a whole. Throughout, arguments increasingly came to address the state's authority to limit women because of their status as problematic laborers due to their physical and emotional characteristics, thereby relying on and reinforcing the implicit male norm of the worker. These shifts in the focal points for analysis and the success of women's protective labor legislation would lead to the next stage of development in which considerations of statutes addressing women's work would come to the forefront of the debate.

The period of specific balancing began with the Supreme Court's ruling in *Holden v. Hardy* that a limitation that Utah placed on the number of hours per day that miners could work was a permissible exercise of the state's police powers. This case confirmed that the arguments about protective labor legislation were shifting toward the analysis of the types of labor and laborers who could be regulated, contrasting with the earlier abstract arguments about the scope and nature of the constitutional guarantees of due process and equal protection. Between 1898 and 1910, cases involving general limits on the terms and conditions of labor dominated the landscape of litigation. While some notable cases involved legislation intended to benefit women, the discussions within the legal community focused on general legislation. The idea that women's legislation required additional independent analysis slowly began to take hold during these years as the reasoning in cases involving general legislation evolved, resulting ultimately in the shift of emphasis from general legislation to women's legislation that would prevail after 1910.

With regard to general legislation, the Supreme Court's ruling in *Lochner* sculpted the federal landscape, confirming the basic thrust of many earlier state cases. Decided in 1905, this case invalidated New York's law limiting bakers to sixty-hour work weeks (*Lochner v. New York*, 198 U.S. 45 (1905)). Nonetheless during these years, the Supreme Court upheld a similar limitation on miners in *Holden v. Hardy* in 1898 (169 U.S. 366); a law preventing barbers from working on Sundays (*Petit v. Minnesota*, 177 U.S. 164 (1900)); a congressional statute limiting federal construction workers to eight hours of labor per day (*Ellis v. U.S.*, 206 U.S. 246 (1906)); and an Arkansas statute regulating payment of employees in the mining industry (*McLean v. Arkansas*, 211 U.S. 539 (1909)). While *Lochner* is at the center of many other analyses of the period, in this interpretation it comes in the middle of the period and simply confirmed argumentative trends that were taking place among attorneys and in the state courts.

On the state level, the two issues that produced the largest numbers of reported opinions were statutes limiting child labor and laws seeking to limit the hours of work of public employees. In many ways, the child labor cases were separate from the main discussion about workers' rights and police power; reformers largely succeeded in persuading the state legislatures and courts that the state had a special protective relationship with children, warranting the validation of strict limits on children's paid work (Zelizer 1985). The eight reported cases dealing with child labor upheld protective measures in seven states, sharply distinguishing the issues at stake from the question of general labor legislation.[2]

The laws addressing states' or municipalities' capacity to limit the labor of their public employees were more controversial; such laws were struck down in Illinois (*Fiske v. People*, 188 Ill. 206 (1900)), Washington (*Seattle v. Smyth*, 22 Wash. 327 (1900)), Ohio (*City of Cleveland v. Clements Bros. Constr. Co.*, 67 Ohio 197 (1902)), and Indiana (*Street v. Varney Electrical Supply Co.*, 160 Ind. 338 (1903)), but one was upheld in Kansas (*State v. Atkin*, 67 P. 519 (Kan. 1902)). The New York Court of Appeals struck down such a statute in *People v. Orange County Road Constr. Co.* (175 N.Y. 84 (1903)) but upheld a later statute after a state constitutional amendment (*People v. Metz*, 193 N.Y. 148 (1908)). Other cases dealt with limits in particular industries and attempts by state legislatures to protect union activities; these measures met with varying degrees of success.

The number of cases concerning women's protective labor legislation began to grow between 1898 and 1910. Before and immediately after the turn of the century, courts continued to hear cases concerning limitations on women's ability to serve alcohol. Before the end of 1904, the highest courts in New Jersey and Colorado and the Supreme Court had joined earlier courts, agreeing that such statutes and ordinances did not limit women's liberties inappropriately (*City of Hoboken v. Goodman*, 68 N.J. 217 (1902); *Adams v. Cronin*, 29 Colo. 488 (1902); *Cronin v. Adams*, 192 U.S. 109 (1904)). After the turn of the century, however, various versions of eight-hour and ten-hour limits on women's hours of labor in different industries began to work their way through the state courts. In 1902, Washington's highest court upheld such a statute (*State v. Buchanan*, 29 Wash. 603), as did Nebraska in 1903 (*Wenham v. State*, 65 Neb. 394), Oregon in 1906 (*State v. Muller*, 48 Ore. 252), and Michigan and Illinois in 1910 (*Withey v. Bloem*, 128 N.W. 913 (Mich.); *W. C. Ritchie*

---

2. The states were California (*Ex parte Weber*, 149 Cal. 392 (1906); *Ex parte Spencer*, 149 Cal. 396 (1906)), Oregon (*State v. Shorey*, 86 P. 881 (Ore. 1906)), Minnesota (*Fitzgerald v. International Flax Twine Co.*, 104 Minn. 138 (1908)), New Jersey (*Bryant v. Skillman Hardware Co.*, 76 N.J. 45 (1908)), New York (*People v. Taylor*, 192 N.Y. 398 (1908)), Indiana (*Inland Steel Co. v. Yedinak*, 87 N.E. 229 (Ind. 1909)), and Louisiana (*State v. Rose*, 51 So. 496 (La. 1910)). This book will not address the battles over child labor legislation, which were distinctive enough to warrant their own independent investigation (Novkov 1997).

& Co. v. Wayman, 244 Ill. 509). New York's Court of Appeals and Colorado's supreme court both struck down statutes of this nature during the same period (*People v. Williams*, 189 N.Y. 131 (1907); *Burcher v. People*, 41 Colo. 495 (1907)).

The Supreme Court also ruled on this question, upholding Oregon's statute in *Muller v. Oregon* in 1908 (208 U.S. 416). *Muller* was significant for confirming the emerging consensus in favor of allowing limitations on women's work. It was noted for the attorneys' effective use in their briefs of the information that interested reformers had been collecting over the last decade regarding women's labor.

The Guarantee of Liberty under the Due Process Clause

During these years, the scope of liberty became a full-fledged node of conflict as the legal community struggled to settle on an understanding of freedom of contract. Lawyers and judges balanced the relationship between liberty and the state's authority to benefit the side of the argument they were supporting, assuming an implicitly male subject of the guarantee of liberty. Those opposing legislation argued that protective measures interfered with the workers' rights to control their own destiny, seeking to tap into the myth of the rugged individual; those in favor of regulation looked instead to the state's authority to limit liberty for the public good. In either case, the specific factual descriptions of the characteristics of the labor and the relationship between employer and employee weighted the preferred side of the balance. Discussions of liberty focused on liberty itself and not extensively on the subject of the guarantee of liberty. With regard to legislation designed to limit women's labor, some lawyers and judges, responding to the growing tide of interest from activists, began to consider women's relationship to liberty independently, questioning the way that female laborers experienced and exercised liberty. As many members of the legal community integrated more pointed factual and scientific information into the analysis, the factual contours of liberty began to emerge with respect to general legislation, contributing to the emergence of a more explicitly male-based standard. In litigation over women's protective measures liberty was also important, but conflicts over its nature with respect to female workers focused growing attention on women's roles as a special category of laborers.

General Protective Labor Legislation and the
Regulation of Male Liberty

If one were simply to read the cases decided in the era of specific balancing, one might get the idea that for the first time the courts were working out the proper role of liberty for a worker within the context of laissez-faire economic commitments. The judges' opinions lay out in painstaking detail the grounded nature of the liberties exercised by employees within a paradigm that assumed a formally equal relationship between employer and employee at the bargaining table. Scholarly opinion, however, nearly universally agrees that the laissez-faire philosophy was firmly rooted by this time, having begun to influence discussions of regulation long before the turn of the century. Why, then, were judges wasting their interpretive energy to explain what almost all institutional players knew and understood about the American economy and the employment relationship?

By the turn of the century, labor agitation and the rise of social scientific investigations combined to challenge the settled belief in the wage contract as a garden-variety contract (Stanley 1998, 97). The discussions of general protective labor legislation thus had to shift from a broad focus on the scope of due process to a more specific consideration of liberty as exercised by male employees and employers as supporters of protection brought these specific claims to the table. Simultaneously, the legal community's debates centered increasingly around the type of labor that male workers were performing, a topic taken up in the next section. This section will outline the growing interest in the precise nature of liberty that male workers held and then explain how this related to the right to contract established in the earlier years. Both of these developments contributed to the sense that the laissez-faire model was under attack; judges' extensive explanations of it in the cases settled its centrality as a paradigm but simultaneously identified the doctrinal places where it could be pressed or even transformed.

The central conflict with respect to general legislation was about how the kind of labor workers performed might provide a reason for allowing protection. At this time, contract freedom was the hallmark of equality and citizenship, and hirelings marked themselves as full members of society and full participants in self ownership by exercising this freedom (Stanley 1998). Attorneys general and others arguing in favor of protective measures had to overcome an increasingly strong conception of workers' individual liberty. As in almost all other areas of law, the implicit subject of guarantees of rights was male, and this implicit gendering of the subjects of law was nothing new. The significant development in these years was the centering of liberty, which led to disputes over liberty's nature. This focus directly on liberty contributed to a more explicit discussion of the right in masculine terms. With a strong conception of liberty at the center of interpretations of due process, the side of the balance holding police power would have to be weighted heavily with specific content to have any effect. In these years, this configuration of the balance with respect to general legislation led to disputes' addressing the nature of the labor that the workers performed.

The trends regarding general protective legislation appeared in the briefs in *Atkin v. Kansas* (191 U.S. 207 (1904)). The attorney for the aggrieved contractor, in seeking to persuade the Court to strike down Kansas's eight-hour law for public workers, focused on liberty and its nature (Pollock 1903, 28). The State of Kansas responded first by asserting that the legislation was in fact an exercise of the employer's liberty, since the state ultimately paid for the labor of public employees even if these employees were subcontractees (Coleman and Loomis 1903, 10). Furthermore, the vaunted liberty of the employees in question masked the employees' dependence upon the contractors (Coleman and Loomis 1903, 18). In their view, this imbalance between employers and employees made construing the relationship between them as one of equality and liberty on both sides disingenuous at best (18). The debate in this case and others thus turned on the nature of specifically grounded understandings of liberty.

Attorneys, in addition to struggling to explain the application of liberty, laid out extensive explanations of the right to contract and its relationship to liberty and property. In these readings, liberty emerged as a fundamentally private and highly individualistic right in line with the accepted understanding of contract as the hallmark of freedom (Stanley 1998). In *Holden v. Hardy* the attorney arguing against the constitutionality of the statute limiting miners to eight hours of work per day refined existing definitions of the right to contract. He identified it as a private right held by employees and broke it down into component elements (Wilson 1897, 46). All of these elements focused on the type of labor in question, maintaining the unquestioned status of the employee as the subject of the guarantee of liberty. The subjects of the guarantee in this view were competent and capable, rational individuals who could protect their own interests effectively in the marketplace (Wilson 1897, 10–11).

As in the period of generalized balancing, many judges relied on liberty, but now, those who struck down legislation grounded their opinions in the claim that liberty was a central right in the political system. The courts that relied on liberty to strike down legislation did not need to define it, because they were relying on familiar conceptions that resonated culturally and politically. This general sense of liberty, as Stanley and Horton have shown, incorporated masculine qualities. The judges employing it envisioned rationally self-interested workers who could negotiate with their employers, assuming that these workers would be male. The earlier debate over liberty's scope had settled the idea that for such individuals, liberty unquestioningly encompassed the right to make contracts, particularly those relating to employment. As addressed later, however, this right was not as extensive for some citizens as it was for others. Concern with the right to contract provided a major source for courts' authority to overturn the legislatures' judgments: of the eighteen cases that invalidated protective legislation, nine relied on the liberty to contract as the central ground for doing so, and one other referred to liberty of contract as one ground. Many judges articulated as the basic point of the liberty of contract that people were to be permitted to work at their chosen occupations without undue interference by the state. In doing so, they provided factual content for the earlier conceptualizations of liberty's role in the constitutional system and its links to freedom of contract. In doing so, they underlined the inherently private nature of the right but unconsciously provoked more controversy over its empirical application. The factual battles in the years of specific balancing would reveal the divergent conceptions of privacy and private right that were taking hold in the political and legal culture at the time.

The federal courts, in such cases as *Holden v. Hardy* and *Atkin v. Kansas* in which legislation was upheld, did not engage in extensive discussions of liberty's scope and operation. These cases focused much more on police power, as explained below. *Lochner*, however, featured a strong reliance on liberty of contract as the main ground for invalidating New York's limitation on bakers' hours. In that case, the Supreme Court explained the liberty of contract as a dual freedom applying equally to employee and employer. Dismissing New York's claims that the law was intended to serve the public interest, the Court construed the question in the case simply as a conflict between "the power of the State to legislate or the right of the individual to liberty of person and freedom of contract" (57). The Court understood this right as "the right of the individual to enter into those contracts in relation to labor which may seem to him appropriate or necessary for the support of himself or his family" (57). The individual in question was the rational, capable, implicitly male individual described in other briefs and court cases opposing protective legislation. Here, as in other cases, the Court echoed the analytical frameworks that state courts were using at the time.

Given the importance of liberty of contract, it is unsurprising that the state courts explored the vital connection between liberty and property extensively. As with direct analyses of liberty, the implicit holder of property was male; even though the latter part of the last century had seen a wave of reforms enhancing women's property rights, judges' language revealed that they were thinking of a male worker as the bearer of property rights in his labor. For state judges seeking to invalidate protective legislation, liberty was not merely the exercise of freedom in some vague sense but the individual's right to control and manage property; it was thus part of the self-ownership that marked meaningful autonomy in the liberal state (Horton 1999). Like liberty, the guarantee of protection for property assumed a male subject. Even judges who supported protective legislation often tended to see liberty's connection to property in this way; a dissenting judge in a New York opinion striking down a state statute regulating bulk sales explained that "Constitutional liberty is the right to act without restraint upon person or property, except such as is necessary or expedient for the general advantage of the public" (*Wright v. Hart*, 182 N.Y. 330, 354 (1905) (Vann, J., dissenting)). With liberty linked explicitly to property, liberty became a private right held by particular rational economic actors and manipulated for their advantage.

Some courts linked the right to contract to management of one's affairs in one's own interests. Illinois's high court, for instance, struck down a closed shop law on this basis (*O'Brien v. People*, 216 Ill. 354, 372 (1905)). All laborers and employees held this authority, and many courts viewed its disturbance for illegitimate reasons as interference with the contracting individuals' civil rights (372). In this view, the right to contract was a private liberty held by both employee and employer, though the courts did not often recognize concrete limitations on the liberty of working class employees (at least with regard to general legislation). Again, the subject of these guarantees was implicitly male, behaving as the stereotypical rational economic actor. As such, the subject himself needed little or no direct analysis.

In considering general legislation, many courts viewed the liberty of contract as a central expression of individuality and self-ownership (Stanley 1998). The Wisconsin Supreme Court claimed that "hardly any of the personal civil rights is higher than that of free will in forming and continuing the relation of master and servant" (*State v. Kreutzberg*, 114 Wisc. 530, 546 (1902)). Work, and the right to agree privately on the conditions and hours of work, were the hallmarks of male individual expression and development. Following on earlier developments, most courts considering general legislation also focused on the guarantee of property rights, believing that labor was a subspecies of property.[3] The relationship between labor and property, as addressed below, was dynamic with regard to the individual whom the courts viewed as the subject of the due process guarantee.

Thus, in analyses of general legislation, liberty was confirmed as a fundamentally private right exercised by individuals who were implicitly male. Courts tended to focus on the guarantee of liberty, contributing to the rise of a node of conflict over its scope and relationship to labor. In particular, they considered how regulations of particular types of labor might interfere with this guarantee. Liberty was the individual's private capacity, free from meddling by the state, to make decisions for himself and to act upon these decisions. Liberty included the right to contract, but the right to contract also had a significant relationship to the right to hold property. The right to contract was both a liberty and a form of property; the property-based aspect of the right to contract further underlined its private nature, as interests in labor as property were not imbued with public significance. It was, in this interpretation, a private possession of the individual who held the requisite liberty to exercise it. The three concepts, then, were fundamentally linked, and all had deeply private elements to them. As debates centered on liberty itself, they did not address extensively the subject of the

---

3. See *In re Morgan*, 26 Colo. 415, 420 (1899); *Gillespie v. People*, 188 Ill. 176, 183 (1900).

guarantee.[4] Instead, the balancing depended upon the empirical categorization of the activities of laborers as either fundamentally private or as having public aspects.

Women as Laborers

While largely persuasive to the legal community, this was only part of the story. In addition to eliminating the possibility of relying on transformative class-based descriptions of the relationship between employers and employees, attorneys and judges focused increasingly in cases involving general legislation on the quality of liberty and the nature of the employment being limited. The implicit reliance on a male laborer as the paradigmatic subject of the guarantee led to discussions of protective labor legislation for women that emphasized (albeit unconsciously) their departure from the standard male liberty bearer. The legal community's lack of interest in men as subjects of the guarantee of liberty paralleled their pointed interest in women as subjects of the guarantee, because the nodes of conflict necessarily turned to what could be debated; women's problematic citizenship raised enough questions to enable the opening of a pressure point for litigants. This in turn encouraged the tendency for courts to consider the laborer rather than the labor in women's cases. As this section and the next will show, activists' focus on women as laborers contributed to the rise of independent analysis of women's liberty within the legal community.

As discussed above, in these years organizations seeking to improve the workplace for women were beginning to turn to legislation as a means to alleviate the difficulties working women faced. Feminists were working out alternative conceptions of feminine citizenship to acknowledge the civic dignity of citizens who had problematic rela-

---

4. William Forbath has argued convincingly that these moves on the part of the courts had an enormous impact on the history of the American labor movement. He shows that, while labor leaders criticized adverse decisions by the courts, they became trapped by adopting the legal and constitutional frameworks the courts established, thus giving up on a strongly class-based socialist critique of the nation's economic priorities (Forbath 1991, 135). These frameworks closed off possibilities for deep or structural change (Forbath 1991). The courts' refusals to consider alternative grounds for constitutionality, including freedom from wage slavery and freedom of association, emphasized their solid support for an understanding of employment contracts as fundamentally private entities. In Forbath's analysis, the courts' definition of labor as a creature of the private economic sphere and labor leaders' acquiescence through the adoption of voluntarist discourse was crucial in the courts' ability to shape and constrict labor reform (168).

tionships to voting and earning, the primary marks of full participation (Nackenoff 1999, 139). Such organizations as the National Consumers' League and the National Women's Trade Union League hoped that protective measures would enhance women's liberty by enabling women to make fairer bargains with their employers (Dawley 1991, 103). Despite the divisions that were emerging between the largely middle-class National Consumers' League and the more working class National Women's Trade Union League, both seemed to agree that abstract commitments to liberty were secondary to the concrete task of ensuring better conditions for women's labor. Maternalist ideology provided the easiest justification to ground protection for women; it was culturally and politically resonant and presented less of a threat to the industrial order than broad claims for class-based justice. This standpoint was logical, since in these years investment in gender-neutral liberty bore little connection to improving women's substantive citizenship rights in the wake of the jurisprudential limits established in the earlier years.

Large and more powerful unions such as the AFL which represented mostly male workers made few attempts to organize women, seeing such efforts as not likely to pay off (Hyman 1985, 23; Kessler-Harris 1985, 274–75). Believing that women would remain unorganized and that employers would then be able to use them to undercut wages, Gompers and other male labor leaders supported protective labor legislation for women while opposing it for men (Dawley 1991, 102). The main concern of the AFL was to promote better working conditions for men through collective bargaining, leading ultimately to a family wage that would keep women mostly out of the workplace and out of competition with men (Dawley 1991, 102).

As a result, the Progressive forces pushing for regulation of women's work spent little time discussing the nature of liberty generally, choosing instead to focus on women's need for protection. To the extent that women's liberty was discussed publicly among these circles, activists argued that protective legislation would enhance rather than diminish women's liberty by enabling them to bargain more effectively with their employers. Because the legal community had to rely on due process, its members could not ignore liberty's relationship with women's legislation. Those who supported such legislation thus developed an interpretation of liberty that focused on women's circumstances in the labor market. This tactic promoted a focus on the female laborers themselves rather than on an abstract definition of liberty, and the background reliance on maternalist conceptions of women's citizenship enabled supporters of such measures to avoid confrontations with the laissez-faire model of employment contracts.

Ultimately, analyses of public and private in general and women's cases began to diverge as well. While the central question with regard to general legislation was whether the type of labor was fundamentally private or if it was infused with public elements, the legal community debated the nature of women's liberty without assuming that their employment was private unless shown to have public elements. Instead, interpretive efforts came to center on women's relationship to the public sphere.

Women's Liberty as an Independent Legal Category

As women's protective labor legislation became an increasingly significant focal point in considerations of due process, the legal community began to debate about women's liberty. (At this point, the scope of this conflict remained largely within the legal community, though in subsequent years it would spill over into the feminist community.) Was it the same as the liberty protected by the due process clause for male workers, or were women different from men in ways that caused them to have divergent rights under due process provisions of the state and federal constitutions? Self-ownership was assumed for hireling men, but women's self-ownership and thus their capacity to dispose of their labor freely was more problematic (Horton 1999, 124). Most members of the legal community recognized that women's relationship with the state differed from the one existing between men and the state because of women's reproductive roles; this difference is the subject of the next section. The legal community disagreed, however, about the scope of liberty for women and the factors that could be construed as providing limits to it.

Attorneys in *Muller* challenging the validity of Oregon's limitation of female laundry workers to ten-hour work days claimed that protective labor legislation limited women's liberty in an illegitimate way. In their view, women had the same right to engage in the free formation of labor contracts as men. These attorneys ridiculed the state's arguments, asking "Upon what theory can the state become her guardian and interfere with her freedom of contract and the right of her employer to contract with her freely and voluntarily, as if she were a man?" (Fenton and Gilfry 1908, 16). In this understanding, women's rights were worthy of the same kind of respect and protection as the rights afforded to men for the simple reason that their rights were the same as men's (Fenton and Gilfry 1908, 27). The real risk, in these attorneys' argument, was that protective legislation would prove to be an additional burden with which women would have to contend, hindered as they already were by a long history of severely circumscribed liberty. As they queried, "Shall her hands be further tied by statutes ostensibly framed in her interests, but intended perhaps to limit and restrict her employment, and whether intended so or not, enlarging the field and opportunity of her competitor among men?" (Fenton and Gilfry 1974, 34). These arguments precisely paralleled the arguments made by attorneys seeking the invalidation of New York's limitation on the hours of bakers in the 1905 *Lochner* case (Field 1905, 653–717).

The brief prepared by Josephine Goldmark and Louis Brandeis benefited from the connections that both had within the Progressive community. Goldmark's lengthy association with the National Consumers' League enabled her to amass an impressive array of data showing the risks of overwork and fatigue and the particular negative effects these conditions had for women. Brandeis helped to incorporate these factual claims into the legal argument that these severe impacts on women's health had a sufficient connection to the public interest to warrant the upholding of statutes that would ameliorate the risks to women. Their connections with the NCL and its aims made it unsurprising that maternalist conceptions of women's proper roles grounded their reasoning. In the voluminous brief, however, Goldmark and Brandeis spent little time discussing liberty or the need to balance public interest against women's rights to make labor contracts with their employers. Instead, they focused on women as laborers. As the next section on police power demonstrates, drawing a tight connection between risks to women's health and the general public interest seemed to be sufficient both for their argument and for the satisfaction of the Supreme Court.

Interestingly, the courts and attorneys who began to develop these legal and factual analyses often relied on *Hamilton Manufacturing* to support their reasoning, despite the fact that this case did not provide any independent analysis of the role of gender. As explained above, in *Hamilton Manufacturing* the Massachusetts Supreme Court simply claimed that the state had the authority to regulate the hours of work as part of its police power, spending little time explaining and defending the extent of this authority (*Commonwealth v. Hamilton Mfg. Co.*, 120 Mass. 383 (1876)). Cases decided near the turn of the century tended to justify the legal legitimacy of protective labor legislation for women by citing *Hamilton Manufacturing* to support the enactment of gendered legislation and *Holden v. Hardy* to support the regulation of liberty in the public interest (*Cronin v. Adams; Wenham v. State; State v. Buchanan; State v. Muller*). After citing *Hamilton Manufacturing*, however, supporters of protective legislation for women engaged in a specifically gendered factual analysis, showing how women differed from the standard male bearers of the guarantee of liberty.

The two federal cases that addressed women's protective labor legislation, *Cronin v. Adams* and *Muller v. Oregon*, did not analyze liberty for women extensively. They simply asserted that women were different from men and left it at that. The *Cronin* Court followed the earlier state-level cases, relying on the state's licensing power to deny a challenge to Denver's law barring women from serving alcohol. In *Muller*, the focus was on women's need for protection. Nonetheless, the Supreme Court explained briefly that women's "disposition and habits of life" tended to prevent them from enjoying the full scope of liberty promised by the due process clause (422). Accepting the detailed arguments made in the Consumers' League's brief about women's precarious position in the labor market, the Court declared that protective legislation would in fact help women to secure meaningful equality with their male competitors and employers in the labor market (422). In this sense too, limits on the hours of labor enhanced women's freedom of contract rather than circumscribing it. The main point on which the Court relied, however, was not liberty but rather the state's authority to regulate on the behalf of public interest.

Similarly, the state courts that upheld laws limiting women's hours of labor did not engage in extensive analyses of liberty. Most of the courts that reported opinions focused exclusively on police power and its scope with regard to women. The Washington high court, which in 1900 had struck down an eight-hour limit on public employees' labor, explained in gender-neutral terms that the increasing complexity of society and employment had led to a greater need for regulation. In doing so, it reasoned in the terms of standard social contract theory, explaining that this need caused a proportional reduction in the natural liberties that individual citizens had held in simpler times (*State v. Buchanan,* 610). The State of Nebraska approached the question carefully, acknowledging that women's labor was indeed property protected by the Fourteenth Amendment and the state's constitution's guarantees (*Wenham v. State,* 401). Nonetheless, women's weaker position in the labor market due to lack of unionization warranted protection to enhance their liberty (405). In both of these analyses, the courts seemed to believe that women's abstract right to contract was the same as that of men, but that women could not exercise their rights effectively in the highly competitive labor markets in which they tended to seek employment. In these analyses, women's actual liberty was enhanced by protective legislation, which prevented unscrupulous employers from taking advantage of them. Furthermore, the courts focused on the particular way that women exercised liberty rather than on liberty itself.

The Illinois Supreme Court, while certainly not prepared to embrace unionization as a solution, addressed somewhat related issues, rejecting in 1910 the earlier ruling in *Ritchie.* In *W. C. Ritchie & Co. v. Wayman,* the court pointed out that women were at significant social and political disadvantages in American society, but the court acknowledged a natural basis for women's disabilities in the tough world of competition. Women's lack of capacity to act effectively and decisively outside of the home "authorizes legislation exempting women from military and jury service and from working upon the public highways or working in mines, and . . . permits men to enjoy, alone, the elective franchise and to hold public office, and fixes their status as the head of the family in exemption and homestead laws" (*Ritchie v. Wayman,* 523). In this court's view, the place of men at the helm of government and at the head of the family justified special protection for women due to their lack of ability to control the economic and political spheres themselves. This analysis provided additional reasons for the courts to hold that women had a different relationship to liberty than men did. Because women did not have political or economic authority, their relationships with employers differed substantially from those of men. Women did not have the same capacity to create free contracts with their employers. Thus, protective labor legislation for women could be understood to enhance women's liberty. As feminist activists sought to rework the boundaries between public and private, maternalist ideology enabled the courts to conceive of protection as something other than an illegitimate incursion into the private realm by the state (Nackenoff 1999, 140–42).

At least one state court saw women's right to contract as precisely equal to that of men, ruling against protective legislation on this basis. The question of women's liberty would become increasingly important in the next period, and part of the impetus for the growing discussion was the 1907 ruling by the New York Court of Appeals in *People v. Williams*, which disrupted the emerging consensus among judges. In this case, the court considered a statute that barred women from working in factories before six in the morning and after ten at night. The majority's opinion criticized the legislature for failing to grant full citizenship to women, explaining that while police power's exercise was appropriate in many instances, "when it is sought under the guise of a labor law, arbitrarily . . . to prevent an adult female citizen from working at any time of the day that suits her, . . . it is time to call a halt" (*Williams*, 134). The court went on to rule that women had the same rights to liberty of contract as those articulated for men, in effect simply applying the analysis developed by earlier state courts and endorsed by the Supreme Court in *Lochner* (*Williams*, 135). In fact, the court cited *Lochner* to support its reasoning (*Williams*, 136).

The *Williams* court construed the statute as an arbitrary limit on women's capacity to work, plain and simple. In language reminiscent of that used by courts striking down general legislation, the court explained that the statute was part of a dangerous trend among state legislatures "to interfere with the lawful pursuits of citizens" (135). Unlike the 1895 *Ritchie* court, however, the New York Court of Appeals did not ignore gender, instead pushing the radical vision of equality described above. The opinion focused on women's capabilities as laborers. In this interpretation, women held the same rights to liberty and exercised the same degree of responsibility in making labor contracts; therefore, they deserved the same kind of respect from the state's laws (137).

The *Williams* court was an aberration in this period. Increasingly, the accepted approach was to question the nature of women's liberty and to compartmentalize it differently than men's with respect to public and private. While most members of the legal community conceived of men's liberty as fundamentally private and insulated from the state's interventions, concern about women's capabilities led many members of the legal community to reason that women could not exercise the kind of independent judgment that was the hallmark of male liberty without the state's help.

Reformers in the feminist community were seeking to reconfigure the concept of public space to enable women to participate more fully in civic life, despite their lack of formal civic rights. In rethinking the boundaries of public and private, they successfully opened new spaces for political participation and influence (Nackenoff 1999, 139–40). Expanded conceptions of feminine agency supported their activities in the public sphere by creating acceptable grounds for arguing that women had a special set of reciprocal rights and obligations with respect to the state. The thrust of these arguments was not that women were an exception that could be fitted within the general rules for the state's interaction with individual citizens but rather that the relationship between women and the state was sufficiently different to require a separate analysis based in maternalist ideology. The creativity of these efforts should not be underestimated. Nackenoff notes that these female reformers were "creating new languages about public space and new visions of the state" (Nackenoff 1999, 141). These changes provoked the legal system to begin rethinking liberty as a right of citizenship when it was exercised by women. Thus, while those considering general legislation focused on the precise scope of liberty and what it covered, members of the legal community addressing legislation limiting women's work considered the way that women exercised liberty, focusing on women rather than on liberty itself. This focus tied in effectively with the dichotomy that was developing in considerations of police power.

While liberty was important in light of these developments, most courts dealing with women's protective legislation expended most of their interpretive energy on police power. The content and operation of police power provided another node of conflict upon which interpretive energy focused. Here too, a gap between general legislation and women's legislation was beginning to emerge as the legal community struggled to apply the principles it had developed in the early period to increasing numbers of cases. As with liberty, the specific factual debates contributed to a growing divide in the frameworks for analyzing different types of protective measures.

Police Power and the Dichotomy between Labor and Laborers

The main gap between general legislation judged according to implicitly (and increasingly explicitly) male-centered standards and legislation regulating women's work was highlighted in analyses of the operation of police power. In the early years, the legal community had applied an antebellum conception of police power in the post-war jurisprudential environment, agreeing that the states had the authority to regulate certain aspects of their citizens' lives but disagreeing about the scope and nature of this authority. In the period of specific balancing, police power's operation on particular types of labor and laborers became the central inquiry. Toward the end of this period, questions about the legitimacy of both general and women's protective labor legislation were turning on the extent to which police power could be used to regulate in the interest of public health. Nonetheless, arguments regarding health were framed in different ways, depending on whether the legislation was general or protected female workers. For general legislation, the concrete factual debate centered on whether certain types of labor were so threatening to workers' health that they had impacts on public health; analytically, lawyers were struggling over exceptions to the general rule that workers' liberty interests outweighed the public's interest in regulation. The analytical framework for female labor, however, was beginning to support a contrary general rule: legislation was valid unless it worked a particular deprivation of rights because women as laborers were more vulnerable than men and also needed more protection for the good of the state.

General Legislation and the Focus on Labor

With respect to general legislation, lawyers and judges increasingly addressed the type of labor being regulated. The early period had demonstrated that most blanket regulations on the hours and conditions of labor were not going to pass constitutional muster without careful justification, so the legal battles began to focus more on the conditions in particular industries. Only through this means would protective measures survive constitutional review, although reactions to *Lochner* hinted that settled beliefs about the appropriate conception of public interest had been seriously disrupted during the rapid industrialization of the late nineteenth century. Such reasons for regulation tied in well to emerging social activism. American socialists and Progressive reformers were beginning to promote better conditions in the American workplace during this period. In their efforts to convince the public that regulation was necessary, reformers worked hard to develop information showing the health hazards in particular industries in the hopes of convincing the legislatures and courts to support statutory limits. Classic examples of this type of work are Jacob Riis's and Lewis Hine's photographs of tenement workers and child laborers and muckraking literature such as Upton Sinclair's 1906 novel *The Jungle,* which documented the life, work, and conversion to socialism of a Lithuanian employee of the Chicago meat-packing plants. The information such reformers gathered quickly became of use to attorneys and courts seeking ammunition to support regulation.

Howard Gillman has demonstrated the importance of police power as a jurisprudential phenomenon during this period. He argues that the judges at the time worked to distinguish between the proper advancement of the states' public interest and the inappropriate efforts of the state legislatures to provide certain workers with particular benefits, which could also lead to unconstitutional limitations on these workers' liberty (Gillman 1993, 9). Industrialization coincided with, and partially precipitated, the rise of political interest groups, which began to demand protection based on workers' vulnerability in particular industries. The courts frequently responded by denying such claims, retrenching their initial standpoint of hostility toward legislation based on membership in a class of any sort (Gillman 1993, 9).

Gillman explains that the fundamental question for the courts during this time was whether the authority to pass a particular statute was within a state's police power. A consensus had emerged in the courts that the states had the authority to pass laws designed to protect the health, morals, safety, or general welfare of the population. This understanding followed the antebellum conceptions of the proper limits to the state's authority to regulate (Ely 1999). By the turn of the century, attorneys realized that if such laws recognized real distinctions between the types of labor that different groups of individuals were performing, the laws could be validated. When such laws readjusted the bargaining position of a particular class, though, they went beyond the state's legitimate authority and therefore violated constitutional guarantees of liberty and, more significantly, equal protection, thereby constituting invalid class legislation (Gillman 1993). Such questions also plagued attorneys, who struggled to define the role of police power, focusing with increasing intensity on breaking down police power into its components and analyzing each. In doing so, the legal community's considerations of police power with respect to general legislation came to focus on the regulated labor and the risks inherent in it or other qualities that set it apart. Determinations of the appropriate extent of police power rested on close factual questions; attorneys used factual analyses to try to persuade judges to place their cases in the analytical category that would benefit them most. As this tendency became evident, the legal community found itself to be increasingly concerned with the nature of the regulations in question and their relationship to the type of labor that the workers were performing.

In *Holden v. Hardy* the attorneys on both sides agreed that, in order to be valid, police regulations had to address the welfare of the community. The attorneys then argued over what constituted the welfare of the community, how extensive the assertions about community welfare had to be, and whether protection based on the particular dangers of the labor could qualify. Jeremiah Wilson, attorney for the mining company, argued that an exercise of police power could not be legitimate if its only purpose was merely to help a particular group of workers (Wilson 1897, 9).[5] In this view, only a regulation that had a direct impact on all or almost all citizens would meet the constitutional standard. The attorneys for the state disagreed, arguing that the public could have a legitimate interest in particularly risky work (Pence and Murphy 1897, 24). The Supreme Court upheld the statute but did not fully resolve the question, leaving it open for further debate.

Because of the serious disagreements about the scope of police power, the regulation of industry to promote the health of workers required substantial justification. The state legislatures, often under pressure from the National Consumers' League or other progressive reformers, had to make specific findings that the work involved was dangerous and posed a health risk. The NCL and other organizations had also begun to muster large banks of facts to engage in litigation,

---

5. He went on to point out that such a limitation worked differently with regard to women and children—for these individuals, "the State has the right, to a limited extent, to exercise control for their *own* good and welfare, and thus indirectly for the welfare of the public" (Wilson 1897, 9).

seeing that the debates had moved to a ground on which such information could be influential. Attorneys seeking to persuade courts to
uphold regulations relied on the protection of health in a particular
industry as a significant factor in their favor. This argument, emerging
in the early period, reached its full articulation between 1898 and 1910
in cases involving general legislation. Attorneys arguing for the statute
at issue in *Holden v. Hardy* claimed that mining was an industry with
generally recognized health hazards warranting state intervention
even under the opposition's understanding of police power (Pence and
Murphy 1897, 12). Their argument depended mainly upon the common
perception of mining work as a particularly dangerous occupation due
to the high risk of crippling accidents; such harms could be limited
through ensuring that mine workers were fully rested when engaged in
labor (Pence and Murphy 1897, 12). Attorneys for the State of Kansas
used a similar framework in arguing that employees working on public construction jobs were in need of special protection, but simultaneously argued that limitations on public employees merely constituted
the state's own exercise of its freedom to contract (Coleman and
Loomis 1903). In both cases the Supreme Court upheld the statutes at
issue, though only in *Holden v. Hardy* was the statute upheld as a valid
regulation of health.

Undoubtedly encouraged by the success of these arguments in
Holden v. Hardy and *Atkin v. Kansas*, Julius Mayer, the attorney for the
State of New York, also relied upon protection of health in a hazardous
occupation as a reason to uphold the sixty-hour work week regulation
at issue in *Lochner*. This argument had convinced the New York Court
of Appeals. Not only was baking a particularly dangerous occupation,
claimed Mayer, but also protecting the health of bakers would advance
the broader interests of the state in maintaining order and good government (Mayer 1905, 732). He reasoned that the Court should permit
the statute to support the state's interest in having strong and healthy
citizens available for civic duties (732). Nonetheless, the main point of
Mayer's argument was to show that baking, like mining, was a particularly unhealthful industry and thus that it warranted regulation by the
state (731). This argument was ultimately unsuccessful, largely because
the Supreme Court rejected the contention that bakery work was particularly dangerous on factual grounds.

Most judges on both federal and state levels followed the employers' attorneys' interpretations, advancing a restrictive vision of police power when addressing general legislation. As with liberty, this standpoint led them to focus on the type of labor that workers were performing. Their principal task was to determine if a particular kind of labor warranted an extension of the state's police power. Police power had always included the authority to regulate the workplace if necessary, simply as part of the power. In some limited instances this could include limiting individual liberty for the good of the public. The early-twentieth-century courts' formula for the exercise of police power generally prohibited its broad exercise but allowed the regulation of certain industries or workers for the public health, safety, morals, or general welfare. The courts struggled to determine how to address police power with regard to general legislation, identifying particular categories of labor as the deciding factor in their rulings. This movement toward reliance on specific descriptions of the type of labor began around the turn of the century on both the federal and state levels but gained additional currency after the Supreme Court's ruling in *Holden v. Hardy*. If a type of labor was particularly hazardous or if it was inextricably linked with the public interest, it could legitimately be regulated, and this largely factual question grounded conflicts over police power in these cases.

The *Holden v. Hardy* Court engaged in a standard review of equal protection and due process but relied on the Utah high court's extensive description of the risks encountered by miners. The Supreme Court explained that while ordinary labor posed no serious threat to health, the kind of work done by miners was particularly harmful, as it was "carried on beneath the surface of the earth, where the operative is deprived of fresh air and sunlight, and is frequently subjected to foul atmosphere and a very high temperature, or to the influence of noxious gases" (*Holden v. Hardy*, 396). The Court continued its explanation by acknowledging the legislature's authority to take into account the unequal bargaining power between employers and employees (397), but characterized its ruling as resting principally on legislative authority to regulate in the interest of health (398). This decision set the stage for subsequent arguments focusing on special industrial hazards or conditions in particular occupations. The Court also decided *Atkin v. Kansas* based on the category of labor covered, but in a different way—the Court found the determinative factor to be the fact that the limitation in question was on work conducted by or on behalf of the State of Kansas (*Atkin v. Kansas*, 219). The type of labor in question—labor for a public entity—thus controlled the outcome in this case.

Lochner also rested partly upon the type of labor addressed by the state statute in the case, but the result was the law's invalidation. The Court, largely accepting Lochner's defense to his conviction, construed the limitation on hours as an affront to workers in an industry that was not particularly unhealthful or dangerous either to the bakers themselves or to the public at large (59, 62). The Court acknowledged the attempts of the State of New York to demonstrate the need to regulate the baking industry, but declared that since baking was not unhealthy either in scientific fact or in common understanding, no such regulation could be sustained (59). Because the labor in question was neither dangerous nor tinged with public interest, the Court saw no reason to permit the interference with individual liberties. In the majority's reasoning, a simple determination that the statute implicated private interests alone was possible because the labor involved had no public significance either in its impact on the workers themselves or directly upon the public at large. Justice Holmes objected strenuously not only to the outcome in the case but also to the Court's framing of the question in this manner; he would have preferred allowing a high degree of legislative autonomy, overturning only those laws that appeared to be manifestly unreasonable (75–76) (Holmes, J., dissenting). Nonetheless, he also focused on labor, claiming that the legislature was the best judge of the risks of particular jobs.

State courts engaged in similar analyses of police power, determining outcomes largely through their reasoning about the type of labor involved in the challenged regulation. The cases upholding limits on mining frequently rested on findings that mining was a hazardous occupation and that the law in question addressed the hazards appropriately. In these detailed analyses, the courts did not merely follow the Supreme Court's ruling in *Holden v. Hardy*, instead engaging in independent analyses of the factual risks involved. In Colorado, the high court objected to a limitation on miners' hours, claiming that the only possible purpose of the law was to protect the health of miners, an illegitimate goal. While the public welfare was a valid aim of legislation, "this maxim cannot be twisted to sustain a law violating private rights which contemplates the promotion of the welfare of less than the entire people" (*In re Morgan*, 26 Colo. 415, 427 (1899)). In this opinion, the court was unwilling to consider any kind of legislation that affected the health and safety only of the workers in a particular industry (428). The Nevada Supreme Court criticized this reasoning, ruling that limits on mining were appropriate because of the highly hazardous nature of the mining industry (*In re Boyce*, 27 Nev. 299, 300–301, 307 (1904)). The California high court followed suit in *In re Martin*, upholding the state legislature's limit of labor in mining and smelting to eight hours per day because of the exceptionally dangerous nature of the work (157 Cal. 51 (1909)).[6]

The New York Court of Appeals in *Lochner* also tied its decision to the labor involved, ruling that the purpose of the statute was to protect the public by helping to ensure the cleanliness and safety of bread products. Because the labor had a direct impact on the public, it could be regulated. The court explained that the legislature had been aiming at public health in passing the statute. The justices accepted the legislature's factual analysis, asserting that "a man is more likely to be careful and cleanly when well, and not overworked, than when exhausted by fatigue, which makes for careless and slovenly habits, and tends to dirt and disease" (*People v. Lochner*, 177 N.Y. 145, 163 (1904)). If hours were limited, the public would be protected from a dangerous product that most people used, now that most baking was no longer done in the home (162). The court also explained that baking was indeed a particularly hazardous occupation for its practitioners, citing the findings of medical authorities that the inhalation of flour created great risks for those working in the industry for lengthy periods of time (165). This opinion fit well within the emerging framework for addressing general legislation. The default position was that legislation limiting the right to contract was not permitted, as it illegitimately limited the implicitly male laborer's liberty. Nonetheless, if the legislature had identified particular distinguishing elements in the type of labor these workers were

---

6. In the cases addressing states' or municipalities' capacity to limit their employees' or subcontractees' hours of labor, state courts disagreed based on whether they saw such limits as addressing a properly constituted class of labor—work conducted for the public. The Washington high court did not endorse such a class in 1900, ruling very briefly that the employment in question was neither illegal nor opposed to the public interest and thus that it could not be regulated (*Seattle v. Smyth*, 329). The Illinois, Ohio, Indiana, and New York high courts used similar reasoning to strike down statutes in their jurisdictions before the Supreme Court's ruling in *Atkin v. Kansas*. New York's Court of Appeals was finally able to sustain such a statute in *People v. Metz*, basing its reasoning in the same principles as those articulated by the Supreme Court in *Atkin*.

performing, the court might permit the legislation to stand. Across the nation, the disagreements over facts thus came to center around the nature of the labor involved.

An exception to the rule that judges primarily addressed the type of labor in cases involving general limits was child labor. Around the turn of the century, a number of cases regarding states' limits on the employment of children reached the state supreme courts; the courts upheld these laws without exception. Regulation of child labor, like regulation of women's work, began to emerge during these years as a form of legislation analyzed through focus on the laborer rather than on the type of labor. As explained elsewhere, child labor regulations garnered the sympathy of the courts because they rested upon the special relationship existing between the child and the state (Zelizer 1985). Because children were future citizens, the state had a particular duty to ensure not only that their health was preserved but also that they were properly educated (Zelizer 1985).[7] Thus, protective legislation for children did not violate their constitutional rights at all, but rather promoted the state's interest in developing the next generation. This reasoning would also carry some weight with respect to women's legislation. Women also had important roles relating to the state's future, and like children, women's differences from the implicitly male worker had to be analyzed and addressed.

In these years, discussions of police power centered more closely on the identification of particular categories of labor that could be regulated. As the tactic of promoting health regulations became increasingly popular among progressive reformers in their attempts to shield their laws from judicial disfavor, attorneys on both sides struggled over the shapes of the categories of labor that could legitimately be regulated in the interest of public health or welfare. By the end of this period, the conflict centering around the factual scope of public health and welfare had contributed to an emerging consensus on a narrow list of types of labor that the states could limit, the principal categories of

---

7. This reasoning supported the understanding that children's rights to liberty and property were qualitatively different from those of adults. For many courts, to use the same kinds of arguments about children's liberty as those used in cases involving adult men was absurd (*Bryant v. Skillman Hardware Co.*, 76 N.J. 45, 47 (1908)). In fact, the courts understood protective legislation for children not to be an infringement upon their liberty, but rather as a proper and wholesome restraint exercised with parental concern (*Commonwealth v. Fisher*, 213 Pa. 48, 56 (1905)). Such restraint was necessary and proper and indeed belonged to the children by right.

which were mining work and public employment. Nonetheless, the emergence of this consensus suggested new targets for argument and debate. The developments regarding women's protective measures began to open a rift between the analysis of general protective labor legislation and women's measures at this point.

Women's Protective Labor Legislation and the Expanding Analysis of Women as Laborers

The battles over preventing women from serving alcohol and over limiting women's hours of work bridged the years in which consideration of women's legislation largely followed the patterns established regarding general legislation and the years in which the women's cases began to drive the development of doctrine. One can see this pattern in a microcosm by considering the relationship between *Lochner v. New York*, decided in 1905, and *Muller v. Oregon*, decided in 1908. Clearly the Court's reasoning in *Lochner* provided much of the background for its decision in *Muller*, but *Muller* was more than a simple modification of *Lochner*'s ruling to accommodate the different situation of women. The case confirmed the special role that public interest was to play in cases involving legislation for women's protection. By 1908, the state courts and the attorneys who litigated cases in them had begun to analyze women's cases in ways that went beyond the application of principles established in general cases. A growing interest in women's health and its relation to the state contributed to the development of an analytical split between women's and general protective labor legislation. This split first became evident in the context of cases addressing women's capacity to work as servers of alcohol. By 1910, the split was firmly established and the legal community was arguing over women's perceived nature as special and different laborers in cases involving limits on women's hours of labor.

Feminist organizations worked on the behalf of laboring women to promote reform through implementing gendered state policies. Reformers' efforts to study working women and develop banks of information about the effect of overwork now began to pay off as attorneys seeking to validate protective labor legislation were able to use these factual materials to support their arguments in the courts. While the National Consumers' League had begun to study particular industries that employed women, the most valuable information for lawyers seeking to uphold statutes limiting women's work was general information about women's health (Brooks, *Consumers' League*). Still, even as reformers were having success in the courts, the organizations themselves were split over class issues. Working-class organizers involved in the trade union movement spent most of their time and effort attempting to induct young women into unions. They often resented the middle- and upper-class reformers who populated the chapters of the National Consumers' League and to some extent the National Women's Trade Union League, who in turn sometimes behaved in a condescending manner toward the working women they were trying to help (Foner 1979, 294–310). The largely middle-class reform organizations, in particular the Consumers' League, began issuing studies and reports that documented the severe health risks that women faced in their labor during these years, encouraging the states to pass labor legislation for women rather than working to organize more women into trade unions.

As Sybil Lipschultz has observed, some feminists began to emphasize women's differences precisely to demonstrate the need for state-sponsored protection for women (Lipschultz 1996). The time was ripe for these efforts, as maternalist rhetoric temporarily displaced masculinist conceptions of manliness, autonomy, vigor, and independence in the public and political spheres (Nackenoff 1999, 156). While these visions could not permanently modify normative conceptions of citizenship, they did enable some women to participate in creating policies that sought to help other women materially (Nackenoff 1999, 165). The reformers could influence the public's and legal community's agendas, but ultimately they could not control these agendas. The courts picked up on research performed by organizations such as the National Consumers' League that were largely run by middle-class female reformers who struggled to improve the lot of working women. The research responded to developments in the legal arena and emphasized women's connection to the state through their roles as mothers. This development was not completely positive; the courts' vision of the female workers these statutes sought to protect was often not the same as the vision held by the reformers (Lipschultz 1996). For many courts, women's need for protection arose from their lesser abilities and capacities, differences that marked them as inherently inferior to male workers. In the period of specific balancing, however, reformers largely ignored troubling hints about how nonfeminist members understood women's civic positions; they were simply elated to achieve victory in the legal arena.

In the early cases involving women, the legal community's analyses had largely paralleled their interpretations in the general protective labor legislation cases. In the period of specific balancing, a subtle shift took place. For those considering legislation aimed at women, women, rather than the labor they performed, moved to the center as the legal community strove to address a growing trend in legislation through a male-oriented mode of interpretation. The central conflict they considered was the extent to which women could be considered a separate class, which would immunize legislation affecting only women from the challenge that it was illegitimate class legislation. As explained above, when attorneys and judges discussed the questions of liberty and privacy in these cases, they initially did so in the same kinds of terms used in the cases addressing general protective labor legislation. After the turn of the century, significant differences began to emerge in the emphases that the legal community placed on certain elements of their analysis. The contrast between applying standard modes of thinking and focusing on women grew sharper as the legal community moved from the early cases regarding women's capacity to work as servers of alcohol to later considerations of a rising tide of limitations on women's hours of labor.

Alcohol, Morality, and the Emergence of an Analytical Split

Within the legal community, attorneys seeking to uphold limits on female servers were the first to connect moral concerns about working women to police power. As the following analysis demonstrates, this focus on moral concerns unconsciously established legal actors' tendency to consider the laborers rather than the labor in their interpretations of police power's reach. In *Cronin v. Adams*, the state's attorneys focused on the question of morality and framed women as both dangerous and endangered moral agents. As explained above, by this time the legal community largely agreed that police power included the capacity to regulate on the behalf of public morals. Groups such as the Women's Christian Temperance Union had worked hard in the previous decades to establish in the public's mind the link between alcohol and immorality, particularly where women were concerned (Tyrrell

1991). The attorneys arguing for the Denver ordinance sought to persuade the Court that the law they supported was clearly permissible
under police power by linking these concepts. They explained: "Laws
prohibiting . . . sale of intoxicating liquors to minors, inebriates and
drunken persons, and like characters, have uniformly been upheld . . .
in the interest of the public morals. If this is true . . . surely it requires no
argument to show that the public morals require such restriction with
regard to women" (Lindsley, Ritter, and Brock 1903, 18). The attorneys
also made much of the fact that only the saloon owner was protesting
the application of the law (24). The Court was being asked to act as
women's savior, protecting them from unscrupulous and evil men who
would otherwise corrupt them, thereby injuring the public morals.

The opponents of the statute took a different view, claiming that
regulating women was not the way to achieve the high standard of
morality sought by the law's defenders. Cronin's attorney explained:
"That woman should be pure and chaste and hedged about by all the
protections possible to insure her exemption from temptation is not to
be accomplished by legal enactment" (Smith 1903, 42). Attempting to
separate the political world on the one hand from the moral and religious world on the other, Smith argued that while the American legal
system operated in accordance with higher moral principles, the
"upbuilding of the moral and religious world" was not within its
purview (41). Furthermore, he found quite troublesome the automatic
linkage between women and alcohol and immorality. Police power, in
his view, could not be exercised to protect the public morals by discriminating against women solely on the basis of sex with no other
explanation or justification (28). In another portion of his brief, Smith
also argued that a more analytically defensible statute would seek to
protect both men and women, since both faced moral hazards in the
presence of alcohol (27–28).

These wide-ranging arguments on both sides regarding the relationship between police power and public morality did not yet have a
great effect in the Supreme Court, however. In *Cronin v. Adams*, the
Court declined the invitation to explore the relationship between
morality and the public interest as these issues related to women. The
justices, citing an earlier precedent, merely explained that the issue of
liquor licenses was "a question of public expediency and public morality, and not of Federal law" (115). Not until 1908 in *Muller* would the

Supreme Court engage in a full analysis of police power's appropriate impact on women.

In the state courts, however, morality quickly became a ground through which the exercise of police power could be justified. As this path became more entrenched, many judges exploited it to uphold protective legislation for women, particularly in the continuing line of cases that addressed statutes barring women from working in places where alcohol was served. These statutes were upheld in all of the reported opinions around the turn of the century; the courts generally ruled that prohibiting women from holding such jobs promoted the public's interest in morality. Alice Kessler-Harris observes that such statutes produced little controversy because of strong beliefs in the need for women to be protected from exposure to immorality (Kessler-Harris 1982, 186). As the Colorado Supreme Court pointed out, such laws were seen as valid acts under the police power since they addressed morality: "That the regulations attacked here are a legitimate exercise of the police power of the state we have no doubt; that their object is to protect the morals of the community, to secure good order, and to advance the general welfare cannot be gainsaid" (*Adams v. Cronin*, 502). However, these themes emerged only after the postbellum legal community had confirmed the state's capacity to regulate in the public interest if it was acting to protect morality. The legal arguments for such regulations generally assumed women to be problematic workers in such an atmosphere and left it at that, establishing a pattern that would carry through to the limits on women's hours of labor.

Courts upholding these policies were adamant, insisting that in permitting such legislation they were doing more than merely discriminating against women on the basis of sex. The Colorado Supreme Court explained that discrimination against women per se was impermissible, but if legislation was based on the prevention of immorality, it could be upheld.[8] The dangers of allowing women to be present in saloons even as servers were obvious, since their very presence was a threat. The court explained, "That injury to public morality would ensue if women were permitted without restrictions to frequent wine rooms, there to be supplied with liquor, is so apparent to the average

---

8. "If a discrimination is made against women solely on account of their sex, it would not be good; but, if it is because of the immorality that would be likely to result if the regulation was not made, the regulation would be sustained" (*Adams v. Cronin*, 496).

person, that argument to establish so plain a proposition is unnecessary" (*Adams v. Cronin*, 496). The court also pointed out that women could constitutionally be excluded from such establishments as patrons, and claimed that this greater power included the lesser power of prohibiting their working in such places.[9] Throughout such analyses, the courts tended to ground their reasoning in women's natures rather than identifying the morally questionable labor as the central point in the analysis.

These laws often had exceptions for the daughters and wives of the owners of the establishments. The courts accepted the argument that the owner could protect such women from immorality and further that the presence of such a woman could make the establishment less subject to the immoral excesses of like places. Furthermore, wives were not employees in any real sense and their presence would encourage good, rather than immoral, behavior (*City of Hoboken v. Goodman*, 221). Presumably, the rowdier elements would be more likely to behave with propriety if the decorum of the owner's home intruded in the workplace. The courts underlined a dichotomy between men and women concerning self-ownership: the male owners could comprehensibly articulate claims that these statutes limited their freedom to contract with female employees, but these claims were denied on the basis of the stronger state interest in morality. The wives and daughters of the male owners, however, were not conceived of as independent agents at all. Rather, they appeared almost as the property of the male owner, as much subject to his control and protection as the barstools and taps. The courts thus relied on such women's status as nonemployees, again demonstrating the problematic nature of female workers and the contradictions inherent between femininity and status as a laborer.

While few members of the legal community would have contested the state's capacity to legislate in order to bolster morality, the interests at stake in the protection of women from the lewd and unsavory atmosphere of bars went beyond this simple desire. Specific factual balancing took place in these cases. If morality had been the only factor weighed in the balance, members of the legal community could simply have

---

9. "Women may therefore properly be excluded from wine rooms as this ordinance provides, and if they have no constitutional right to insist upon being admitted to places there to be supplied with liquor, when the effect would be demoralizing to society, a fortiori, the saloonkeeper may be prevented from furnishing them facilities for contributing to that result" (*Adams v. Cronin*, 497).

based their arguments in the questionable moral status of alcohol use and sale per se. Instead, these cases drew on the earlier tendency to base arguments for the legitimacy of such laws in the public need to protect morality by preventing a state's women from becoming debauched through exposure to alcohol. They also initiated the growing tendency to analyze women's position in the workplace when considering protective labor legislation for women. The danger the courts feared arose from women's particular moral risks rather than simply from the nature of the labor itself.

Hours of Labor and the Special Risks
of Female Workers

While the state courts developed reasoning concerning the relationship between police power and morality, in the period of specific balancing the legal community also addressed limits on women's hours of labor. These cases continued the trend established in the litigation over women's capacity to serve alcohol, focusing on women's special needs and relationship to the state. The leading cases of the previous period, *Hamilton Manufacturing* on the one hand and *Ritchie* on the other, had provided precedents to ground future decisions but did not themselves provide models of reasoning applied specifically to limits on women. In this period, the legal community began to puzzle out this relationship, developing the bases for analysis that would ground the shift of focus to women's legislation after 1910.

The most noted arguments regarding women's differences were those constructed by Goldmark and Brandeis in their companion brief to persuade the Supreme Court to uphold Oregon's ten-hour-per-day limit on female laundry workers. Like the attorney arguing for the limit on hours at issue in *Lochner*, Goldmark and Brandeis sought to persuade the Court through the use of empirical data. Unlike the New York attorney, however, they focused on female workers rather than on the particular hazards associated with laundry work. Relying on the reams of information collected by the National Consumers' League over the years and additional studies from overseas, they built an argument based in police power that justified regulating women's labor by differentiating women from men in two ways. First, they expressed the general understanding that women, unlike men, had a particularly important role not only in bearing but also in rearing the next generation of citizens. Second, they argued that women's physical structure was different from men's, rendering women's reproductive capacities more vulnerable to damage from overwork. The lengthy brief was devoted mostly to demonstrating the physical differences, allowing the brief for the State of Oregon (of which Brandeis was also a coauthor) to draw the connection between these differences and the legitimate exercise of police power by the state. Their maternalist emphasis derived both from their connections to the National Consumers' League and from their belief that these arguments would most effectively convince the Court to depart from its ruling in *Lochner* only three years earlier.

Relying on evidence from the medical community, Goldmark and Brandeis documented the threats of overwork to women's delicate and complicated reproductive systems. Women whose line of work required them to stay on their feet were at particular risk: "The long hours of standing, which are required in many industries, are universally denounced by physicians as the cause of pelvic disorders" (Brandeis 1908, 93). Even if a woman stopped working upon marriage, her reproductive system was not safe from the ravages of overwork (and thus was not safe for the developing citizens in her womb), since "The evil effect of overwork before as well as after marriage upon childbirth is marked and disastrous" (101). Limiting women's hours of labor would thus help to prevent damage to their ability to bear children successfully.

The physical differences that Goldmark and Brandeis cataloged went beyond the reproductive organs. Again relying on evidence from physicians and information developed by the National Consumers' League, they argued that due to women's special structure and function as mothers, they had less natural endurance than men:

> Besides these anatomical and physiological differences, physicians are agreed that women are fundamentally weaker than men in all that makes for endurance: in muscular strength, in nervous energy, in the powers of persistent attention and application. Overwork, therefore, which strains endurance to the utmost, is more disastrous to the health of women than of men, and entails upon them more lasting injury. (Brandeis 1908, 83)

Women's lack of endurance, they asserted, made women far more prone to suffer a variety of workplace injuries when they worked too long. Therefore, the state would be justified in providing special protection for them for the same reasons that the Court had upheld the protective statute for miners at issue in *Holden v. Hardy* (Brandeis 1908, 83). The need for protection, however, was rooted in women's bodies rather than in the labor itself.

Tying in some of the themes that had emerged in the cases addressing liquor licenses, Goldmark and Brandeis also asserted that overwork presented special moral threats to women. They explained, "Laxity of moral fibre follows physical debility. When the working day is so long that no time whatever is left for a minimum of leisure or home-life, relief from the strain of work is sought in alcoholic stimulants and other excesses" (Brandeis 1908, 109). While this argument could apply equally to men and women (and would, in the years and briefs to come), in the *Muller* briefs, the abuse of alcohol and its subsequent moral hazards appeared as a particular risk for weaker-willed women.

Ultimately, all of these differences and particular potential harms related to women's connection to children. The substantial risks of harm to women alone were bad enough, threatening to initiate a period of decline in the physical, mental, and moral state of the entire community (Brandeis 1908, 112). The real harm, though, was that this deterioration would persist in the next generation, passed on by the overworked and damaged women of the current generation. Goldmark and Brandeis warned that when women were consistently permitted to work too long, "Infant mortality rises, while the children of married working-women, who survive, are injured by inevitable neglect. The overwork of future mothers thus directly attacks the welfare of the nation" (Brandeis 1908, 112). The inevitable conclusion was that the state had the authority, if not the duty, to protect itself against the impending catastrophe.

In the brief for the state, the attorneys summarized Brandeis and Goldmark's extensive array of factual information, claiming that arguments in favor of women's freedom of contract were revealed as "mere sophistry" when balanced against the factual record of difference (Manning et al. 1908, 48). The attorneys went on to paint a picture of women as marginal and strained workers who deserved the protection of the state (56). The state's ability to exercise police power to protect the public interest, they argued, clearly included the authority to regulate women's work. Given the particular risks that women ran when they overworked and given women's vital role in reproducing and raising the next generation, the state ridiculed the idea that a law limiting women's hours "is not a law involving the safety, the morals, nor the welfare of the public" (56). Throughout this analysis, the brief's authors focused consistently on women and their physical risks; an uninformed reader would have had some difficulty discerning that the case was about laundry work.

Attorneys for Curt Muller, the laundry owner, attempted to counter this onslaught of factual evidence. They sought to use the strategy that had succeeded in *Lochner*, claiming that laundry work was not particularly dangerous to women's health, and that the statute rested instead on the illegitimate theory that women were in need of special protection solely on account of sex (Fenton and Gilfry 1908, 29–30). They argued that in addition to resting on inaccurate assumptions regarding women's differences from men, the ultimate result of the statute in question would be to injure women's ability to succeed in the labor market by making them unable to compete effectively with unregulated men (34). Much of their argument, as discussed above, rested on the assertion that women were men's equals in their capacity to work and make contracts and on an expansive understanding of women's liberty under the ruling in *Lochner*. In doing so, they constructed women as holders of the abstract right to contract endorsed by the legal community in the period of generalized balancing. Nonetheless, because they were responding to the state's placement of women at the center of the analysis, the argument still took place on the basis of women's nature as laborers. Fenton and Gilfrey directly engaged and sought to refute the argument that women were problematic laborers in need of special consideration rather than focusing exclusively on the nature of laundry work.

The significance of the attorneys' debate was that it confirmed the shift in analysis for women's cases, both in terms of the focus and of the approach. The briefs all centered around women as laborers rather than the nature of laundry work and its particular hazards, following the patterns of litigation developed in the state courts, where judges and attorneys initiated the focus on female laborers in the context of the cases addressing alcohol servers. Goldmark and Brandeis's brief also forced the opponents of the law to respond to a dense factual debate, confirming that scientific evidence and factual arguments, rather than formal legal categories, would be the interpretive battleground for this case and for future cases.

The arguments against the limit on women's hours were ultimately unconvincing to the Supreme Court, which adopted Brandeis and Goldmark's arguments practically wholesale. The Court summarized the amicus brief quickly, citing the "abundant testimony of the medical fraternity" to support its assertion that the state had the authority to limit women's labor in order to protect its interest in "preserv[ing] the strength and vigor of the race" (*Muller v. Oregon*, 413). Reiterating the arguments made on the state's side, Justice Brewer went on to explain that regulating women's work benefited the entire populace and not only the women thus limited (421). The discussion of public health relied equally on the health of individual women as potential child bearers and rearers and the health of the body politic through its continuation in the next generation (421). It further confirmed the public significance of women and of their bodies particularly.

Following the trend already established on the state level, the Court further endorsed the idea that with regard to protective statutes addressing women's work, the laborer herself was the significant factor. The justices explained, "Differentiated by these matters from the other sex, she is properly placed in a class by herself, and legislation designed for her protection may be sustained, even when like legislation is not necessary for men, and could not be sustained" (*Muller v. Oregon*, 422). Here and in its explicit statement that its decision in no way raised questions about *Lochner*'s status, the Court demonstrated its implicit determination that male labor was the norm and female labor was a significant exception that warranted its own rules and ultimately its own jurisprudence. Such statements confirmed the move toward developing arguments specifically addressing women's situation rather than continuing to apply reasoning developed with regard to male-centered legislation like that at issue in either *Holden v. Hardy* or *Lochner v. New York*.

The outcome and reasoning in *Muller* were notable for their national significance, not for their novelty. The state courts, through their analysis of whether women's legislation automatically constituted illegitimate class legislation, had already moved toward considering women's position in the labor market in order to justify upholding limits on women's work. With increasing frequency, courts permitted the exercise of legislative control over women's work by articulating a state interest in women's health. Whether the courts upheld or struck down legislation, they mostly argued over whether women were in need of special protection, leaving the basis of discussion as the laborer rather than the restricted labor. Likewise, judges increasingly framed their opinions in terms of their beliefs about women's concrete capacities and the relationship between these capacities and the state. To make these kinds of claims, they relied on the scientific and social scientific evidence developed specifically for the cases.

The fear of these courts, like the federal courts, was that women's excessive work would have ill effects for children. Six years before *Muller*, the *Buchanan* court held Washington's limitation on women's hours to be clearly in the public interest because it dealt with the common public health issue of women's overwork: "It is a matter of universal knowledge . . . that continuous standing on the feet by women for a great many consecutive hours is deleterious to their health. . . . [T]hat which would deleteriously affect . . . the mothers of succeeding generations must necessarily affect the public welfare and public morals" (*State v. Buchanan*, 610). The court apparently believed the connection between women's reproductive roles and the public interest to be self-evident. At this time, most judges making arguments of this nature felt that no evidence had to be presented to support this most obvious of observations about the connection between lengthy hours of labor and women's health. Other courts, including supreme courts in Nebraska, Oregon, Illinois, and Michigan, reasoned in a similar fashion *(Wenham v. State; State v. Muller; Ritchie v. Wayman; Withey v. Bloem)*.

The Illinois judges' ruling used such arguments to overrule the court's earlier pronouncement in *Ritchie v. People* (155 Ill. 98 (1895)). They claimed that the original case had been wrongly decided and that subsequent developments in jurisprudence regarding women's labor laws had revealed the need to address such laws differently *(Ritchie v. Wayman)*. The court criticized the earlier decision's failure to take differences between men and women into account. The obvious nature of such differences warranted the earlier case's reversal. The judges reasoned, "It is known to all men (and what we know as men we cannot profess to be ignorant of as judges) that woman's physical structure and the performance of maternal functions place her at a great disadvantage in the battle of life" *(Ritchie v. Wayman*, 520–21). Unlike the statutes involving male labor, statutes addressing women's work could rest on the legislature's ability to recognize real difference and adjust for it in the statutes they enacted. Like the *Muller* Court, the *Ritchie v. Wayman* court acknowledged both physical and functional differences between women and men (530).[10] The Illinois court thus changed its position as a result of its careful analysis of women as laborers.

Like the Supreme Court in *Muller*, the late-nineteenth- and early-twentieth-century state courts focused on women's lack of strength and stamina due to their reproductive functions as the major physical differences between women and men as the main justifications for upholding protective legislation for women. Women could not labor as long as men could: "Certain kinds of work which may be performed by men without injury to their health, would wreck the constitutions and destroy the health of women, and render them incapable of bearing their share of the burdens of the family and the home" (*Wenham v. State*, 405). Because women were constitutionally weaker than men, they could be understood to constitute a special class in need of protection for health-based reasons. The Nebraska Supreme Court endorsed this position, stating, "The state must be accorded the right to guard and protect women, as a class, against such a condition; and the law in question, to that extent, conserves the public health and welfare" (405). In this analysis, the court recognized that the hours of physical labor for a woman were not limited to the hours she spent on the time clock, another factor balancing against a radical conception of equal individual liberty for women. Not only were women the weaker sex, but they also had additional (and more important) responsibilities in the home further straining their physical resources.[11] Other state courts also echoed this reasoning in upholding limits on women's hours of work.

The two cases during this period that invalidated limits on women's hours of labor engaged in the discussion of health regulations and implicitly accepted the idea that women's work could be regulated in the public's interest. The problem for both courts was that the connection between the regulation in question and women's health was

---

10. The Illinois Supreme Court identified four differences that justified limiting women to ten-hour work days: "(1) The physical organization of woman; (2) her maternal functions; (3) the rearing and education of children; (4) the maintenance of the home" (*Ritchie v. Wayman*, 530).

11. While the recognition of women's dual responsibilities may sound familiar to twenty-first-century ears, it was not the same critique as that advanced by feminists in the 1970s and 1980s who pointed out that women's labor in the home represented an unpaid "second shift." Rather, the well-ordered domestic domain was a right of free men and was part and parcel of the set of contractual entitlements that marked the full-blown rational male citizen. Women's inability to manage housework and childcare effectively was thus as much, if not more, of an injury to their husbands as to them (Stanley 1998, 161–64).

not drawn closely enough. The year before the Supreme Court ruled in *Muller*, the Colorado high court in *Burcher v. People* refused to allow a limitation on female laundry workers because the legislature had not made a specific finding that labor in a laundry was particularly dangerous or injurious (503). Like Illinois's first ruling, the *Burcher* decision did not refer to gender specifically, holding to the paradigm for general labor legislation by considering the nature of the labor involved (rather than the laborers) in gender-neutral terms (503). *Burcher* was thus an anomaly during this period. In contrast, the *Williams* court in New York, considering a ban on night work for women, followed the growing trend to take a woman-centered approach. The court reasoned that the statute in question did not even purport to protect women's health "except as it might be inferred that for a woman to work during the forbidden hours of night would be unhealthful" (*Williams*, 134). The court could have accepted a limit on women's hours of labor if such a limit were properly linked to the health interests accepted elsewhere (134), but as the statute stood, the connection between the limitation on women's work and the interests of the state was too vague.

In the early years of the period of specific balancing, few within the legal community attempted to explain the scope of women's difference from men. Change was coming, as a few members began to make the argument that women were equal to men in their possession of abstract rights to liberty, an argument that would have been a nonstarter in any legal setting fairly recently. Nonetheless, in these years most lawyers and judges simply assumed that the differences existed, detailed them briefly, and moved on to a consideration of how these differences influenced considerations of the legitimacy of legislating for women's benefit. The node of conflict around the proper application of police power with respect to women encouraged factual discussions about women's differences. When such differences were accepted, most legal analysts simply concluded that the state's intervention was warranted on women's behalf since the laws in question could not be understood as class-based legislation. Using difference as a basis for analysis contributed to the shift toward considering the laborer rather than the nature of the labor in cases involving women's legislation; these trends reinforced each other. As the massive factual records popularized by the introduction of Brandeis-Goldmark briefs began to dominate the legal scene, unquestioned assumptions gave way to more extensive explanations of the sources and scope of difference. At the same time, the legal community, in addressing cases involving statutes limiting women's work, increasingly came to focus on the female laborer rather than on the nature of the work involved. In leading cases such as *Muller*, the attorneys and courts spent practically no time analyzing the precise nature of work in the regulated occupation, focusing instead on medical evidence about women's differences from men and their particularly delicate natures.

The New Separation between General Legislation and Laws Limiting Women's Work

In the years around the turn of the century, the discourse concerning protective labor legislation became more sophisticated and more contentious. Now that the legal community had established a role for the Fourteenth Amendment, conflicts arose over the precise shape and scope of that role. Between 1898 and 1910, increasing numbers of state courts had to grapple with the difficult problem of specifically balancing liberty under the Fourteenth Amendment against the states' rights to regulate through the exercise of police power. The legal community had accepted both that police power was limited and that the guarantees of equality and liberty could not be easily gainsaid; the challenge was thus to explain under what circumstances regulations could be permitted or disallowed.

This change took place as the legal community acknowledged the growing influence of legal realism. Social scientific evidence began to make inroads against formalist logic, opening up a new ground for interpretive analysis with additional lay actors' ability to shape the process of litigation. As arguments grew more factually detailed, the legal community's focus shifted from basic discussions of the role of due process to more pointed disagreements about the proper relationship among liberty, labor, and property. In defining the substantive question of rights under due process, liberty became the center of the analysis, provoking specific discussions of its scope in briefs and in the case law. The concept of liberty of contract began to appear frequently, and the comfortable consensus about liberty of contract's role within a generally accepted laissez-faire economic model was under attack. The growth of litigation over equal protection has been noted by other scholars; this analysis points out the ways that the elevation of liberty in the analysis of due process was refined during this period through interpretive battles over its meaning and scope. Further, these discussions of liberty implicitly and sometimes explicitly addressed a male subject of the guarantee. Rather than simply arguing about due process, members of the legal community now placed men's liberty prominently in their discussions, contributing inadvertently to a gendered split among the cases.

Debates over police power also heated up, coming increasingly to center around the question of health regulations. During the period of specific balancing, social reform organizations such as the National Consumers' League and the National Women's Trade Union League began to generate information for attorneys and judges to use in their discussions. They generated alternative conceptions of the state's power and of the interplay between public and private, and they did so in explicitly maternalist terms. By the end of this period, due process analysis was focused tightly on the balance between liberty and police power, and the legal community questioned whether particular types of labor or laborers warranted state intervention in the public interest.

The nodes of conflict had shifted to more factual disputes. In part, this shift was due to legal realism's impact, but it was also due to the nature of the nodes of conflict. The initial disputes were largely over formalistic questions about the definition and scope of liberty and police power, but once the legal community had reached some degree of consensus, the center of conflict shifted to the further articulation of these concepts in concrete, empirical contexts. Attorneys and increasingly activists sought to expand or limit the reach of the doctrinal categories through the presentation of factual arguments; many judges were now more ready to hear these arguments in light of the ascendancy of legal realism in elite academic and legal circles.

Conflict continued in the context of cases involving general regulations, but it was increasingly confined to factual disputes within these legal categories. The analytical strategy of manufacturers and others opposing protective measures had two main elements. First, they sought to establish as a general rule the principle that protective measures were presumed to be invalid interferences in the fundamentally private relationship between employer and employee. They delineated the private nature of this relationship in terms of their belief in a formal and abstract equality between employer and employee that would brook no interference from the state. Drawing on the developments of the earlier period, they emphasized the cases that had invalidated protection for workers in various industries, interpreting these cases as establishing broad principles rather than as setting rules for particular industries. Second, they read the cases that did allow protective legislation as addressing industries that had particular characteristics warranting a higher degree of state intervention.

With regard to general legislation, the legal community increasingly came to analyze the relationship between liberty and police power in terms of the type of labor the state was seeking to regulate. The stock subject of the due process clause's guarantee of liberty was an implicitly male rational economic actor who, under ordinary circumstances, could successfully negotiate his own labor contracts to his advantage. Lawyers and activists seeking to persuade the courts to validate general protective labor legislation could not undermine this figure's authority to act on his own behalf; they thus turned to showing that the labor in question was exceptional for one reason or another. The conception of particularly problematic types of labor could exist alongside an understanding of hirelings' self-ownership that depended upon freedom of contract without directly challenging laissez-faire. Those supporting such legislation took advantage of the realist revolution by relying on detailed factual information about the labor in question, producing empirical arguments for why particular types of labor had to be regulated for the public good.

During these years as well, actors in all phases of the legal process began to analyze women's work independently. Some public interest organizations argued that for various reasons women were in particular need of protection in the labor market. Attorneys increasingly focused their arguments on the extent to which women were different from men in legally cognizable ways. Both courts and attorneys gradually moved toward considering the nature of the labor addressed by general statutes while considering the nature of the laborer in statutes protecting women and children.

In cases involving laws limiting women's work, the focus was on women as laborers rather than on the nature of liberty itself and its interaction with police power. Reformers and the legal community articulated explanations for the extent to which female laborers differed from the paradigmatic male subjects of the guarantee of liberty. In arguing about the scope of police power in these cases, the legal community gradually shifted toward an analysis of the extent to which female workers had to be limited for the public good. Rather than collecting and presenting data about the hazards of particular industries, those arguing for such regulations focused on women's physiology, psychology, and social roles.

The two leading Supreme Court cases of the era, *Lochner v. New York* and *Muller v. Oregon,* highlighted the tensions of this period and demonstrated the split between cases involving general legislation and cases involving protection for women. Both involved challenges to state statutes limiting the hours of workers—New York had limited (male) bakers to sixty-hour work weeks, and Oregon prevented female laundry employees from working more than ten hours in a day—and *Muller* was decided only three years after *Lochner.* Nonetheless, the Supreme Court invalidated New York's statute and upheld Oregon's. The gender of the limited workers was the most obvious difference between the cases, but a closer look shows that the analyses in the two cases diverged on other grounds as well. These differences rested upon each case's position within different nodes of conflict.

Lochner is justifiably famous for establishing nationally the primacy of freedom of contract and thus the doctrinal and political significance of substantive due process (Rowe 1999). Within the development of nodes of conflict, *Lochner* was significant because it confirmed particular trends, not because it established them. The New York legislature, responding to the developing rule that protective measures had to be based on broadly defined threats to public health, ensured that they based the statute explicitly on the hazards of the baking industry to individual bakers and on the health risks that the general public faced from eating bread produced by unhealthy bakers. In doing so, the legislature relied on factual elaborations of two emerging legal principles: that some types of private labor were dangerous enough to the workers to warrant intervention and that some types of private labor had sufficient public significance to allow regulation. The Supreme Court confirmed that the threshold for justification under both of these principles was high indeed.

Muller was a key moment in the period of negotiation, but its significance went beyond the national establishment of the principle that measures protecting women were constitutionally valid despite the ruling in *Lochner.* The case marked the Supreme Court's public endorsement of legal realist reasoning through the justices' reliance on a factual brief submitted by a noted progressive attorney and reformer and an officer of a national group seeking protection for workers. The success of

Louis Brandeis and Josephine Goldmark in convincing the Supreme Court to uphold Oregon's limit on the hours of female laundry employees confirmed that reformers could have a significant role in the legal process, contributing to the further development of vigorously contested nodes of conflict. In future years, support for challenged protective measures would not come solely from the attorneys general who defended them on the states' and Congress's behalf. Furthermore, the line between legal advocacy and political advocacy would continue to blur as activist attorneys became more involved in efforts to validate protective measures.

These developments would shape the next phase of the period of negotiation. After 1910, cases involving women's legislation came to the fore as general legislation faded into the background. Activists, lawyers, and judges all reacted quickly to the success of the National Consumers' League in *Muller v. Oregon*, gearing up for a pitched battle over women's legislation, a battle to be fought with extensive factual information rather than with legal rhetoric.

Chapter 4

Laborer-Centered Analysis: The Ascendancy of Women's Legislation

This period of the study encompasses the most active time for consideration of women's protective labor legislation and marks the point at which arguments over laws protecting women began to drive the development of doctrine. During these years, groups advocating for protective legislation worked directly in the legal arena, developing their agendas for research to address the legal categories that judges and attorneys had established to address protective measures. The period began with the rise to ascendancy of women's legislation after 1910 and ended just before the Supreme Court's decision in *Adkins v. Children's Hospital* in 1923, which will be addressed in the next chapter. This period was one of laborer-centered analysis as the legal community focused not only on statutes involving women's protective measures but also specifically on the laborers themselves that these statutes protected. In contrast to their focus in the period of specific balancing, most members of the legal community, while still concerned with factual analysis, centered their interpretive energies on the subjects of the guarantee of liberty rather than on the tension between liberty and police power. The arguments and rulings of this period confirmed that the major division that would undergird constitutional development with respect to regulation in the 1920s and 1930s was a gendered division rather than a separation between the working and capitalist classes. In the period of laborer-centered analysis, the legal community largely committed itself to an independent interpretive framework for statutes involving women's work; this framework would occasionally influence considerations of general protective measures. During these years, the doctrinal developments generated a growing tension between gendered and purportedly gender-neutral reasoning regarding protective legislation, but now this tension was coming from a context in which the principles developed to address women's protective measures became the norm.

In these years, members of the legal community assimilated the developments of the previous period. With the focus on laborers rather than on the labor they performed, legal actors developed dense factual records demonstrating the effects of labor generally upon women. Interpretations of women's reproductive roles took on increasing significance. Those supporting protective measures sought to define the sources and consequences of women's weak position in the labor market precisely. While many of these arguments were deeply gendered in their connection to reproduction, some could logically extend to male workers. Toward the end of this period, a few members of the legal community attempted to shift the analysis to a gender-neutral basis, but had little success. Throughout these years, the legal and lay communities promoting protection for women became increasingly intertwined.

By 1910, the focus on types of labor was firmly established in cases involving general legislation, while the cases addressing women's protective measures emphasized women's roles as laborers. The period encompassing the 1910s would see three major developments. First, the framework articulated to address cases involving women—the focus on the laborer and her relationship to the labor marketplace—would become the dominant paradigm as the cases involving women's labor took the center stage in the courts. Second, groups seeking reforms, in particular the National Consumers' League, adjusted their political and research agendas to tie in with litigation more directly. Finally, some attorneys and judges began to apply the modes of analysis used in cases involving women to cases involving general protective labor legislation. The period started with the reactions among members of the legal community to *Lochner* and *Muller* and ended on the eve of the Supreme Court's ruling in *Adkins v. Children's Hospital*.

The years of laborer-centered analysis saw women's increasing participation in labor and civic life. As protective labor legislation addressing women's work came to dominate the legal scene, the fight for women's suffrage reached its climax; in 1919, the Nineteenth Amendment was ratified, granting the right to vote in federal elections to adult women. World War I also took place during these years, with resulting mass disruptions of the labor market and greater opportunities for employment for women. World War I also raised significant questions about the possibilities for regulation; during the war, national regulations that previously would have been unthinkable were put into place as emergency measures. To many observers' surprise, however, the changes in the scope for federal authority were temporary, not permanent, as the Taft Court actively promoted a return to normalcy, defined as the prewar balance of power between the federal government and the states (Post 1998).

The final battles for and passage of the Nineteenth Amendment in the state legislatures had promoted unity among women's groups but could not completely mask growing differences regarding both tactics and goals. In the decade after 1910, some feminist activists concluded that supporting protective labor legislation aimed specifically at women was no longer a wise tactic. Others remained convinced that only support for such legislation would lead to the adoption of universal legislation. Still others began to express the view that while universal legislation was desirable, women would always need a higher degree of protection than men (National Women's Trade Union League 1923).

Such disagreements were compounded by growing tensions in other areas. Socialist women seeking class-based justice became increasingly frustrated with middle-class liberal feminists' focus on women's individual rights, such as the right to vote (Kessler-Harris 1985, 277). The National Consumers' League continued to support increased legislation staunchly, while women's trade unions pushed for greater organization, each questioning the other's priorities (Newman 1912b, 7). Most seriously, after suffrage had been achieved, the National Woman's Party openly declared its backing for an equal rights amendment, infuriating those who feared that such an amendment would eliminate special legislation for women (National Women's Trade Union League 1922; Blatch and Beyer 1923).

Driven by the success of Goldmark and Brandeis in *Muller*, attorneys and activists developed arguments that relied increasingly on evidence from the social sciences. Many crafted arguments designed to manipulate legal categories through an analysis of facts, but as in the *Muller* case, the facts on which many attorneys and activists relied had little to do with the individual plaintiffs and defendants in the cases. By 1912, Goldmark had pulled together the factual record she had used to develop the brief in *Muller* and published it as a book entitled *Fatigue and Efficiency;* later attorneys then cited this book as evidence of the ill effects of labor on women in their attempts to convince judges that regulating women's work was in the public's interest. In these years, however, the scientific factual evidence helped to support the development of the legal framework described above. Increasingly, facts could do more than drive the outcome in particular cases; the new method of presenting facts had caused a fundamental shift in legal categories by grounding an independent framework for the analysis of women's protective measures.

The power of this development was nowhere more evident than in the efforts of Josephine Goldmark and Felix Frankfurter in support of Oregon's efforts to establish minimum wages for its workers. Still intent on pursuing their strategy of using protective measures for women to pave the way for general protective legislation, Goldmark and Frankfurter produced factual briefs for the two Supreme Court cases of *Stettler v. O'Hara* and *Bunting v. Oregon.* The briefs explained in lavish and voluminous detail the reasons that protecting laborers served the public's interests. The argument of the briefs was at bottom a claim that earlier rulings of state and federal courts had fundamentally misconceived the relationship between constitutional principles and the modern labor market because of a misunderstanding of the realities of modern industrial society.

The Universe of Cases between 1911 and 1923

Like the years between 1898 and 1910, the period of laborer-centered analysis was a time of ferment in the courts over protective labor legislation. Forty-nine cases were reported, seventeen on the federal level and thirty-two on the state level. Even more than in the previous period, courts were more likely to uphold than to strike down protective labor legislation, approving 82 percent of the statutes and disapproving 18 percent. The lopsided nature of these outcomes, however, can be partially explained by the high proportion of women's cases. Over half of the rulings involved challenges to women's measures, almost all of which turned out favorably for the legislatures that had passed them. Sixty-seven percent of the general cases upheld protective legislation, as compared to 93 percent of the cases dealing with protective legislation specifically aimed at women.

The federal courts were upholding more of the general measures as the individuals promoting these statutes developed them more carefully and defended them more consistently in terms of the type of labor they regulated. Nonetheless, judges remained stricter with regard to general legislation, invalidating laws in nearly half the reported opinions. In cases involving women, they continued to view the statutes in a more positive light, invalidating only one.

The state courts continued their high level of activity, considering thirty-two cases during these years. They were becoming less hostile toward protective legislation; during these years in their reported decisions they upheld over 85 percent of such laws. Nonetheless, statutes involving women had a better chance of surviving state court review than general statutes. Between 1911 and 1923, only one state court—the high court in Wyoming—reported a decision invalidating protective legislation for women. In this period, three state high courts invalidated general legislation.

During these years, the main focus was on women's legislation as the courts on both the federal and state level addressed the various justifications for protecting female laborers. In a reversal of the earlier pattern, the cases involving general measures gradually became a sideshow to the main event: consideration of the legitimacy of limits on women's hours and minimum wages.

TABLE 10.   Decisions in All Cases Involving Protective Labor Legislation, 1911–23

	Upheld Protective Legislation	Struck Down Protective Legislation	Total
All cases	40 (82%)	9 (18%)	49
General cases	14 (67%)	7 (34%)	21
Cases involving women	26 (93%)	2 (7%)	28

TABLE 11.   Decisions in Federal Cases Involving Protective Labor Legislation, 1911–23

	Upheld Protective Legislation	Struck Down Protective Legislation	Total
All cases	12 (71%)	5 (29%)	17
General cases	5 (56%)	4 (44%)	9
Cases involving women	7 (87.5%)	1 (12.5%)	8

Brief Overview of Nodes and Litigation in the Period of Laborer-Centered Analysis

As chapter 3 suggested, *Lochner* and *Muller* were watershed cases not so much for their reasoning or outcomes, both of which were unremarkable, but simply because they were decided by the Supreme Court. Because of their visibility and binding impact on other state and federal courts, *Lochner* and *Muller* set the stage for the next round of litigation. Future litigants would focus on the largely factual inquiries that each case unconsciously encouraged, providing powerful incentives to litigants to develop information through social scientific studies rather than simply through analysis of the circumstances of the named plaintiffs and defendants.

This period saw the most direct conflict over two different visions of the labor market and the relationship between employers and employees. The loose consensus about the proper relationship between public and private and between legitimate state action and individual liberty was never completely solid even before the period of negotiation began, but now the consensus itself began to break down along gendered lines. After 1910, the legal system held two models of the employment relationship in a largely unconscious fashion. One—that which applied to male labor—was what modern scholars would recognize as the traditional laissez-faire model. In this model, a hard separation existed between the public and private spheres with most matters of employment falling on the private side of the line. Individual decisions about employment, whether those of the employer or the employee, were fundamentally private choices with little or no social or political significance. Male workers and their employers exercised autonomy freely through their arm's-length negotiation. As a general rule, intervention by the state into this relationship constituted an ille-

TABLE 12.   Decisions in State Cases Involving Protective Labor Legislation, 1911–23

	Upheld Protective Legislation	Struck Down Protective Legislation	Total
All cases	28 (87.5%)	4 (12.5%)	32
General cases	9 (75%)	3 (25%)	12
Cases involving women	19 (95%)	1 (5%)	20

gitimate incursion of the public realm into the private. This model was well rooted in the liberal economic and political theories of the eighteenth and nineteenth centuries. While it was still firmly grounded by legal conceptions of contract and liberty, its cultural and political resonance had begun to wane under the twin pressures of labor agitation and social scientific research (Stanley 1998, 97).

The second model rested upon a different understanding of the relationship between public and private. In this model, the public interest had a wider scope that allowed for state intervention in the relationship between employer and employee because the relationship was not presumed to be fundamentally private. New thinking about alternative feminine forms of citizenship drove this analysis, which addressed women's work (Nackenoff 1999). The public significance of women's work existed on two levels. Women themselves were creatures of public significance because of their role in childbearing and child rearing; as the producers and nurturers of the next generation of citizens, they warranted the state's interest and protection. This alone, however, did not require the generation of a different model for the relationship between employer and employee. Those supporting regulation could simply have argued that women's roles in effect amounted to a thumb placed on police power's side of the balance between liberty and police power.

The second level was the belief that the relationship itself between women and their employers had public significance. In this emerging model, the differences between men's labor and women's labor were obvious and consequential. In particular, many within and outside of the legal community were beginning to believe that women had a different relationship with their employers than men did due to women's lack of autonomy. In this emerging view, women's bargains with their employers were not simple agreements over the price of labor but rather incorporated women's reproductive burdens, both physical and psychological (an insight rediscovered by feminists in the 1970s). While a male employee and his employer were determining the value of his labor, a female employee incorporated her duties to her family and her physical infirmities as part of the bargain. A consensus was emerging that the relationship between a woman and her employer thus contained elements that affected the public interest deeply. A female employee's health and welfare were significant for the state, and thus the employment relationship itself was imbued with public interest, allowing for the state's intervention in circumstances that would not warrant intervention for male workers. This model allowed feminist activists and male policymakers to use the gendered rhetoric of citizenship for closely related but diverse ends. Feminists promoted this rhetoric to achieve maternalist protection of working-class women by middle-class reformers. Policymakers seized upon these arguments to promote the preservation of home and hearth in the name of future citizens and to provide the working-class male with access to middle-class norms of the private domain of the well-regulated home (Nackenoff 1999; Stanley 1998).

The reasoning in the briefs and opinions shows that the legal community's engagement with cases involving women's protective labor legislation had resulted in the establishment of these cases as a separate category within analysis of due process. Once most members of the legal community had settled for themselves the question of whether women indeed constituted a separate class, they began to work through the implications of this conclusion. Cases involving women's protective labor legislation continued to address women's status as somewhat problematic laborers, presenting detailed information that resonated culturally and about which most observers would agree. Specifically, the legal community focused on women's roles as mothers, their physical and role-based difficulties, and their exploitation in the labor market as reasons for protecting them through the law. All of these issues depended upon the advocates' ability to connect women's status as laborers to the public interest in some way. The cases addressing general protective labor legislation during this time still occasionally focused on the scope of liberty and its relationship with police power, but as time went on, they occasionally adopted the new frameworks articulated in the cases involving legislation for women.

The attorneys and judges producing and evaluating these arguments did not appear to recognize the degree of disagreement that was emerging within the feminist community over the role of difference. The legal community did not acknowledge the advocates of equality within feminism; to the extent that feminism had an impact, it was on the side of those seeking to validate laws protecting women. The central role of maternalism encouraged even the advocates seeking stronger rights of citizenship for women to rely on immutable differences. Even as more lawsuits challenging minimum wages began to work their ways through the court systems, most members of the legal community maintained their focus on women's biological differences from men and these physical differences' impact on women's health. Goldmark and Frankfurter's reliance on the relationship between women's socioeconomic position and the need for protection was not picked up by the broader legal community until the decision in *Adkins* and the economic crisis of the 1930s forced the consideration of new arguments.

Having succeeded for the most part in convincing the courts that women needed protection due to their roles as mothers and their physical fragility, attorneys advocating for regulation also began addressing industrial conditions and women's lack of bargaining power due to their poor economic positions. These arguments were sometimes specifically related to women but at other times were general in their framing. The courts hearing cases before 1923 largely ignored such arguments, relying on the well-established explanation that women were physically vulnerable and could be protected on that basis.

Courts' acceptance of women's difference as a valid argument had strong roots in the culture of the time. Erickson points out that this focus on difference became evident at the end of the nineteenth century as analysis in cases and legal treatises turned from social and moral explanations to biological explanations (Erickson 1989, 230). Laws that could have been applied to both sexes were applied only to women because such laws could then be framed as protecting motherhood; this had the possibly unintended consequence of reinforcing differential beliefs about the rights of citizenship belonging to men and women after the turn of the century in the United States. Upholding such laws for women and not for men emphasized the dependence on women's difference at the cost of recognizing the real costs of industrialization (Wikander et al. 1995, 9). Greater protection came at the cost of entrenching a differential conception of women's citizenship (Horton 1999). Thus, it would not be so easy for interested reformers to turn the arguments around to benefit all workers.

Women's protective labor legislation had taken the center stage in the decade before 1920, and by the end of the decade, the outcomes and reasoning in cases involving women's protective labor legislation were driving the legal community's considerations of due process and police power. The Supreme Court heard several cases involving women's protective labor legislation during these years, upholding limits on women's hours in four cases (*Hawley v. Walker*, 232 U.S. 718 (1914);

Miller v. Wilson, 236 U.S. 373 (1915); *Bosley v. McLaughlin*, 236 U.S. 385 (1915); *Dominion Hotel v. Arizona*, 249 U.S. 265 (1919)). Oregon's minimum wage for women survived a challenge in 1917 (*Stettler v. O'Hara*, 243 U.S. 629 (1917)). A lower federal court struck down a minimum wage for female workers in the District of Columbia, a decision the Court would approve in *Adkins v. Children's Hospital* (261 U.S. 525 (1923)).

None of the Supreme Court cases produced extensive opinions, though the justices writing in *Miller* and *Bosley* spent some time laying out responses to worries about due process. Pro- and antiregulatory interests closely watched *Stettler*, but the Court, reduced to eight members by Justice Brandeis's recusal, could not produce a majority opinion. An additional ruling in *Riley v. Massachusetts* upheld an enforcing mechanism for a protective labor legislation statute: the Court approved the conviction of a factory owner for allowing his employees to work five minutes later than the posted lunch hour mandated by statute (*Riley v. Massachusetts*, 232 U.S. 671 (1914)).

The state courts continued to consider, and for the most part to uphold, limits on women's hours of work. Between 1910 and 1913, courts in California, Massachusetts, Illinois, Washington, New York, and Oregon upheld a variety of statutes limiting women to a certain number of hours per day or per week in particular fields of employment (*Ex parte Miller*, 162 Cal. 687 (1912); *Commonwealth v. Riley*, 97 N.E. 367 (Mass. 1912); *People v. Chicago*, 256 Ill. 558 (1912); *Washington v. Somerville*, 67 Wash. 638 (1912); *People v. Kane*, 139 N.Y.S. 350 (Kings Co. Sup. Ct. 1913)). Between 1915 and 1920, New York's Court of Appeals upheld statutes providing for rest periods for women and banning night work by women, and Arizona upheld limits on women's hours (*People v. Charles Schweinler Press*, 214 N.Y. 395 (1915); *People v. Warden*, 109 N.E. 1088 (N.Y. 1915); *Dominion Hotel v. State*, 17 Ariz. 267 (1915)). The *Schweinler* case overruled New York's earlier determination in *People v. Williams* that limits on women's night work were unconstitutional. Only Wyoming struck down a limit on women's hours during this period (*State v. LeBarron*, 162 P. 265 (Wyo. 1917)).

Toward the end of the century's second decade and into the 1920s, courts began to consider the question of minimum wages for women, again upholding them most of the time until the Supreme Court's decision in *Adkins v. Children's Hospital* in 1923. Such statutes were approved in nine cases taking place in six states between 1913 and 1920.[1]

Most minimum wage provisions established a commission or board that was charged with investigating economic conditions in the industries and areas covered by the statute. The commission would then promulgate regulations, usually establishing a minimum weekly wage with which employers in the affected occupations had to comply. The reasoning in these cases followed the framework established to address regulations mandating limits on the hours of women's labor. While those opposing these regulations challenged the operation of such commissions on the ground that they inappropriately exercised legislative power, the main argument levied against minimum wage boards was that the mandated minimum wage itself violated women's and their employers' rights to due process (see, e.g., *Holcombe v. Creamer*, 120 N.E. 354 (Mass. 1918)). Questions about the legitimacy of the minimum wage were to consume the legal community during the 1930s as disagreements immediately developed over the Court's reasoning in *Adkins*. The next chapter will take up this conflict and minimum wages more generally.

As far as general legislation was concerned, the federal courts considered varied topics and had mixed reactions. An evenly divided Supreme Court upheld Oregon's ten-hour-per-day limit on labor, citing the possibility for overtime pay (*Bunting v. Oregon*, 243 U.S. 426 (1917)). The Court also upheld measures prohibiting company stores in mining towns from paying their employees in scrip, establishing a system of workers' compensation, and mandating various controls on railroad employees, including limitations on hours of labor (*Keokee Coke Co. v. Taylor*, 234 U.S. 225 (1914); *Jeffrey Mfg. Co. v. Blagg*, 235 U.S. 571 (1915); *Wilson v. New*, 243 U.S. 332 (1917)). During the same period, however, the Court struck down two congressional statutes limiting child labor and a state statute outlawing yellow-dog contracts (contracts that barred employees from joining unions) (*Hammer v. Dagenhart*, 247 U.S. 251 (1918); *Bailey v. Drexel Furniture Co.*, 259 U.S. 20 (1922); *Coppage v. Kansas*, 236 U.S. 1 (1915)).

On the state level, the issues were not as diffuse. Nearly half (five)

---

1. Minimum wages were approved in Ohio (*Ex parte Hawley*, 98 N.E. 1126 (Ohio 1913)), Oregon (*Stettler v. O'Hara*, 139 P. 743 (Ore. 1914)); *Simpson v. O'Hara*, 70 Ore. 260 (1914)), Arkansas (*State v. Crowe*, 130 Ark. 272 (1917)), Minnesota (*Williams v. Evans*, 139 Minn. 32 (1917); *G. O. Miller Telephone Co. v. Minimum Wage Commission*, 177 N.W. 341 (Minn. 1920)), Massachusetts (*Holcombe v. Creamer*, 231 Mass. 99 (1918)), and Washington (*Larsen v. Rice*, 100 Wash. 642 (1918); *Spokane Hotel Co. v. Younger*, 113 Wash. 359 (1920)).

of the state cases addressing general legislation concerned statutes limiting workers' hours of labor. Two of the statutes were upheld and
three were struck down, though the Alaska statute was not invalidated
on due process or equal protection grounds (*State v. J. J. Newman Lumber Co.*, 102 Miss. 802 (1912); *State v. Barba*, 61 So. 784 (La. 1913); *State v.
Bunting*, 139 P. 731 (Ore. 1914); *Commonwealth v. Boston & Maine R.R.*,
110 N.E. 264 (Mass. 1915); *U.S. v. Northern Commercial Co.*, 6 Alaska 94
(1918)).[2] Toward the end of the period, the Kansas high court heard
challenges to industrial commissions established to regulate particular
industries such as mining and meatpacking; the operation of both commissions was upheld (*Court of Industrial Relations v. Charles Wolff Packing Co.*, 109 Kan. 629 (1921); *State v. Howat*, 109 Kan. 376 (1921)). Like
minimum wage boards, such commissions were becoming a common
feature across the nation at the time.

Applications of the New Conceptions of Liberty

In these years, property dropped almost entirely out of the picture; the
central point of analysis concerning individuals' rights had become liberty, and a node of conflict developed around its operation with respect
to men's work. By 1915 or so, the legal community had settled on framing liberty as a largely male-centered right of self-ownership, arguing
over its particular application in general cases. The role of liberty
remained somewhat in flux in cases regarding protective labor legislation for women, however, and this discussion became increasingly contentious between 1911 and 1923. As Stanley has shown, configuring
women as owners of themselves was problematic particularly in reference to contract; the widespread acceptance of maternalist rhetoric in
the realm of public policy highlighted this tension (Stanley 1998). By
the time of the Supreme Court's consideration of California's eight-
hour limit on women's labor in *Miller v. Wilson* and *Bosley v. McLaughlin* in 1914, attorneys and courts were articulating conflicting explanations for how women could and did exercise liberty. As in the earlier
years, the main focus was on how female laborers related to the guar-

---

2. The Mississippi and Oregon courts upheld limits on labor, while the Louisiana
and Massachusetts courts struck them down on due process or equal protection grounds.
The Alaska statute failed because the legislature improperly submitted it to the public for
a popular vote.

antee of liberty, but in the period of laborer-centered analysis, additional arguments about women's difficulties in the workplace began to emerge, arguments that could ultimately be generalized to address men's workplace struggles as well. The legal community debated two major issues involving liberty: the nature of women's liberty and the impact of protective labor legislation on women's liberty. Discussions about the nature of women's liberty were now mostly gendered and incorporated an understanding that it did not have the strongly private nature based in self-ownership that opponents of protective measures commonly attributed to male liberty. While arguments over the impact of protective labor legislation on liberty had the potential to transcend gender, judges did not immediately recognize this potential. Instead, they largely continued to see women's bargaining power as qualitatively different from that of men and thus as allowing greater leeway for public intervention.

Attorneys arguing against the validity of these statutes claimed that the state legislatures had gone too far in protecting women, but by this time even the opponents of protective labor legislation acknowledged that the limits for men and women were different. Widespread acceptance of difference led even the opponents of measures protecting women to articulate a limited scope for women's liberty. Arguing against California's eight-hour limit for women, the attorneys for the employer claimed that the legislature had the right to pass laws protecting both women and men: "it is the right to legislate when the employment becomes *dangerous*" (Flint and Van Dyke 1914, 40). The only difference was that for women, the scope of danger was broader. Thus they claimed that her personal liberty of contract, though subject to more extensive limits, was the same as that of men, and that women exercised liberty in the same way that men did (40). The internal construction of liberty was identical, though women faced more external limits. In these attorneys' analysis, California had strayed too far from the basic principles established to address general protective labor legislation (84). They argued that this tendency to move away from the bedrock right of liberty at stake in cases such as *Lochner* masked illegitimate attempts to use the states' police power to achieve outcomes that would be better reached through individual bargaining or through private labor organization (123). These actions were damaging to individual women, the attorneys asserted, because they undermined the individual female laborer's right to bargain on her own behalf, thereby limiting her liberty. Such liberty appeared very much like the laissez-faire image of private autonomy at stake in *Lochner*.

The attorneys arguing for the validity of the statutes at issue in *Miller* and *Bosley* challenged these views of the effect of women's protective labor legislation upon women's liberty. They endorsed a gendered conception of women's liberty relating to women's weaker positions in the marketplace. In their view, protective laws, far from limiting the freedom of individuals, provided greater liberty for those members of the labor marketplace who had less initial freedom. In this interpretation, the state was perfectly justified in protecting such laborers: "The right of the state to protect its citizens, particularly its women and children, from oppressive bargainers has been repeatedly recognized by this and other American courts" (Webb, Denman, and Arnold 1914, 25). Because women and children were particularly at risk of being exploited by unscrupulous or greedy employers, the state's action in setting minimum standards for employment contracts ensured that such workers would not become embroiled in particularly unfair contracts. In this interpretation, the evolution of considerations of protective labor legislation from basic repetitions of male-centered conceptions of liberty to a deeper questioning of how such liberty was exercised by nonparadigmatic (i.e., female) workers was an advance, not a negative development. Nonetheless, such arguments relied on portraying women as special cases for regulation and as different from the normative male worker.

Three years later, Josephine Goldmark and Felix Frankfurter sought to convince the Supreme Court to uphold Oregon's minimum wage for women. Part of their argument concerning liberty was even more deeply gendered than the claims in the California cases. Picking up on claims that had succeeded in state courts, they grounded their discussion of bargaining power on the particular characteristics of female workers rather than in the structural imbalance of power between employers and employees, regardless of gender. They claimed that the justification for protecting women rested comfortably upon women's inability to negotiate effectively and equally with their employers (Frankfurter and Goldmark 1916, A44). This imbalance existed for a variety of reasons; for instance, they claimed that women were more inclined to accept any kind of work, regardless of the poor conditions, in order to maintain their families. They also argued that women were less psychologically suited to drive effective bargains with their employers (A44).

Other parts of their argument focused more generally on the impact of protective legislation on the laborer's liberty. These claims were not as deeply gendered. Frankfurter and Goldmark began their discussion of liberty by questioning the framing of liberty interests by opponents of the Oregon statute. "What, then, is the 'liberty' which these plaintiffs assert and show to be really curtailed? It is nothing but the 'liberty' of not being required to get leave of the Commission before making contracts below a living wage" (Frankfurter and Goldmark 1916, A20). They then argued that the free market actually inhibited workers' capacity to exercise liberty: "When no limit exists below which wages may not fall, the laborer's freedom is in effect totally destroyed. He has no reserves upon which to draw and hence must accept any terms, regardless of his value" (330). The use of the male pronoun in this sentence suggests the generalizability of this argument to minimum wages for male workers as well as women. Their critique of the labor market assumed the basic legitimacy of markets but questioned the fairness of the existing baseline, in some ways prefiguring arguments that constitutional scholar Cass Sunstein would make several decades later (Sunstein 1993).

In this understanding, protective labor legislation strengthened all laborers' rights to contract freely with regard to their labor. This was still a transitional argument, as it did not challenge the primacy of liberty of contract. Goldmark and Frankfurter engaged in an internal critique of the concept, arguing that what their opponents labeled liberty of contract was in fact a sham, providing only a cover for employers to abuse their employees freely (Frankfurter and Goldmark 1916). This analysis too was framed in gender-neutral terms: "True freedom of contract is established, rather than impaired, by such restrictions. Their very purpose is to assure the parties an equal basis for bargaining, so that they may be *free* to bargain on the merits" (A47–48, emphasized in original). Nonetheless, the argument retained a fundamentally gendered thrust: by raising women to a more equal footing with their employers, the state could help women to emulate the fairer contracts generated by male employees and their employers, particularly when the male employees were unionized. The brief thus conceived of women's liberty as depending upon public concern and regulation. This dual strategy enabled Goldmark and Frankfurter to advance arguments that could ultimately apply to male laborers, while relying on the kinds of arguments that had convinced the courts for the last several years to uphold legislation for women.

Most courts that heard challenges to women's protective labor legislation upheld the legislation, rejecting arguments that the statutes in question limited women's liberty in inappropriate ways. The federal courts did not rise to the challenge of analyzing women's liberty extensively in gendered terms or of determining precisely the relationship between protective legislation and laborers' liberty. At this time, federal judges had not yet begun to pick up on the state courts' fuller analyses of liberty, though attorneys' and state judges' interpretations were shaping the arguments that the federal courts would later validate. In these years, however, the Supreme Court paid little attention to elaborate arguments over women's liberty, following *Muller* by simply claiming in most cases that the individuals' liberties were overridden by the proper exercise of police power in the public interest. For instance, in *Bosley v. McLaughlin*, the Court concluded that the overriding risks to the health of the female student nurses warranted limiting their hours of labor (392). Concerns about women's physical conditions continued to interest the courts during these years, maintaining the push toward modes of analysis that depended upon difference for their success. Only in the first stage of the challenge to the District of Columbia's minimum wage for women did the federal courts discuss liberty in any great degree, and in that case, the court relied upon the understandings of male liberty that had prevailed earlier.

The district court that heard the *Adkins* case on the trial level relied on precedents addressing general legislation to show that the right to liberty necessarily overrode the minimum wage in question. While the case consolidated separate challenges to the minimum wage by the Children's Hospital with another case, the court focused on the plight of one Willie Lyons, an elevator operator in the District of Columbia Congress Hotel (*Children's Hospital v. Adkins*, 284 F. 613, 614–15 (D. D.C. 1922)). She had bargained with the hotel for a monthly wage of thirty-five dollars and two meals a day; the minimum wage board issued an order barring female hotel employees from earning less than $71.50 per month (614–15). As a result, explained the court, Lyons had lost her position to a man who could work for a lower wage than that fixed by the minimum wage board (618). The court excoriated this development, chastising the legislature for its paternalistic action: "Take from the citizen the right to freely contract and sell his labor for the highest wage which his individual skill and efficiency will command, and the laborer would be reduced to an automaton—a mere creature of the state" (623). The universally male gender-neutral language of the majority underlined its reasoning, which simply applied the generally understood guarantee of liberty to the female workers affected by the statute. Such reasoning relied on the implicitly male-centered conception of liberty of contract developed in the previous period, merely replacing the male subject of the guarantee of liberty with a female subject. In his dissent, Chief Justice Smyth argued that gender did matter. He praised Congress's investigation into women's special situation and relied upon the health interests at stake to argue that the statute should have been upheld (634–37).

On the state level, no protective law aimed at female laborers was invalidated in the period of laborer-centered analysis on the ground that it violated women's liberty of contract. This did not mean, however, that the state courts ignored the role of liberty in these cases. As in the years of specific balancing, courts relied upon women's roles in reproduction, child rearing, and homemaking as well as on their weaker positions in the labor market (see, for instance, *Schweinler*). Unlike their federal counterparts, state-level judges were beginning to accept the argument that protective labor legislation had the capacity to enhance women's liberty of contract. Ultimately this would have implications for considerations of protective labor legislation in the next period: rather than returning to discussions of liberty and trying to work out the precise scope of liberty, courts during the 1920s and 1930s would focus on the extent to which the restrictions placed upon women constituted proper exercises of police power and simultaneously increased liberty by enlarging bargaining options.

Several state courts endorsed the kinds of arguments that Goldmark and Frankfurter would make to the Supreme Court in 1916. They reasoned that the negative conditions women faced in the labor market led to severe limits on their liberty, not through governmental interference with the right to make contracts, but rather because of the penury that led disempowered workers to accept almost any offer of employment, no matter how exploitative. A New York court, citing the large influx of women and children into the labor market, explained that such laborers were unable to compete successfully with men, "com-pell[ing] them to submit to conditions and terms of service which it cannot be presumed they would freely choose. Their liberty to contract to sell their labor may be but another name for involuntary service cre-ated by existing industrial conditions" (*People v. Kane*, 357).[3] The only way to enhance women's exercise of liberty was thus to limit their abil-ity to agree to horrible bargains (*People v. Kane*, 357). The Oregon high court sustained a minimum wage for women along the same lines, claiming that women working for inadequate wages had no choice but to accept their employers' offers, leaving them with substantially less liberty in the absence of state intervention (*Stettler v. O'Hara*, 139 P. 743, 749 (Ore. 1914)). In Minnesota, the state supreme court also ruled in favor of a minimum wage for these reasons, claiming that their find-ing was solidly backed by the findings of public investigators: "women in the trades are . . . not paid so well as men are paid for the same ser-vice . . . in many cases the pay they receive for working during all the working hours of the day is not enough to meet the cost of reasonable living" (*Williams v. Evans*, 139 Minn. 32, 40 (1917)). Women's inability to extract a living wage from their employers marked them as funda-mentally unfree. Thus, establishing a minimum wage set a ground level for negotiations, enabling women to drive fairer bargains for themselves and thereby enhancing their liberty of contract (*Williams v. Evans*, 40).

On the state level, the discussion of liberty in cases involving women's protective labor legislation had shifted to a more specific analysis of the nonantagonistic relationship between women's liberty and the public interest. In keeping with the tendency that had emerged in the previous decades to consider women's legislation separately, the legal community focused its arguments on how women exercised lib-erty and on the precise interaction between such statutes and women's liberty. These issues were the central points in contention in the node of conflict around women's liberty. In these laborer-centered analyses, those supporting protective labor legislation began to articulate the notion that protective laws enhanced women's liberty by making it eas-ier for them to bargain effectively with their employers. For these indi-viduals, protective laws in effect raised women to a more equal plane

---

3. While such arguments with respect to male hirelings could not yet succeed in the legal arena, they had been popular in class-based critiques of the economic system since the abolition of slavery (Stanley 1998, 70).

with men, enabling them to begin their negotiations from a stronger baseline. Opponents, who argued both that such adjustments were inappropriate and that they limited, rather than enhanced, women's freedom of contract challenged this conception. The growing acceptance of a connection between poor bargaining conditions and liberty had important implications for police power.

Deeply Gendered and Potentially Broader Arguments about Police Power

While cases were still taking place within the general constitutional framework of the due process clause, most of the legal community's analysis between 1911 and 1923 was more narrowly focused on police power. The debate addressed particularly the question of what factors in women's lives justified the exercise of police power to protect them from the vicissitudes of the labor market. These arguments rested largely on the factual research that organizations advocating reform had conducted. Like the arguments concerning liberty, the claims about police power were somewhat conflicted in their uses of gender. Uncertainty about the significance of women's roles as mothers for the purposes of determining the extent of police power generated one set of arguments. In this context, laypeople, attorneys, and courts all considered the extent to which the state's interest in mothers and mothering was a legitimate public interest, but the motivations driving these actors differed greatly. Advocates for statutes and judges upholding them also relied on general claims about the physical risks of overwork and work for low wages, but while such claims were often gender-neutral on the surface, they masked a gendered conception of physical debility. Finally, those supporting protective measures relied upon structural economic arguments. While these arguments had the potential to reach beyond women's protective labor legislation, they were most often framed in gendered ways.

Generally, these arguments took place within an emerging sense that women's work and women's agreements with their employers were not fundamentally private but imbued with public significance. Advocates for protective labor legislation had sought primarily to promote the constitutionality of the legislation, not to change the fundamental legal framework, but their actions ultimately reconfigured the way that the legal system conceived of the nature of the labor market.

Police Power and the Protection of Mothers

The most convincing justification for protective labor legislation for
women was that it accommodated women's special status as mothers or
potential mothers. In these years, the legal community focused on the
effect of women's roles as mothers rather than working to differentiate
women from men. Such arguments were nonetheless necessarily based
on women's differences from men and portrayed women as problematic laborers because of their primary service to society as the source of
the next generation. Through laborer-centered analysis, advocates for
protective labor legislation gained full benefit from female-centered and
feminist groups' research on mothers and mothering, using the information the groups had gathered to advance their legal agendas. Due to
realist advances in the prior decade, the legitimacy of factual and social
scientific claims was now well established throughout the legal community. The agendas of advocates, however, did not always completely
match the goals for which reform-minded groups had compiled the
information, and this section will explore this process.

As Theda Skocpol and other scholars have demonstrated, concern
for motherhood and mothers was a powerful tool for activists in the
Progressive Era and immediately afterward (Skocpol 1992, 321–73). By
emphasizing women's roles as mothers, reformers could tap into
maternalist sentiments common during the time and encourage the
legal community to view protective labor legislation favorably.
Motives for relying on motherhood to advance the cause of protective
legislation were mixed. Many individuals, including members of
prominent labor unions, the National Consumers' League, and the
National Women's Trade Union League, saw the approval of protective
labor legislation for women as the first step toward validating protective labor legislation for all workers and used motherhood simply as
the most effective argumentative strategy to achieve the first stage of
regulation (Skocpol 1992, 376–78). Others, as discussed below, believed
that women needed particular protection regardless of what happened
in other areas. In this view, motherhood was a marker of women's special nature, which needed protection above and beyond that of the normative male worker. In the period between 1923 and 1937, as chapter 5
will show, the subterranean tensions among activists with these differing agendas would give way to open hostility.

Throughout the second decade of the century, the National Consumers' League and its local chapters, emboldened by their success in *Muller,* worked tirelessly to demonstrate that excessive labor was harmful to mothers and that such harm had definite repercussions for the rest of society. In their view, women's roles as mothers were both cause and effect of the harms that women suffered in the workplace from overwork and low pay. The Connecticut chapter explained that mothers, due to their devotion to their children, were more subject than men to exploitation in the labor marketplace. Women would gladly accept low wages that men would scornfully reject because of their tender interest in children and family; this natural inclination superseded the economic law of supply and demand (Consumers' League of Connecticut 1919, 5). Even young women who were not yet mothers would feel this kind of responsibility toward their families, working long hours to ensure the health and safety of younger siblings as well as to save up enough money to marry and indulge their maternal instincts directly (Consumers' League of Connecticut 1919, 5). Because women had a biological need to protect and defend children, actual or potential, they would accept almost any wages offered. Because of this tendency, argued advocates of protection for women, statutory limits in the form of both restrictions on hours and minimum wages were both appropriate and necessary.

Members of the Women's Trade Union League of Chicago claimed that women's roles as mothers justified the state's intervention on the behalf of the race (loosely understood as white melting-pot Americans). In a 1919 pamphlet, the trade union league members claimed that protective legislation was necessary, for without it, "How shall the State in its own interest see that these women, the mothers of our citizens of the future, are preserved in health so that they may perpetuate a vigorous and virile race?" (Women's Trade Union League of Chicago 1919, 3). By 1919, this and other statements evinced the inroads that the legal battle for protective labor legislation had made in public discourse: lay advocates had learned that to be successful, they had to frame their arguments in the legal terms of the state's permissible public interest. In doing so, they focused on motherhood as the strongest argument, even though it was not readily translatable into a basis for extending regulation to male workers. As earlier cases had demonstrated, interest in women as a class of reproducers could justify regulating their labor; thus the reform-minded groups researched and spoke on this theme. This argument in its most stark and eugenics-based form, common among attorneys and courts in the century's second decade, appeared in some feminist publications during these years.[4] The feminist community would hotly contest such notions during the later 1920s and 1930s.

As in the period of specific balancing, the National Consumers' League continued to provide information and litigation support to reformers who sought to promote legislation mandating protection for workers. In the Oregon minimum-wage case, *Stettler v. O'Hara*, Josephine Goldmark (then the publication secretary) coauthored the lead brief with Felix Frankfurter. They argued that women's pivotal roles as mothers justified the security of a mandatory minimum wage. Since women were "the future mothers of the Republic," their overwork would have dire consequences for the nation as a whole for generations to come (Frankfurter and Goldmark n.d., 99). Throughout their brief, Frankfurter and Goldmark elaborated on this argument by tying their evidence about women's health to the need to protect the race (Frankfurter and Goldmark n.d.). This connection justified the link between protection of women and the public interest. In their analysis, however, they emphasized women's needs to fulfill both their roles as mothers and their roles as workers, claiming that these roles were often intertwined. While they focused on women as workers, the problem they addressed was how the state could accommodate female laborers by ensuring that their capacity to bear and raise children would not be endangered.

In contrast to this approach, nonfeminist advocates of protection portrayed women as marginal and deeply problematic workers because of their roles as mothers. Nonetheless, they also argued that women's work was fundamentally a matter of public concern. In nonfeminist advocates' view, the problem that protective legislation addressed was the simple fact that women worked outside the home

---

4. Such beliefs and statements were by no means the exclusive province of reform-minded women's groups. Typical of union attitudes during this period was that of the American Federation of Labor, which believed that while female workers were entitled to equal pay for equal work, "Women workers must not be permitted to perform tasks disproportionate to their physical strength or which tend to impair their potential motherhood and prevent the continuation of a nation of strong, healthy, sturdy and intelligent men and women" (American Federation of Labor 1919). The AFL had endorsed early the concept that women, like workers who performed particular kinds of hazardous labor or worked in particularly difficult situations, needed statutory protection—unionization, in the AFL's view, would never be a good solution to the special problems that female workers faced (Foner 1979, 212–56).

for wages. In arguing for the constitutionality of the statutes at issue in *Miller v. Wilson* and *Bosley v. McLaughlin*, California's attorneys claimed that while women increasingly worked for wages outside the home, their primary contribution to society was not their paid labor, but their work in the home (Webb, Denman, and Arnold 1914, 28). The attorneys then expressed their concerns about the decline of the so-called native population and the rising tide of immigrants unfamiliar with American values; this development threatened the entire nation (28–29). Rapid social and cultural degeneration was attributable to one factor: the widespread entry of women into the paid labor economy. As women entered the labor market, they lost their power of biological and cultural reproduction to the various hazards of the workplace (28–29).

For these supporters of minimum wages, the preservation of this "American" stock was of vital importance, because only these individuals could preserve and translate cherished American values to the next generation without distortion. This risk to America's future justified limiting women's work severely in the interest of parrying the dangers to civilization (Webb, Denman, and Arnold 1914, 25).[5] While few attorneys made such direct anti-immigrant arguments, the fear of a rising tide of immigrant culture underlined many lawyers' claims about the importance of protecting motherhood. Such arguments demonstrate that many members of the legal community used maternalist arguments not to enhance women's status in the workplace or to nurture more fertile ground for general legislation, but rather to push women out of the workplace. In this view, when women returned to the home, they could revivify a semimythical past in which women generally performed only wholesome household labor and raised large families, eschewing involvement in the outside world. Women's reentry into the home would also strengthen traditional conceptions of male workers' freedoms through the re-creation of an ordered private realm free of labor for men (Stanley 1998).

The Supreme Court in the years before 1920 seemed to be satisfied with both types of explanations, deeming them uncontroversial (or

---

5. The attorneys went on to hint that a racial catastrophe was in the making: "It is not our purpose to engage in a discussion whether our feverish economic activity is the *causa causans* or the *causa sine qua non*, or any cause at all of what, if it is not checked, means the speedy extermination of Anglo-Saxon stock in America, and the substitution in its place of the Mediterranean and West Asiatic races. Nor does it concern us whether the substitution may or may not be racially advantageous" (Webb, Denman, and Arnold 1914, 29).

uninteresting) enough to warrant little discussion. In *Miller v. Wilson*, the Court upheld an eight-hour-per-day limit on female hotel workers on the authority of *Muller v. Oregon*, claiming that women's maternal functions and role in preserving the strength and vigor of the race were ample considerations for allowing the regulation (*Miller v. Wilson*, 380). Believing that the analysis in *Muller* had addressed the issue completely, in most of the cases, the Court simply made reference to *Muller* and left it at that.

Not so with the state courts. Setting the stage for later litigation in the federal courts, they delved into the legal and factual questions raised by such laws. In justifying their acceptance of the link between women's physical fragility and the dangers to the future generation, the judges often examined the relationship closely and explained it carefully, particularly in the years immediately after 1910. The Illinois Supreme Court took judicial notice that "on account of woman's physical structure and maternal functions her health, and that of her offspring, was subject to be injuriously affected by requiring her to perform long hours of labor" (*People v. Elerding*, 254 Ill. 579, 583–84 (1912)). This link was crucial in providing a public interest "hook" on which to hang an argument based in police power. The state exercised its police power through its regulation of women in the public interest. Women's liberty was bounded by a direct public health interest in them, by public interest in children and reproduction, and by a more generalized public interest in them. In their embrace of this broader conception of public interest, they largely accepted the nonfeminist advocates' conception of women's paid employment as an occasional necessary evil. For such judges, these factors combined to create a powerful public force that outweighed weaker countervailing interests in women's liberty, which as demonstrated above, was often enhanced by protective legislation.

Referring to the volumes of data amassed by the state and various research organizations, the New York Court of Appeals declared that safeguarding women's health was a matter of "vital importance" not so much for the women's own benefit, but rather "for the sake of the children whom a great majority of them will be called on to bear and who will almost inevitably display in their deficiencies the unfortunate inheritance conferred upon them by physically broken down mothers" (*Schweinler*, 406). Other high courts in various states, including Illinois, Washington, California, and Arkansas, based their rulings at least in part on statements about the physical risks to children attributable to women's poor working conditions (*Elerding*, 583–84; *Somerville*, 644–45; *Ex parte Miller*, 697; *State v. Crowe*, 130 Ark. 272, 278–79 (1917)).

Women's social roles as mothers also provided a powerful ground for allowing them to be the subjects of special protection. Alice Kessler-Harris and others have discussed the ways that references to motherhood justified upholding legislation that would otherwise fall (Kessler-Harris 1982, 184). Courts often linked this distinction to women's responsibility for maintaining the household for the family. The California high court relied on such reasoning to uphold an eight-hour limit on women's labor in certain occupations, explaining that women who worked also had household duties, resulting in a much longer working day than the hours on the time clock (*Ex parte Miller*, 697). Clearly, if women had to be available to raise children and maintain the household, their ability to work long hours would be inhibited. This social difference perceived by the courts translated into a legal difference, justifying the separation of women into a single class of workers, regardless of what kind of labor they performed.[6] Women's individualistic right to liberty was mitigated by their social duty as the caretakers for children. Further, their duty to their children limited their ability to drive bargains with their employers, again raising the possibility that protective labor legislation would give them more liberty rather than restricting them.

The arguments regarding motherhood thus enhanced the image of women as problematic workers. This reinforced the tendency for the legal community to focus on laborers rather than on the work they performed. By tapping into maternalist and eugenicist concerns about female laborers, advocates for protective legislation could convince courts to uphold the laws. Not all attorneys, however, were promoting the feminist agenda of improving women's circumstances in the workplace with their arguments. Feminist activists and attorneys who were mostly concerned with enabling women to work shorter hours for higher wages promoted arguments that were equally useful to attor-

---

6. This broad interest in protecting women was not universal, however. Many statutes had specific exclusions for cannery workers and domestic labor, leaving the most vulnerable and lowest-paid workers unprotected. These exclusions largely affected women of color and the most recent immigrants. Since such women had even more marginal claims on citizenship than white, nonimmigrant women, states' unwillingness to protect them was unsurprising analytically. Practically, such women had few powerful political allies among reformers.

neys and judges who saw women principally as mothers and only secondarily as workers; some of these individuals expressed dismay at women's mass entrance into the paid labor market. Thus, while references to women's roles as mothers were effective in supporting protective legislation for women, this technique had implications that would trouble advocates for equality after 1923.

The gendered arguments for protecting women also advanced a conception of the relationship between employer and employee that departed from the laissez-faire beliefs prevalent with respect to protective measures for men. Maternalist efforts to reconceive women's citizenship were beginning to have some impact in the legal arena (Nackenoff 1999). In this view, labor itself had public implications in its effects upon the laborer, since the laborer herself had a public role in her connection to the next generation of citizens. These developments coincided with the high-water mark for feminist activism in the early twentieth century as women achieved the ballot in federal elections. Maternalism had grounded a new understanding of the state as a partner for citizens, assisting them to achieve fuller lives through its protective efforts (Nackenoff 1999). While it applied most directly to women, this conception of the public significance of laborers' conditions and labor legislation could be extended beyond female workers, and the advocates for wide-scale reform of working conditions were quick to recognize and exploit this possibility.

Potentially Broader Arguments Based on Police Power: Physical Risks and Roles

Motherhood provided a justification for protective labor legislation for women, but did not help with the broader aim of achieving protection for all wage laborers, both male and female. Arguments about the physical risks of labor had this potential. In the period of laborer-centered analysis, activists, lawyers, and judges often discussed the various physical risks inherent in working for wages. In order to succeed in court, reformers and interested members of the legal community focused these arguments on the physical risks that women faced. Attention to women's differences enabled advocates to separate laws protecting women from the general laws aimed at men—the default position for general laws was still that they were invalid, but the default position that had emerged for women's laws was that they were valid. Furthermore, significant doctrinal differences undergirded the nature of the relationship between male employees and their employers and female employees and their employers. Nonetheless, the specific arguments about women could sometimes be generalized to other workers. In discussions of physical risks, the juxtaposition between arguments addressing women's situation and statements about the general risks of labor became increasingly contradictory. Organizations struggled to come to terms with whether they were ultimately in favor of special legislation for women, regardless of what level of protection men ultimately achieved. While arguments based on the physical risks to the laborer had the potential to apply beyond women, when such arguments appeared in women's cases, they largely portrayed a problematic laborer who was definitely gendered female. Nonetheless, even without a conscious strategy for litigation, reform-promoting organizations saw their new conception of the American worker's public significance beginning to spill over to affect general legislation as well.

Many advocates based their estimation of the special risks to women directly on women's biological differences from men above and beyond women's capacity to bear children. One such advocate claimed, "Women cannot be made men by act of legislature or even by an amendment to the United States Constitution. That does not mean women are inferior or superior to men. Refusal to recognize the biological differences between men and women does not make for equality" (Blatch and Beyer 1923, 116). This view, which the Supreme Court had acknowledged in *Muller*, emphasized women's particular unfitness for the physical strains associated with industrial labor. The National Consumers' League also emphasized women's biological limitations, claiming that arguments for parity in legislation ignored reality (National Consumers' League 1922, 3). By this time, the National Consumers' League was beginning to exhibit some frustration with advocates for equality, claiming that these differences would always necessitate special treatment for women: "This is no matter of today or tomorrow. The inherent differences are permanent. Women will always need many laws different from those needed by men" (3). As the years passed, advocates on both sides would become even more polarized, as the next chapter will demonstrate.

Likewise, some feminist advocates for protective labor legislation highlighted the special physical risks they believed women faced when working long hours. The state chapters of the Consumers' League in particular emphasized this argument, relying on their own studies and on studies conducted by states or the federal government. In a 1922 pamphlet, the Consumers' League of Connecticut argued that ten hours of work in a day was harmful for women, because women were naturally more frail than men. Women were thus more subject to workplace injuries, with all of the grave consequences for the household attendant upon such injuries. The Consumers' League claimed that women tended to be in greater danger of injury both because they did not have men's physical strength and because they would continue to work even when fatigued or ill, something that men would not do (Consumers' League of Connecticut 1922). None of these consequences boded well for healthy home life for the female employees or for their families. Physical difference combined with women's household responsibilities to create a particular need for regulation: women's lesser physical abilities led them to neglect their household duties, leading to serious problems, while women's household responsibilities taxed their strength and endurance, leaving even less energy for the workplace. While feminists saw this primarily as a limit on women's liberty, others construed it as damaging men's rights. As Stanley has shown, women's inability to maintain the household could be understood as a limit on men's access to idealized freedom, since the classical model assumed an ordered home life into which the male laborer could retreat after his daily struggle for subsistence was complete (Stanley 1998, 161–64, 195). Regardless of their focus, however, like the legal community the lay advocates maintained a focus on female workers and the dangers and harms they faced in the workplace, not on the type of labor they were performing.

In the years of laborer-centered analysis, attorneys arguing for protective measures in the Supreme Court did not worry about the tensions between general arguments about the physical strains associated with the workplace and specific arguments relating to women's particular risks. They simply used both kinds of arguments to justify the challenged legislation on the basis of the laborer's needs and liberty interests. The Supreme Court's ruling in *Muller* had encouraged later attorneys to emphasize the role of women's health in their briefs even when the attorneys were not connected with reform-minded groups. Thus, in his arguments in favor of upholding an employer's conviction for allowing his female employees to work five minutes into their statutory lunch break, the attorney for the State of Massachusetts claimed that *Muller's* reasoning about women's health clearly applied to the *Riley* case (Swift 1914, 4). Work in factories posed both mental and physical risks to the health of the female employees, justifying rigid enforcement of breaks (16). In Swift's argument, the loss of adequate meal time carried significant health risks for women in particular (26). The response to these arguments was that the criminal conviction of a man for allowing women to work five minutes longer than the statute allowed bore no substantial relationship to protecting women from injury (Jennings and Brayton 1914, 8–9).

The challenges to the limitations at issue in *Miller v. Wilson* produced more conflict about how women's physical condition was threatened and the subsequent capacity of the state to regulate. The argument between the opposing sides simultaneously hinted at the possibility of reading physical risks more broadly. Citing Goldmark's work in the *Muller* brief, the California team defending an eight-hour limit for female workers declared, "The relationship between fatigue . . . and . . . health . . . is so well recognized that it is not necessary to refresh the judicial knowledge of the court with citations from medical authorities and the reports of public investigation" (Webb, Denman, and Arnold 1914, 6–7). The gender-neutral phrasing could have served as well for a case involving general legislation, particularly since much of the information Goldmark had compiled applied to both men and women.

The attorneys challenging the regulation in *Miller* appeared not to understand that a significant shift had taken place with respect to women's legislation. They attempted to use the earlier male-centered framework, which required the legislature to articulate a relationship between the type of labor being regulated and public health (Flint and Van Dyke 1914, 25–26). Rather than focusing on whether the state had the authority to regulate women's labor, they argued instead that the measure passed by the State of California, which covered women in a variety of occupations,[7] was far too broad in its scope. They complained that "one of the most comprehensive, diverse and varied fields of economic activity, the employment of women—a field in which one perfectly distinct class of business activity differs by a whole pole from

---

7. The law limited women to eight hours of labor in manufacturing firms, mechanical or mercantile establishments, laundries, hotels, restaurants, telephone companies, or transportation companies and had a specific exemption for cannery workers (*Bosley v. McLaughlin*, 236 U.S. 385 (1915)).

another—[was] covered in a small page and a half of crude legislation" (Flint and Van Dyke 1914, 34). Such a blunderbuss approach, in their view, demonstrated that the legislature was not really interested in women's health, but rather was seeking to impose its own views concerning the balance of industrial power, tipping the scales in favor of employees (16). Their attempt to shift back to the general framework rather than using the framework that had developed regarding women's laws was not successful.

In the companion case of *Bosley v. McLaughlin*, which addressed the same law, the attorneys arguing against the law also charged that the state assembly had attempted to legislate on the basis of economic class interests rather than in order to protect health. Unlike their fellow counselors, they tried to use the new framework. They claimed that to justify such a regulation, the legislature would have had to demonstrate the concrete difference between men and women it sought to address and additionally to show how the law would protect women against the ill effects of that difference (Wheeler and Bowie 1914, 68). This the legislature had not done, and therefore, argued Wheeler and Bowie, the statute should be struck down since it was not properly related to health (68). Nonetheless, like Flint and Van Dyke, they claimed that without an investigation of the health risks inherent in the regulated labor, limitations on the laborers could not be approved. The Supreme Court ultimately disagreed with these arguments in both cases, focusing on the female laborers' health and ruling that the statute's relationship to health was both clear and close enough to warrant its validation *(Miller v. Wilson; Bosley v. McLaughlin)*.

Fighting the challenge to Oregon's minimum wage, Frankfurter and Goldmark also argued that concern for women's health necessitated the support of protective labor legislation for them. Their arguments largely followed the same lines that advocates for limits on hours had firmly established. They connected women's health risks to the roles women played in the household, including women's need to keep up household appearances. They claimed, among other things, that women faced greater health risks than men because of their greater need to maintain their social positions (Frankfurter and Goldmark n.d., 77). This analysis hinted at a sense of self-ownership and autonomy for women that paralleled the commonly accepted and unanalyzed conceptions of the connection between men's liberty and autonomy. Nonetheless, this parallel conception of selfhood was grounded in difference. Much of their voluminous brief in this case was dedicated to detailing the risks to women's health faced in industrial work writ large; their arguments largely differentiated women from men, showing that for various reasons, women were more subject to injury from low wages than men were. These arguments generally emphasized the need for public oversight of the workplace and conceived of the terms of contracts between employers and employees as matters of public concern.

The federal courts, persuaded by these types of arguments, often relied on concrete evidence about women's physical risks to uphold protective legislation, accepting the argument that women's health and the impact of labor contracts on their health were valid subjects for the state's concern. The emphasis in this analysis was on the existence of real difference, or differences between men and women that were obvious and undeniable to the courts deciding these cases. These differences could then ground a broader range for the exercise of police power. For example, *Bosley v. McLaughlin* largely turned on the physical risks inherent in the regulated labor, which in that case was the work of student nurses and pharmacists under California's eight-hour law. In this case, the Court quoted lengthy passages from a U.S. Bureau of Education study on student nursing, using this information to show the tiring and risky nature of the work as it related to women's physiology (392–94). This careful survey of a particular industry, however, was atypical. More frequently, the Court simply referred to generalized but definitely gendered physical risks and left it at that. Even in *Bosley*, which was as close as the justices came to implementing the male focus on labor in a case involving female workers, the Court's analysis suggested that the decisive factor was not the nature of the labor itself but the fact that women were performing this tiring and draining labor.

As they had with respect to motherhood, the state courts engaged in more searching analyses of physical differences than the federal courts did. In the state courts, many members of the legal community focused on women's physical differences from men as reasons for accepting the argument that women's health needed more protection than men's health. Thus, the Illinois high court ruled that a ten-hour limit on female hotel workers was acceptable since "working long hours day after day . . . has a tendency to weaken and impair the health of women that would not attend shorter hours of employment" (*Elerding*, 583). The court made much of the demands placed upon female hotel employees, emphasizing both women's particular vulnerability and their lack of ability to handle periods of heavy labor and rest (583). While the opinion did discuss the strain of hotel work, it clearly relied on the relationship that such work bore to women's particular physiological infirmities.

The common belief in particular health risks to women mattered to the judges deciding these cases. Numerous courts accepted without question the assertion that women were physically more delicate than men, taking judicial notice of the differences between the sexes (*Elerding*, 583). This pattern occurred frequently, and also included courts who accepted without question the evidence quoted by the Supreme Court in *Muller v. Oregon* about women's differences.[8] Some courts used other measures of public acceptance of difference, pointing to the varieties of protective legislation for women that had already been upheld on the basis of women's differences from men (*People v. Kane*, 355). Many courts vacillated between emphasizing the risks that women faced and emphasizing women's differences from men that rendered them more vulnerable to workplace injuries.

Nonetheless, the focus throughout remained on the laborers, not the labor; this fit in well with the growing tendency to rely on information from experts regarding women's conditions. In upholding a minimum wage for women, Oregon's Supreme Court cited a number of recent studies showing the negative effects of overwork and low pay on women in particular (*Stettler v. O'Hara*, 748–49 (1914)). The California court looked to information from groups of reformers to conclude that women's household duties warranted judicial recognition, "considering the delicate frame of women as compared with men" (*Ex parte Miller*, 697). This difference, in addition to immunizing the legislation from equal protection review, provided a logical ground for public intervention to protect women's health.

Women's health was identified with public health not only because the public had an interest in the health of its individual citizens. Because the courts recognized women's roles in the home as the key to perpetuating the existence and high quality of life that the state wished to inculcate (albeit primarily for full male citizens), the courts

---

8. "We have thus quoted at length from the opinion of the learned justice [in *Muller v. Oregon*] because we think his argument is convincing and unanswerable, and that it supports the validity of the statute now under consideration" (*Washington v. Somerville*, 646).

allowed the state to express and act upon a public interest in preserving the health of women (Stanley 1998, 195). For most courts, this interest had no parallel in considerations of men's health or men's roles as citizens with lives outside the workplace. Women's lives outside the workplace, while formally private, were imbued with public significance to a far greater degree than those of men. The California Supreme Court made this connection in a case involving a ten-hour limitation on women's work, stating that such laws' application to women alone was permissible on the grounds that women were physically weaker than men and burdened with bearing children. As a result, "the health and strength of posterity and of the public in general is presumed to be enhanced by preserving and protecting women from exertion which men might bear without detriment to the general welfare" (*Ex parte Miller*, 695). Again, while the court recognized the need to regulate to protect against physical harm, the phrasing of the protection would apply only to women.

Among activists, attorneys, and judges, the physical risks of the workplace became a significant element in considerations of protective labor legislation as women's laws came to the forefront. These arguments largely addressed women's particular health risks, with reproduction as a central concern but encompassing more. While such arguments had the potential to apply outside of the context of women's laws, they were framed in deeply gendered terms. Concern with the physical risks of work could have fit into either a consideration of labor or of laborers, but in keeping with the now-dominant framework, discussions of physical risks focused on the nature of the laborers in question and their particular vulnerabilities.

After about 1915, the question of limiting women's hours of labor seemed to be sufficiently settled. Courts and attorneys were no longer extensively discussing such statutes, turning instead to the question of minimum wages for women and applying the same argumentative framework. Here as with the laws limiting hours, judges and attorneys noted the wealth of sociological information that women's groups and other reformers had accumulated. The Arkansas Supreme Court acknowledged these efforts in its case upholding minimum wages for women in 1917, claiming that "it is a matter of common knowledge . . . that conditions have arisen with reference to the employment of women which has [*sic*] made it necessary for many of the States . . . [to] make a detailed investigation of the subject of women's work and their wages" (*Crowe,* 281). The court then developed a detailed explanation of the connection among overwork for women, women's duties in the home, and public interest. These concepts began to shade into a third argument for regulation, that of women's position in the labor market as victims of rapid industrialization.

Workers' Victimization by the Economic Structure

Arguments connected directly to women's biological differences from men were the main justifications for allowing protective legislation for women. Nonetheless, some members of the legal community focused on other differences as well. More social and economic in nature, these other differences had not received as much attention from the courts in the years preceding the emergence of the minimum wage as a main focus. Still, as they would come to play a larger role in the later debates, they are worth noting here. Driven largely by activists' arguments, the legal community in the second decade of the century initiated discussions about whether the exploitation inherent in the labor market itself might provide a basis for protection. Like physical risks, exploitation could be framed either as an argument about women's particular need for protection or about the necessity of comprehensive protection for all workers.

The feminist community engaged in an increasingly acrimonious debate over women's subordinate position in the labor market and the appropriate solution to the problem. Some feminists had begun to question openly the wisdom of relying on maternalist ideology. The fundamental disagreement was whether women's disabilities in the labor market were due to women's particularly vulnerable natures and status or to the structure of the labor market itself. Attorneys connected to women's organizations and outside of them drew on this debate to develop gender-neutral and gendered explanations concerning structural economic risks. At this time, most judges were unwilling to engage in gender-neutral analysis, but their acceptance of the gendered arguments provided the logical framework for continued debate over the public significance of the labor market's structure and operation.

A theory among some reformers was that women's failure to organize effectively was largely responsible for the difference between women's and men's positions in the workplace. Pauline Newman, noted New York organizer, thus argued in 1912 that the real solution to

women's lower wages and long working hours was the swift unionization of working women, not the passage of the protective legislation
promoted by women's club reformers:

> [T]o shorten the workday and raise wages is, or SHOULD BE, the
> business of the working woman herself. No one can or will do it
> better than she herself. If the minimum wage should amount to
> anything at all, the working woman will have to *determine* as to
> what the minimum scale of wages and the maximum scale of
> hours should be; and it will have to be done . . . on the basis of col-
> lective bargaining. . . . And so, why not concentrate all efforts to the
> organizing of the working woman? I'd rather you girls would
> organize and demand your own. Why not show these philan-
> thropists that you can take care of your own interests? How about
> joining your union? (Newman 1912b, 7, emphasized in original)

Newman argued further that the real responsibility for enforcing provisions and agreements for shorter working days should rest with
female workers, not with the state; as long as the state was solely
responsible for enforcement, violations would be rampant. She claimed
that in order for provisions limiting working hours to function effectively, working women would have to police their own conditions of
labor actively (1912b, 7). Newman argued that empowered workers
backed up with union contracts would be able to enforce workplace
standards more effectively than state statutes that would require governmental inspections. In Newman's view, organization among working-class women, not legislation promoted by middle-class reformers,
would ultimately achieve the safer and more economically viable
workplace that working women needed. Labor organizers such as
Newman recognized that the embedding of gender-based difference in
the law could easily supplant efforts to organize all workers on the
basis of class. Like race, gender could thus divide the working class and
fragment its interests through workers' conceptualization of themselves primarily on gendered, rather than class-based, grounds.

Newman's views, however, were not adopted by the more prominent and well-heeled reform organizations. In the earlier cases, the
courts had practically foreclosed widespread organization on class
grounds through invalidating protective measures, granting injunc-
tions against labor activism, and upholding measures that limited

unions' ability to organize (Orren 1991). Advocates for protective measures saw maternalism as the only way to achieve their agenda of protection. They acknowledged the organizational and class-based difficulties faced by female workers but framed such difficulties through the lens of gender to push for legislation. In doing so, they largely adopted gendered explanations of the economic risks that workers faced. Members of the National Consumers' League argued that women as a class were unable to unionize effectively and that this deficiency added to their natural disadvantages in the workplace (Blatch and Beyer 1923, 116). In this analysis, women's inability to organize had led to employers' ability to impose individual contracts on naive young women who had no bargaining leverage. Such advocates argued that as long as women were in this position, talk of freedom of contract would only mask the employer's greater ability to exploit female workers (Blatch and Beyer 1923, 116). In this understanding, protective labor legislation was a form of empowerment for women.

For the middle-class reformers, a strong argument for the minimum wage was that women faced particular moral hazards from low wages. Such arguments portrayed women as the helpless victims of their economic circumstances. Low wages and long working hours, in this interpretation, created risks for women that men did not face. These advocates relied upon reports from various public service commissions to support their argument that women who received wages below a certain level were at risk of turning to prostitution to supplement their incomes (Union News Items 1913, 7). They argued further that cities should undertake studies to determine what level of wages would protect young women coming from rural areas to the cities from moral risks (Union News Items 1913, 7). These discussions began to provide factual grounding for both gender-neutral and gendered arguments regarding women's victimization in the labor marketplace. Advocates would continue to develop these arguments in the coming struggles over minimum wages that would consume the courts of the 1920s and 1930s. In the later years, many attorneys would adopt both types of arguments.

Before 1920, these arguments were beginning to creep into attorneys' analyses on both sides. Those opposing protective legislation for women sometimes mentioned that attempts to ameliorate exploitation in the marketplace were inappropriate state interventions into conflicts between the laboring and capitalist classes. In *Miller v. Wilson*, the attorneys arguing against California's eight-hour law accused the state of having illegitimate economic motives. They claimed that such laws were plainly "bald attempts at economic betterment under the guise of the police power—that is, attempts to use the government, in the case of women, as a substitute for the organized associations of labor in the case of men" (Flint and Van Dyke 1914, 123). Such arguments cheerfully acknowledged class as the primary division in the labor market but rejected any efforts on the part of the state to act on the behalf of the working class. In their view, such activity was harmful and dangerous, upsetting the balance between employer and employee by imposing the state's heavy thumb on the employee's side of the scale.

Goldmark and Frankfurter provided the only comprehensive argument but in doing so initiated a trend that would dominate the next period. Basing their analysis on gender rather than class as the primary division among workers, they agreed that protective legislation could take the place of union activity for women, but saw this in a positive light. Framing their argument in largely gender-neutral terms, they argued that employers had an economic, as well as an ethical, obligation to pay their employees enough money to enable them to subsist (Frankfurter and Goldmark n.d., A29). They explained that because most employees depended upon one employer for their livelihood, that employer should have to pay the minimum wage, which was the minimum amount calculated by the board to sustain a working woman. Paying less than the minimum wage not only was damaging to the employee but also endangered the employer, who would not be able to maintain employees at a lower economic level (Frankfurter and Goldmark n.d., A29). To the charge that most women were only working to make a little extra money to cover frivolous household expenses, Goldmark and Frankfurter cited governmental studies showing that the majority of female laborers were supporting themselves or assisting substantially to support their families (Frankfurter and Goldmark n.d., 290). Ironically, this argument could not yet succeed as a justification for paying minimum wages to men as well as to women.

Goldmark and Frankfurter developed additional arguments that could apply explicitly beyond the field of women's work and that addressed class-based oppression more directly and comprehensively. Prefiguring modern critiques of *Lochner*-era jurisprudence, they argued that the entire framework failed to recognize the serious imbalances of power and lack of neutrality inherent in the status quo of the economic system in place at the time. For them, exploitation in the labor market was a general harm that required redress by the state. In their view, the statutory establishment of minimum wages was necessary to mitigate the worst competitive feature of the labor market: the driving of wages below the subsistence level in certain sectors. The problem of low wages was in effect an instance of market failure that the state had the authority to address. They sought to convince the Court that minimum wages corrected a labor market that was not properly establishing the cost of labor; minimum wages thus enabled workers to bargain with their employers on a basis of fairness (Frankfurter and Goldmark n.d., A47–48). When wages were driven below the subsistence level, workers would accept jobs at any wage offered in order to stave off starvation; this ultimately would lead to a downward spiraling of wages and the destruction of the base of the capitalist system (Frankfurter and Goldmark n.d., 330). This argument did not rest on women's differences from men; the only significance of difference was that women were more likely to end up in jobs that paid substandard wages due to the various social restrictions on women's choices of occupations and options.

Again, though, Goldmark and Frankfurter hedged their bets by including arguments that relied explicitly on gender. In their analysis, another evil consequence of the unregulated labor market affected women disproportionately: the decline in morality and the risk of women's turning to prostitution and dissipation. While Goldmark and Frankfurter were not bold enough to claim that women's low wages were the primary cause of women's choice to lead "an immoral life," they asserted a definite connection between substandard wages and the destruction of morality (Frankfurter and Goldmark n.d., 114). Women seeking to support their families and facing dire straits for themselves and their children might yield to the lucrative temptation to become prostitutes; alternatively, deadened by long working hours and low wages, they might turn to alcohol for solace. Both of these dangers, in Goldmark and Frankfurter's views, were directly attributable to the unregulated labor market for women. In this regard, the public interest in women was both in preventing harm to them and in preventing them from becoming dangers to society. Ultimately the state would have to step in one way or another. States could either mandate minimum wages or be forced to subsidize industry by providing public aid to underpaid workers. It was thus up to the state to protect its own direct interests by enforcing a minimum wage on all employers. Without this kind of protection, the exploitative nature of the labor market would injure all of society in the long run.

While Goldmark and Frankfurter crafted both gender-neutral and gendered arguments regarding women's victimization by the labor market, the courts were largely unprepared to consider such claims at this stage. As Robert Post has shown, after the end of World War I the Supreme Court was largely concerned with containing the potentially wide-ranging effects of the wartime upheavals and thus retreated into drawing boundaries between public and private (Post 1998). The Supreme Court's efforts along these lines echoed the state courts' earlier endorsement of such divisions; the result was that many judges were willing to consider the public significance of work only as it touched on women's particularity. Thus, instead of addressing the implications of arguments about the structural oppression that women faced in the labor market, the federal courts relied instead on the standard discussions of motherhood and physical differences. In considering limits on hours and minimum wages for women between 1911 and 1923, the Supreme Court did not comment on women's victimization by the economics of the labor market until *Adkins* was decided. The only federal case to address these issues was the Washington, D.C., District Court's ruling in *Adkins* in 1922. In that case, the court took a dim view of such arguments, claiming that "the equal wage paralyzes ambition and promotes prodigality and indolence. It takes away the strongest incentive to human labor, thrift, and efficiency, and works injustice to employee and employer alike, thus affecting injuriously the whole social and industrial fabric" (*Children's Hospital v. Adkins*, 621). The majority also pointed out that immorality was as prevalent among the wealthy as among the impoverished (621). The dissenter in the case, Chief Justice Smyth, protested that the legal question was not about economics but rather about Congress's prerogatives, and that minimum wages generally promoted a more stable economy (627, 632) (Smyth, J., dissenting). He also characterized the act as "a measure to prevent the confiscation of a working woman's labor by those who have the economic power to do it" (637), but neither his colleagues nor ultimately a majority of the Supreme Court justices were convinced by his reasoning.

The state courts also continued to advance explicitly gendered analyses, looking to the problems created by industrialization as weighing with particular force on women rather than characterizing them as broad market failures. With regard to limits on hours, some state courts claimed that such regulations were justified to address the changes that had taken place in the economy that particularly affected women. For the Washington high court, the need to use police power to protect against threats to the public welfare had grown substantially along with the developing economy, but this necessity applied particularly to women because of the health risks they faced (*Somerville*, 643).

Arguments regarding morality provoked little comment from the state courts, many of which simply asserted that regulations of hours or wages promoted the public morals. The Oregon court cited a study showing that underpaid salesgirls who did not have families upon whom to rely in difficult economic times sometimes turned to prostitution (*Stettler v. O'Hara*, 748 (1914)). This explanation, however, was somewhat anomalous at this juncture.

In these years, the lay activists and attorneys arguing for legislation began to address structural features of the labor market, analyzing the role of women's lack of unionization and the ill effects of exploitative employers upon their employees. Most of these discussions were framed in gendered terms, focusing on the particular evils that women faced in the labor market. Tension began to emerge over whether women's negative experiences were qualitatively different from men's. In the next period, those arguing against protective legislation would claim that women's experiences were not fundamentally different from men's and thus that women could no more be protected through legislation than men could. During the years of laborer-centered analysis, however, these arguments were not major factors, largely because judges had not yet begun to address them in any systematic way. Instead, advocates maintained in the background of their analyses a primarily private conception of liberty in relation to general legislation while endorsing an understanding of women's liberty as imbued with public significance. This analytical commitment further reinforced the tendency to focus on laborers rather than labor.

Like the analysis of liberty, the analysis of police power in these years was more focused, depending heavily on factual contentions derived from social scientific research and centering on laborers rather than their work. The central concern among activists, attorneys, and the courts was the state's authority to limit women's labor because of women's particular status as mothers, as physically weak laborers, and as economically marginal employees. Considerations of motherhood's connection to police power emphasized women's differences from men by their very nature; activists and some attorneys used these arguments to improve women's position in the labor marketplace, while nonfeminist attorneys and some judges saw them as a tool to drive women out of the workforce. Discussions of physical risks relied on explanations of women's differences from men, but some of these considerations were framed in gender-neutral terms toward the end of this period. The arguments that had the greatest potential for application to men's situation were those concerning the exploitative nature of the labor market. These claims had the potential to promote a reconceptualization of the state and its proper role in the economy, but their universal application would be problematic because of their introduction on gendered grounds. The next section will explain how some members of the legal community began to apply the lessons they had learned in the context of the women's cases to analyze men as laborers, hoping to expand the conflict over the public significance of the exploitation and subordination of workers.

Shifting Modes of Analysis in Cases Involving General Legislation

These developments in the analysis of statutes protecting women initially affected only that category of cases. While some attorneys were venturing onto broader ground, federal and state courts largely continued to see such cases as a separate category, judging them within their own framework. Judges by and large focused on women as laborers, identifying justifications for protective legislation that were connected to women's bodies, roles, or particular situations within the labor market. These arguments implemented a conception of the labor market as a space in which individuals made decisions that had public significance and thus as a space subject to the regulation of the state. While this conception of the labor market initially applied only to women, it would ultimately affect general legislation as well. As mentioned above, many reform organizations that supported protective labor legislation for women hoped that achieving such laws for women would ultimately advance protection for men as well (Foner 1979; Skocpol 1992). In the years of laborer-centered analysis, the principles used to support women's legislation occasionally began to invade discussions of general legislation within the legal community. Often the same types of arguments were used, but occasionally the focus on laborers would turn to developing reasons why male laborers needed particular protection. In these interpretations, members of the legal community promoting protective measures argued that men, like women, could face risks as laborers; many attorneys began to rely on laborer-centered arguments rather than developing specific factual claims about the regulated labor itself. The most obvious arguments used in women's cases that could apply to general legislation were those addressing the structure of wage labor and the inherent inequalities between employers and employees. Another class of claims included gendered arguments about men's civic roles as a basis for protection.

Attorneys' Tentative Embrace of the Standard Developed for Women's Statutes

Just as arguments regarding the structure of the labor market and the inequality between employer and employee became more standard in the cases involving female workers, they also began to appear occasionally in discussions of limits applying mainly to male workers. In several cases, attorneys argued consciously that the labor market was a legitimate subject for the state's regulatory concern even insofar as this concern touched the relationship between employer and employee. In *Keokee Coke Co. v. Taylor,* one of the arguments advanced to support Virginia's law barring coal companies from paying their employees in scrip was the structural inequality between coal miners and their employers. Attorneys for the State of Virginia asserted that freedom of contract required equal relationships between employers and employees; this type of relationship "certainly does not exist between coal diggers and their employers" (Noel and Duncan & Cridlin 1914, 5). In this line of reasoning, this lack of equality would lead to circumscribed freedom of contract for desperate employees. The opponents of the law found this argument to be specious, asserting that payment in scrip prevented "shiftless, thriftless, spendthrift" miners from wasting their wages, thereby improving their situation (Irvine and Bullitt & Chalkley 1914a, 27–28). In their more standard analysis, the statute simply violated the workers' right to contract for payment in scrip rather than cash (27). Nevertheless, both approaches focused on the workers and their interactions with employers rather than on the nature of coal mining. Part of the reason for the attention to miners was the issue in the case, a regulation affecting payment, not the conditions of labor, but the arguments nonetheless could have centered around the coercive circumstances of company mining towns rather than on the workers themselves.

Attorneys for the State of Kansas had less success making similar arguments about the negative impact of the modern industrial economy for the individual laborer in *Coppage v. Kansas,* in which the Supreme Court ultimately overturned Kansas's law barring yellow-dog contracts. Proregulation attorneys claimed that unionization was a powerful equalizing factor in the constant battles between employers and employees, and without potent labor unions, the employee was left at a substantial disadvantage in the struggle for subsistence (Dawson and Sheppard 1914, 17). The opponents of the statute advanced the view that labor unions were strictly private class-based organizations, a position that advocates for women's protective legislation were beginning to challenge implicitly in their observations that women's lack of unionization contributed to their victimization in the labor market (Vermilion and Evans 1914, 46). Here too, though, both supporters and opponents of the statute focused on workers and the legitimacy of exploitation as a specific harm rather than on the type of labor in question.

Goldmark and Frankfurter experimented with the idea of expanding the analysis of labor's physical risks to include male workers' potential harms. In doing so, they developed their previous factual arguments more fully. As with women's legislation, the most complete statement of the physical effects of the industrial economy came indirectly from the National Consumers' League. Goldmark and Frankfurter marshaled massive quantities of evidence to support their claim in *Bunting v. Oregon* that long working days were dangerous for male industrial employees. Much of their one-thousand-page brief was devoted to convincing the Court that fatigue was damaging not only for individual workers, but also for the state as a whole. First, they showed that fatigue was problematic not only in "dangerous" work such as mining, but in ordinary manufacturing as well (Frankfurter and Goldmark 1916, A63). Thus, they argued, courts should not only recognize the dangers in particular industries but should also allow protective legislation more generally for all industrial workers.

Long working hours not only increased the risk of industrial accidents on the job but also lessened the worker's resistance to dangers outside of the workplace. Here, Goldmark and Frankfurter explained the specifically gendered risks that men faced from overwork. In an argument paralleling their concerns with female workers' moral risks, they claimed, "Laxity of moral fiber follows physical debility. After excessive labor, the overtaxed worker is left stupefied or responds most readily to coarse pleasures and excitements" (Frankfurter and Goldmark 1916, A404). They argued further that the commonly perceived and much maligned workingman's proclivity for drinking resulted from long work days. When employees were on the job too long, they would turn to alcohol to relieve the physical and mental strains after their shifts were over: "Among industrial workers the desire for drink is often due to the physical incidents of factory work, such as exposure to extreme heat, or the inhalation of dust or fluff in the many trades involving such hazards. Intemperance often results also from the worker's craving for some stimulant or support for exhausted energies" (Frankfurter and Goldmark 1916, A414). This attempt to shift the blame for alcoholism from the working-class individual to his greedy employers was a common motif in reformers' pamphlets as well (Kelley n.d.).

Ultimately, overwork of male employees damaged the state directly, in Frankfurter and Goldmark's view. This argument confronted head-on the earlier consensus on the private nature of the contractual relationship between employers and employees. They reconfigured understandings of state action and inaction, presenting an image of the individual as fundamentally intertwined with the modern state and its apparatuses; unlike Sunstein's late-twentieth-century analysis, however, they did so in part on a gendered basis. Men, like women, had particular gendered responsibilities to the state with which excessive labor could interfere, and thus their relationships with their employers were not purely private. Long hours of labor deprived workers (including male workers) of precious time with their families and left them with no opportunity to better themselves by going to libraries or attending public lectures. While women could not perform their duties toward children, who were future citizens, men could not manage their duties connected with current citizenship if they were permitted to work too long (Frankfurter and Goldmark 1916, A452). Meaningful self-ownership and full citizenship thus depended upon the state's willingness to provide a bulwark against the pressing demands of economic need. In a supplementary brief filed for the State of Oregon, state officials echoed this sentiment, claiming that Oregon in particular needed to have an educated and active citizenry because of its reliance on initiatives and referenda for state legislation. Because of this practice, "In order to discharge his duty as a citizen and a legislator, it is necessary that each and every voter of the state devote a certain amount of time to the subjects before the people" (Brown and Bailey 1916, A72). Lengthy hours of work would prevent men from exercising their civic responsibilities by robbing them of the necessary time and energy to inform themselves about the great public issues of the day (Brown and Bailey 1916, 72). This brief thus shifted the terms of the argument, challenging the framework generally used to address general legislation. While the Court did not invalidate Oregon's statute, it was evenly divided and could not articulate any binding response to these arguments, which thus remained in play for some time to come.

Opponents of the Oregon statute relied on standard arguments against general protective labor legislation, claiming that the statute bore no substantial relationship to public health or welfare (Fulton and Thompson 1916, 18). Their analysis promoted the maintenance of a rigid split between public and private, with the relationship between employers and employees firmly on the private side of the line. They argued further that the regulation did not fit into the accepted categories of addressing a particularly dangerous kind of employment or a particularly vulnerable employee (Fulton and Thompson 1916, 18, 21). They heatedly opposed any attempt by the state legislature to intervene into the economic structure for the benefit of the working class, claiming that setting wages for standard (male) employees in safe industries bore absolutely no relation to health, the only acceptable justification, and was thus invalid (Fulton and Thompson 1916, 32). They thus reinforced the standard analysis of general legislation, decrying the lack of specific justifications for the state's intervention into the bargaining process. Nonetheless, because they were responding in the context of a conversation about men as laborers, they could not concentrate exclusively on the nature of the labor involved.

Attorneys' arguments on both sides thus showed the extent to which the standards developed to address women's protective measures had begun to come into play in cases involving general statutes. Following the successful models presented in cases involving women's measures, attorneys arguing for regulation sought to convince the courts in both gender-neutral and gendered terms. Those promoting general measures argued that men faced the same kinds of structural imbalances of power as women and also claimed that men had particular needs for protection relating to their social and functional roles as heads of households and citizens. Those opposing such measures often responded within the same framework, claiming that male laborers were not particularly at risk either in a gender-neutral or a gendered sense. In these arguments, laborers increasingly became the central point in the analysis, and some attorneys began to challenge the idea that male employees' relationships with their employers were fundamentally private. These arguments largely prefigured the discussions that would take place in the federal courts in the next period, but the Oregon high court's ruling in *Bunting* grounded the adoption of the framework developed for women's statutes to analyze general measures.

The Courts' Gradual Shift toward Considering Male Laborers

In the period of laborer-centered analysis, the federal courts addressing general labor legislation did not address men's status as laborers to any great degree. In effect, the Supreme Court seemed to have forgotten its pronouncements in *Holden v. Hardy* that inequality in bargaining power was a factor worthy of consideration. The Court in *Coppage v. Kansas* took the opposite tack, justifying a high degree of economic inequality and subsequent restrictions on bargaining power as an outcome of the constitutional guarantees of liberty and property (*Coppage v. Kansas*, 236 U.S. 1, 17 (1915)). The dissenters objected to this characterization, claiming that the Kansas statute properly addressed an inappropriate degree of coercion, but this view gained few adherents on the Court in the short term (*Coppage*, 38 (Day and Hughes, J. J., dissenting)). In both cases, however, for the most part the Court continued to apply the framework developed to address general legislation.

Courts addressing general protective labor legislation on the state level wavered between using the frameworks dominant in the period of specific balancing and the frameworks developed in response to women's legislation. The federal courts would eventually pick up on this development, shifting their analyses as well in the next period. In 1912, the Mississippi high court adopted a forward-looking argument, claiming that legislation had to acknowledge the changing relationship between employers and employees (*State v. J. J. Newman Lumber Co.*,

102 Miss. 802, 828 (1912)). The court did not, however, follow this pro-nouncement with a discussion of the laborer and his position. Instead, it followed the strategy of the *Holden v. Hardy* Court and described the specific strains associated with the restricted labor (*Newman Lumber*, 834). In 1913, the Louisiana high court also focused on the nature of the restricted labor but reached the opposite conclusion, striking down a limit on the hours of men working to keep boilers running in manufac-turing plants. The court explained simply that the labor was not excep-tionally taxing or dangerous (*State v. Barba*, 61 So. 784, 786 (La. 1913)). Such analyses largely applied the reasoning developed during the ear-lier years, maintaining the default position of invalidating regulation and allowing for special justification for male workers only if the work involved was somehow out of the ordinary.

The ruling in *State v. Bunting*, which a divided Supreme Court upheld in *Bunting v. Oregon* a few years later, was an exception to this pattern. The state court largely accepted the broader arguments advanced by the National Consumers' League, upholding limits on hours and wages on the basis of health (*State v. Bunting*, 732). The court began with a standard statement that the police power could be exer-cised to protect health, but construed this power broadly to cover indi-vidual citizens, rather than limiting it to groups of citizens with special relationships to the public interest (734). The judge then explained that his analysis of general limitations rested on reasoning that had already been accepted in the context of legislation protecting women: "Legisla-tive regulations of the hours of labor of men and that of women differ only in the degree of necessity therefor" (735). He found that the rea-sons for limiting the hours of men's labor were sufficient. In supporting the regulation, the court relied on general risks to the employee rather than a specific analysis of regulated industries, asserting that lengthy physical labor caused both physical and mental decline (735). This analysis paralleled interpretations exercised in cases addressing women's legislation by painting a clear picture of the risks of overwork to men's health in particular. This ill effect had dangerous implications for the future of the state: "The safety of a country depends upon the intelligence of its citizens, and if our institutions are to be preserved the state must see to it that the citizen shall have some leisure which he may employ in fitting himself for those duties which are the highest attributes of good citizenship" (735). The court thus adopted and mod-ified arguments that had worked for women's legislation, citing the public role that male citizens played in maintaining the democratic institutions of the nation.

The court's ruling was a significant development. This reasoning placed male laborers at the center of the analysis, not discussing the type of labor to any great extent. Its emphasis was on the laborers' participation in the state as citizens, which then served as the required connection to the public interest to justify the state's action. The court, however, did not engage in a simple balancing of men's liberty against the state's authority to act in the public interest, instead conceiving of the relationship of employment itself as directly affecting the state.

The *Bunting* decision, however, was not adopted widely as a pattern for reasoning yet. It provided some hope to those seeking to promote general legislation, but concern with women's legislation would dominate the next period, as the Supreme Court radically changed the playing field with its decision in *Adkins* in 1923. Nonetheless, the Oregon court's ruling in *Bunting* showed that even in cases involving general legislation, courts could look to the laborer and his or her relationship to the economy and the state in determining the fate of protective labor legislation.

In these years, the legal community began to shift from considering labor to analyzing instead the laborer himself. These arguments often played out in gender-neutral ways, as the claims that were succeeding for women's measures attracted the attention of those advocating for general legislation. Sometimes they also appeared in gendered form, focusing on men's particular responsibilities to the home and the state. This phenomenon would appear anomalous if taken out of context: why would an attorney or a court claim that male workers were in need of protection as men during the years in which *Lochner* still reigned supreme? When considered as an extension of the framework developed to analyze women's measures, however, this analytical move made perfect sense. The fact that it was possible and coherent testifies to the extent to which the modes of analysis developed to address women's protective statutes had quietly supplanted the general framework developed before the turn of the century and endorsed in *Lochner*.

The Expanding Analysis of Laborers around 1920

Women's cases were now the main focus of attention, which contributed to some significant changes in the way that the legal community addressed questions concerning the states' rights to protect workers. In these years, the central issue in the analysis of due process became a question about the proper justifications through which states could limit the right to contract in order to protect workers' health broadly defined, a large interpretive shift from the broader questions common only twenty-five years earlier. Rather than a simple question of balancing private liberties against public interest, the nodes of conflict over liberty and police power encouraged focus on the nature of the relationship of employment and in particular on its public significance.

In addition, activists and the legal community considered closely women's position in the labor market. Did women actually have less liberty to begin with because of their particularly poor standpoint in the bargaining game? How could protective labor legislation for women actually increase their freedom to make fair and reasonable labor contracts, given their roles as mothers, their physical disabilities, their tendency to settle for poorer bargains than men due to the pressures of supporting their children, and their lack of unionization? Could any of these justifications be extended to male laborers? Throughout the analysis, the shift from focusing on labor to focusing on laborers was largely confirmed.

At this point, the nodes of conflict involved full participation and communication among the activists, attorneys, and judges. In the previous period, activists were becoming fully involved in the process of litigation, but by century's second decade, their direct participation in the process was evident and effective. The attractiveness of litigation as a forum for pressing a liberal agenda of expanding rights for the downtrodden spurred on existing organizations and encouraged the formation of new organizations. It is no accident that the years between 1909 and 1920 saw the establishment of the American Civil Liberties Union, the American Jewish Congress, and the National Association for the Advancement of Colored People, all of which depended heavily upon the courts to promote their interests in securing expanded civil rights and liberties (Epp 1999, 265).

Groups promoting protective legislation worked directly on litigation, and the lines between activists and attorneys became increasingly blurred. With their greater legal savvy and their interest in achieving victory in the courts, reforming groups adjusted their researching efforts to address the legal categories that judges had established in the early years of the twentieth century. If judges were convinced that only a strong showing of risk to the public's interest would justify upholding protective measures, these groups were determined to provide enough social scientific evidence to prove risk. Beyond these efforts, however, the groups sought to stretch the legal category of public interest sufficiently to establish the presumptive legitimacy of protective measures.

The debate over minimum wages that emerged toward the end of this period provided a focus for disagreement not only for the legal community but also for feminists. In the years preceding the Supreme Court's decision in *Adkins*, many women's groups publicly endorsed conceptions of difference that would ultimately provoke controversy within the women's movement (Kelley 1923). Before the passage of the Nineteenth Amendment, much of the disagreement within the feminist community over the role of equality for women remained underground as activists focused on convincing state legislatures to ratify the amendment. After its passage, the differences of opinion concerning the value of gendered protective labor legislation could no longer be quietly maintained. Feminists had moved away from the loose consensus developed during the struggle for suffrage. The first sallies of the acrimonious battles over equality as a goal for women had taken place; the stage was set for a serious rift during the next period (Blatch and Beyer 1923). At the same time, women with diverse goals continued to work within the legal system, for the most part trusting that it might, with proper persuasion, be convinced to act on the behalf of the progressive interests that many feminists held dear.

Attorneys continued to develop modes of legal reasoning that would accomplish their ends of persuading courts to strike down or uphold protective labor legislation. Even those who supported protective labor legislation did not always have the same motives as feminist reformers. Assisted in some cases by laypeople, they focused on analyzing women's roles in the workplace, struggling to produce convincing explanations of when the use of police power to protect them was justified. They also worked to explain women's nature and roles in the rapidly changing industrial context, usually generating gendered explanations for their support or opposition to protective labor legislation.

Judges often believed that women's relationship to liberty was different from men's because of their physical and social detriments and their important role in bearing and raising the next generation. The courts' understandings of police power, often linked to their beliefs about the public's legitimate interest in women, combined to convince the courts to allow extensive protections for women. The courts generally analyzed the statutes by considering women's place in the labor market rather than by questioning the type of work they were performing.

The justifications presented by advocates for protective legislation were women's roles as mothers, the harms women faced in the unregulated workplace as a result of their physiques and their social roles, and the dangers to women from economic exploitation. Motherhood was a well-established justification during these years; maternalist arguments succeeded. Such arguments, by their nature, were limited to women. Arguments about the physical risks of the workplace and the interplay between home life and labor might apply to both sexes. Both men and women could face serious injuries if they overworked, and men and women had different civic responsibilities with which work could interfere. As the courts construed these arguments, however, they were mostly based in women's role as homemakers and in the particular physical differences from men that rendered women vulnerable in the workplace. Similarly, some activists and attorneys argued from a gender-neutral standpoint that exploitative employers caused harms that were serious enough to warrant statutory redress, but had difficulty persuading the courts to adopt these contentions. These arguments, whether focused specifically on women's particular vulnerabilities to exploitation or generally on the nature of the labor market, did not yet make much of an impression on either the state or federal courts.

The rising dominance of laborer-centered analysis ensured the continuance of divisions between workers on the basis of gender. Even when arguments for protecting men were advanced, they were advanced in gendered terms. Earlier courts had largely foreclosed the legal recognition of workers as a class through a myriad of rulings thwarting the right to organize and exercise collective power. Middle-class reformers, either through expedience or conviction, promoted protection in the arena in which it could succeed without threatening the legal community's consensus that regulations protecting workers on the basis of their class status were inappropriate. Even as arguments about market failures and economic exploitation began to make some headway, they did so in the form of claims about individual laborers' interactions with the economic system. Claims about the structural exploitation of the working class were not cognizable within this framework, but at least the framework enabled attorneys to argue successfully for the protection of some individuals.

The next period would see an even sharper focus on the question of women's roles in the workplace. The courts would have to deal not only with more statutes seeking protection for women, but also with a rapidly changing social and economic context. The boom period of the twenties, followed by the Great Depression in the thirties, created new challenges for actors from all standpoints in the continuing battle over protective labor legislation.

Chapter 5

Gendered Rebalancing: Minimum Wages and the Battle over Equality

This chapter addresses the final portion of the period of negotiation. The final period began with the Supreme Court's controversial ruling in 1923 that the District of Columbia's establishment of a minimum wage for women was unconstitutional. This ruling initiated a sustained debate over the legitimacy of minimum wages, which took place in the larger context of the question of whether the state had the legal capacity to regulate the terms and conditions of labor for all workers. Settled understandings were upset, requiring the legal community to rethink the balance between laborers' rights and the state's authority to regulate, primarily by questioning the extent to which the two concepts were actually in tension. The litigation of the previous decade had confirmed that the legal debate would center on laborers and their relationships with their employers, with the labor market generally, and ultimately with the state. Litigation over minimum wages would confirm the final death knell of the laissez-faire model of airtight private relationships between employers and employees, ushering in the general acceptance of the state's interest and involvement in the labor market. This development took place on the basis of gender primarily rather than class; the period of laborer-centered analysis had drawn the doctrinal lines in such a way as to concentrate focus primarily on questions of women's characteristics and only secondarily on their issues as members of the working class. The legal system grappled with the problem of women who were workers, not with the problem of workers who happened to be female.

These years saw all players in the legal negotiations struggling to reconceive the balance between liberty and police power in light of the problem of the minimum wage for women. Gendered rebalancing, however, meant more for these actors than figuring out the appropriate weight of liberty and police power. For feminist activists, it meant weighing the opportunities against the dangers of relying on maternalist ideology to ground substantive efforts to improve women's conditions in the workplace. For attorneys, it meant adding into the balance the public implications of economic exploitation in the labor market, albeit in gendered terms. For judges it meant reconsidering the operation of the framework established to accommodate women's particular circumstances as workers in light of the Supreme Court's decision in *Adkins v. Children's Hospital.* Many judges faced the difficult task of attempting both to show respect for the precedent set in *Adkins* and to address increasingly persistent and prevalent arguments about the public need for gendered regulation.

The battle over minimum wages, which reached national prominence with the Court's ruling in *Adkins* and lasted until the Court's ruling in *West Coast Hotel,* took place within the feminist community as well as outside of it. Advocates for minimum wages for women advanced an essentialist vision of women's particular physical and psychological infirmities and how these infirmities limited women's liberty in the labor marketplace, while feminists promoting equality rejected the notion that women as a group were less able than men to wrest fair contracts from their employers. As in the previous decade, feminist and nonfeminist attorneys conducted the debate in legal terms, which influenced the ways that judges reasoned in the cases. As this process took place with respect to minimum wages, two major developments occurred. First, advocates for minimum wages used both gendered and gender-neutral arguments in their focus on the labor marketplace, ultimately endorsing a legal and factual framework that applied effectively to men as well as to women. This development rested upon the prioritizing of laborer-centered analysis in the previous period. Second, the contest over minimum wages culminating in *West Coast Hotel* provided the grounding for the legal legitimation of the state's widespread intervention in the labor market. In this sense, the case was not only a new beginning but also a culmination. By the end of this chapter, it will be clear that *West Coast Hotel* did not emerge simply from the justices' fears of Roosevelt's Court-packing plan or from the Court's greater satisfaction with the statute's framing. Rather, the ruling was forged in a crucible heated by the intensive battles over the outcome in *Adkins* and the fate of women's minimum wages. *West Coast Hotel* is significant for its outcome, but the ruling's greatest significance is its framing of the proper relationship among employers, employees, and the state, a framing that derived directly from over a half century of debate concerning women's protective labor legislation.

While the courts considered a few other issues in their reasoning about due process during the years between 1923 and 1937, the bulk of the discussion centered around minimum wages for women, and the public focused attention on these cases. In these years, all parties analyzed laborers, addressing female laborers and their capacities in particular. Much of the debate that took place between *Adkins* and *West Coast Hotel* questioned whether women were enough like men to warrant treating them the same as men, but arguments that could apply to both men and women became increasingly common. By the end of this period, the reversal initiated in the second decade of the century by Goldmark and Frankfurter was complete: the courts were using arguments about workers' experiences in the labor market that had initially applied only to women to uphold protective measures for all workers.

At the same time, activists, attorneys, and judges went back and forth between framing arguments in terms specific to women and terms that could apply to men as well. Arguments that a few attorneys and activists had made tentatively in the years of laborer-centered analysis were now appearing on all levels. The question addressed only peripherally by judges, but weighing on the minds of many members of the legal community was whether, if protective statutes were justified for women, the same arguments could result in their acceptance for male workers as well. The extension of reasoning applicable to women would lead to a complete revision of the public/private split as it related to the labor marketplace, closing the gulf that had emerged between the background framework of cases involving male labor and cases involving female labor. This gendered rebalancing would set the stage for the more widely heralded rebalancing between national and state-based authority.

At the beginning of this period, the women's movement seemingly should have been having its finest hour. After a long and arduous battle, the Nineteenth Amendment had finally become part of the Constitution, bringing several laggard states into line with what progressive forces had achieved elsewhere. The major women's organizations knew that they had played a key role in this process, and several had now begun to focus on national policy, pushing for more federal attention to the "special" issues of women (Mink 1985).

The major cloud in the sky, which soon burst into a storm of discontent, was protective labor legislation, which contradicted the push for full equality. The National Woman's Party, which had briefly discussed disbanding after the Nineteenth Amendment had gone into effect, had instead discovered a new goal upon which to focus: a comprehensive equal rights amendment that would ensure that women had the same rights as men (Lipschultz 1996). Active, articulate spokeswomen for equal rights soon began pressuring Congress to consider the amendment, and the members of the National Woman's Party began writing letters and newspaper articles explaining why a drive for equality was the next logical step in the women's movement (National Woman's Party 1926).

Members of some other women's organizations viewed this process first with apprehension, then with alarm. The National Consumers' League and the National Women's Trade Union League in particular, two high profile organizations with branches in several states, felt that now was certainly not the right time to be pushing for equal rights (Swarts 1924). Since the NWTUL had come fully on board in favor of statutory protections for women, both organizations had worked hard and successfully in several states to secure laws limiting the number of hours that women could work, preventing night work by women, and setting minimum wages for women (Foner 1979, 303–24). In the view of these women, the proposed constitutional amendment endangered these gains, and the clubwomen wanted no changes that meant any possibility of a return to the unprotected days of the late nineteenth century (Kelley 1923).

As with many internecine conflicts, the two sides descended into mutual distrust and hostility, with each side claiming that they truly represented the desires and interests of working women. The National Woman's Party secured endorsements of the equal rights amendment from an impressive array of business women's and professional women's groups, in addition to some of the unions organized around the particular trades that women generally practiced (National Woman's Party 1936). For their part, members of the National Consumers' League and the National Women's Trade Union League encouraged their state organizations to drum up support for protective labor legislation and engaged in letter-writing and speaking campaigns against the amendment. Newspapers featured debates between the two sides (Perkins and Baker 1926).

Throughout this battle each side clung to particular images of women to make its point. The advocates of equality presented the image of the independent woman, who did not deserve to be classed with children and other incompetents in terms of her ability to bargain regarding her labor. She was strongly encouraged to gain better circumstances in the workplace through the formation of more potent unions, rather than relying on the protective power of the state, which she could not fully trust. The advocates for protective legislation, on the other hand, presented the picture of the exhausted mother who worked (often at night) more than eight hours per day for wages that could not support her adequately and then had to come home to the innumerable tasks of the household. For this woman, equality was a wonderful theoretical goal, but in practical terms she needed assistance from the state to wrest a living wage and reasonable working conditions from her greedy or desperate employer. Her wretched circumstances were a direct result of her very womanhood, the quality that also justified the state's direct interest in her well-being.

The passage of the equal rights amendment was never a serious possibility (or threat) during this period. The members of the National Woman's Party and the National Consumers' League and the National Women's Trade Union League agreed far more than they disagreed about a variety of issues. Even with regard to protective legislation, both camps felt that the best solution would be for protective legislation to cover both men and women. Both sides also agreed that equality was a significant long-term goal and that working to reduce the instances of sexism in the current law was necessary. Neither side, though, was willing to compromise on the issue of protective labor legislation for women; thus the movement must have seemed diffuse and impotent to outside observers.

By the end of the period of negotiation, although both sides had won in a sense, their arguments were not faithfully translated into legal discourse. While advocates for equality were pleased that protective measures now applied to both men and women, women were still subordinate. Those who had supported women's protection all along could be happy that the protections would continue, but most members of the legal community had endorsed a construction of female workers as pathetic and helpless. With the doctrinal battles over the legitimacy of protective measures now settled, consideration of women in the workplace returned to being a minor sideline in the main thread of jurisprudential development concerning labor and employment, just as due process had largely disappeared as a ground for striking down measures delineating and supporting the creation of the modern welfare state. The end result of gendered rebalancing was the shunting of women's concerns and issues away from the mainstream of jurisprudential inquiry as questions about the extent of national authority and the proper workings of the now legitimated welfare state came to replace them. Likewise, space for labor interests was finally achieved in national politics, but the labor interests finally accepted were significantly different from their radical forebears of the late nineteenth century.

The Universe of Cases

This period was much less active than the previous decades. Between 1923 and 1937, the courts considered only eleven cases on the federal level and seven on the state level directly addressing the constitutionality of general protective labor legislation or legislation aimed specifically at women. This group of cases represents a significant drop in the number of reported opinions on these issues. Nonetheless, even more than in the years of laborer-centered analysis, cases involving women's legislation dominated the scene. Furthermore, the public had become increasingly sensitive to the activities of the Supreme Court, which raised the political stakes for the individual decisions.

The courts were more hostile to protective labor legislation than in the earlier years, particularly on the federal level. Seven cases supported protective legislation under the state and/or federal constitutions, while eleven invalidated such laws. The difference between the rates of upholding these measures generally and upholding them for women persisted; however, even women's protective labor legislation did not fare well during this period. For the most part, the only laws to be upheld by the courts during the 1920s and the early New Deal were safeguards for women, mostly minimum wages. The single exception, *Stevenson v. St. Clair*, was a challenge to a statutory minimum wage for minors that was upheld by the Minnesota Supreme Court in 1925.

Outcomes in the federal courts confirm the common picture of reformers' frustration with the judiciary—individual judges and panels struck down most of the protective legislation they considered. Nonetheless, courts continued to uphold protective legislation for women more frequently than other types of protective legislation. The only protective labor laws that made it past the "Four Horsemen"[1] and their federal colleagues were acts involving women's work.

The state courts in this period were not nearly as active as they had been in previous decades. Another difference from the earlier periods was that the state courts were substantially less active than the federal courts: between 1923 and 1937, the states disposed of only seven cases in published opinions. Their pattern of decision making was somewhat different from the federal pattern. They split evenly on general legislation, upholding one general statute and striking another down. In the five reported cases involving legislation for women, they struck down two statutes and defied the Supreme Court's ruling in *Adkins* to uphold three.

Both sets of figures show that the battle over regulation of the workplace and wages took place around the issue of protective labor legislation for women. Other cases were of course important: the *Schechter* case

TABLE 13.   Decisions in All Cases Involving Protective Labor Legislation, 1923–37

	Upheld Protective Legislation	Struck Down Protective Legislation	Total
All cases	7	11	18
General cases	1	4	5
Cases involving women	6	7	13

TABLE 14.   Decisions in Federal Cases Involving Protective Labor Legislation, 1923–37

	Upheld Protective Legislation	Struck Down Protective Legislation	Total
All cases	3	8	11
General cases	0	3	3
Cases involving women	3	5	8

1. The Four Horsemen who were largely responsible for the Supreme Court's apocalyptic (in the Roosevelt administration's view) treatment of New Deal legislation were Justices Butler, McReynolds, Sutherland, and Van Devanter.

struck down the National Recovery Act, and *Carter v. Carter Coal* invalidated the Bituminous Coal Restoration Act (*Schechter Poultry Co. v. U.S.*, 295 U.S. 495 (1935); *Carter v. Carter Coal Co.*, 298 U.S. 238 (1936)). Nevertheless, the courts maintained their focus on female laborers and their relationship with their employers and the labor market.

Brief Overview of Nodes and Litigation in the Years of Gendered Rebalancing

Now that the legal community had settled the legitimacy of limits on women's hours of labor, the broad contest over the proper scope of state intervention in the labor market largely came down to a single issue: the state's legal authority to establish minimum wages for women. Three issues shaped the battle over the legitimacy of minimum wages in this period and contributed to a gendered rebalancing of the tension between liberty and police power that largely dissolved the tension. First, feminist activists and members of the legal community argued over whether minimum wages enhanced or undermined women's liberty. Second was continued debate over what kinds of risks to laborers warranted the state's exercise of police power; in particular, this argument addressed the role that wage supports played in the labor market. Finally, the legal community disagreed over the extent to which the framework for analyzing women's work should also apply to male labor. In some instances, the conflicts in the period of gendered rebalancing brought into the mainstream of the legal community arguments that had been made only on the fringes in the previous years.

The question about women's liberty was largely factual in its nature and thus was well suited to investigation by lay groups of activists and their associated attorneys. The debate over the significance of women's physical and psychological differences from men initiated in the early years of the twentieth century was modified by the entry of feminists promoting women's equality. Concern over women's liberty coalesced around two questions. The first question was an inquiry about the extent to which women were essentially different from men in ways that warranted the state's intervention to enhance their liberty; this question was not new. The second question arose from the specific focus on minimum wages but also had essentialist elements to it. This question was about the kind of factual information that was relevant to protecting or enhancing liberty; specifically, activists and members of the legal community argued over whether imbalances in bargaining power constituted significant limits on liberty.

The conflict over the scope of police power related closely to these questions about liberty. The general question about police power was what factors mattered in determining whether legislation was legitimately in the public interest. The factual basis on which this question was debated was the proper relationship between the state and the labor market; was the labor market so inherently exploitative to women that the state could step in to protect them and thus to protect its own interests? Some arguments were limited strictly to women and depended upon differentiating women from men, while others could be generalized to embrace male workers. In the cases addressing minimum wages for women, some advocates for the laws portrayed women's neediness in the labor market as a function of their very femininity, but others argued that imbalances in bargaining power between employers and employees were the key factors. Even if women's particular characteristics rendered them unequal in the relationship between employer and employee, this justification for regulation could extend to male workers if advocates could present convincing factual arguments about men's lack of access to bargaining power.

Justifications based on factors involving the laborer rather than the type of work were commonplace by this time. By 1936, women's groups and their associates were filing extensive briefs on opposite sides of cases, each claiming that it represented the true interests of American working women (Matthews and Greathouse 1936; Heffner and Crary 1936). This discussion also spawned an earnest consideration among judges of the extent of women's equality. Equality was important for future cases, because later corporate attorneys would rely on women's inherent differences from men to seek the containment of protective measures to women. Even if women were different from men, the key question was the extent to which these differences justified maintaining separate legal frameworks for adjudicating cases addressing protective measures for all workers and for women specifically.

The final issue was the extent to which these arguments were generalizable. Generalizing the gendered arguments about the labor market would mark the rejection of the framework based in the rigid separation between public and private that was the hallmark of the laissez-faire model used to analyze protective measures for men at the turn of the century. Instead, the labor market's relation to the state's interests would be confirmed and the question of the state's ability to regulate it would lose its relevance. The labor market itself would no longer be conceived of as a private preserve subject to limited intervention by the state.

The debate over these nodes of conflict would reveal the problematic nature of feminists' arguments for and against protective labor legislation. Advocates for women's interests had finally achieved the ability to have meaningful direct effects on the process of litigation but found themselves at odds with each other. These conflicts between feminists, however, masked the fact that their increasing influence in the process of litigation was not necessarily leading to the advancement of women as a class. While most feminists on both sides sought to advance women's position in the labor market and to make the workplace better for men as well as for women, many members of the legal community had different interests. These interests played out in the process of litigation. Ultimately, they led corporate attorneys and representatives of the state to use women's circumstances to advance their competing agendas for and against regulation, while advocates for feminist groups on both sides saw the battle over minimum wages as a staging ground for different visions of women's advancement. These nodes also led directly to the ruling in *West Coast Hotel*, narrowing the contested issues sufficiently to enable the Supreme Court to validate women's minimum wages in a way that would ground the permissibility of a wide variety of other statutes. This analytical development depended on the confirmation of the shift from the earlier male-centered mode of analysis to the more recent female-centered approach.

Unlike most of the earlier rulings of the Supreme Court concerning protective labor legislation, *Adkins v. Children's Hospital* countered the trends that had emerged in the state courts during the previous period. Following the lead of many states, Congress had passed a law establishing a mechanism that would set minimum wages for female workers in particular jobs. Like most minimum wage statutes of the time, this one created a minimum wage board, which was charged with conducting an investigation to determine the lowest amount per week on which a single woman could live (*Adkins v. Children's Hospital*, 261 U.S. 525, 539–41 (1923)). This amount would then be used as a guideline for setting the level for the minimum wage. One of the parties in the case was a female hospital worker who claimed that the law deprived her of her rights to liberty and property without due process of law (*Adkins*, 542–43). The Supreme Court, in a five-to-four decision, upheld her claim and struck down the congressional statute (*Adkins*, 559). This decision disrupted the landscape of litigation over protective legislation, since it appeared at first to cut directly against the Court's 1908 ruling in *Muller v. Oregon*, in which a statute limiting female laundry workers' hours of labor to ten per day had been upheld. Up to this point, as explained earlier, most courts on both the state and federal levels had rejected claims that women's freedom of contract required the invalidation of legislation regulating the terms and conditions of their labor.

By 1923, several states had established minimum wages for women only. All of these laws, both state and federal, were called into question by the Supreme Court's order. The state courts soon responded to the Supreme Court's ruling. The first challenge to such a law during this period occurred peripherally in Massachusetts, where the high court decided *Commonwealth v. Boston Transcript Co.* in 1924. The Massachusetts minimum wage differed from the regulation struck down in *Adkins*; rather than setting a required minimum wage and turning to the state for enforcement, Massachusetts's commission merely recommended the appropriate minimum wage (*Commonwealth v. Boston Transcript Co.*, 249 Mass. 477, 479–80 (1924)). In this case, the court considered Massachusetts's requirement that newspapers publish the findings of the commission and ruled that this requirement was unconstitutional (482). It did, however, comment that it believed Massachusetts's establishment of a minimum wage to be constitutional even in light of the *Adkins* decision, since the state's minimum wage was not mandatory (486).

In 1925, the Supreme Court of Kansas invalidated Kansas's minimum wage for women (*Topeka Laundry Co. v. Court of Industrial Relations*, 119 Kan. 12 (1925)). The statute, much broader in scope than the District of Columbia's statute at issue in *Adkins*, had created an industrial welfare commission to determine the appropriate wage for women's maintenance and apply that minimum wage in any industry or occupation in which women worked. Supporters of the law tried to show that the statute directly addressed the health and welfare of female workers, but the court interpreted the statute as having the same basic purpose of fixing wages that *Adkins* had condemned (*Topeka Laundry*, 17).

In 1935, New York's minimum wage statute received its first hearing in court, where it was upheld at the trial level. Joseph Tipaldo, a laundry manager in Brooklyn, was convicted for violating the requirement to pay a minimum wage by underpaying his female employees and then falsifying his account books to conceal the transgression (*People v. Morehead*, 270 N.Y. 233, 235–36 (1936)). The supreme court (New York's trial court) found that the law had been carefully crafted to avoid the constitutional problems faced by other minimum wage statutes (*People v. Morehead*, 282 N.Y.S. 576, 579–80 (Kings Co. Sup. Ct. 1935)). The New York Court of Appeals disagreed and, in a much-criticized decision, ruled that the statute was unconstitutional because it was similar enough to the District of Columbia's statute to warrant invalidation (*People v. Morehead*, 238–39 (1936)). The justices pointedly sidestepped the issue of whether they agreed with the reasoning in *Adkins*, explaining that their principal reason for invalidating the statute was its incompatibility with the Supreme Court's precedent (237).

Finally, in 1936 Washington's supreme court upheld its minimum wage, which covered all female workers and used an industrial welfare commission to investigate living conditions and make recommendations about the appropriate wage level. The case arose when Elsie Parrish, a chambermaid at the defendant hotel, made a claim for back wages she was owed from the differential between her pay and the minimum wage established by the commission (*Parrish v. West Coast Hotel*, 55 P.2d 1083, 1084 (1936)). In effect, the Washington Supreme Court threw down the gauntlet, challenging the U.S. Supreme Court to find that the law was "a plain, palpable invasion of rights secured by the fundamental law and has no real or substantial relation to the public morals or public welfare" (1090).

On the federal level, the Supreme Court's first case addressing protective labor legislation for women after *Adkins* was *Radice v. New York*, which considered New York's prohibition against women's working at night. The case resolved tensions over night work for women dating back to the *Williams* decision in 1907, which had struck down the state legislature's first attempt to regulate such labor (*People v. Williams*, 189 N.Y. 131 (1907)). The owner of a restaurant in Buffalo was convicted for employing women after ten o'clock at night in violation of the statute

(*Radice v. New York*, 264 U.S. 292, 293 (1924)). Justice Sutherland, who had written the opinion in *Adkins*, explained that the ruling in *Adkins* had not been meant to foreclose regulations of women's work that only addressed the public's concern about women's health and welfare (294–95). The Court thus upheld the statute.

In 1925 and 1927, the Court validated unreported state decisions that struck down minimum wages for women in Arizona and Arkansas respectively (*Murphy v. Sardell*, 269 U.S. 530 (1925); *Donham v. West Nelson Mfg. Co.*, 273 U.S. 65 (1927)). In both of these opinions, the Court relied on *Adkins*, choosing not to address appellants' arguments that the statutes in question differed substantially from the District of Columbia statute.

In 1936, the Supreme Court finally settled the fate of Joseph Tipaldo, ruling that the Court of Appeals's interpretation of New York's statute bound it to rule that the minimum wage was unconstitutional under the authority of *Adkins* (*Morehead v. New York*, 298 U.S. 587 (1936)). In what seemed to be almost an invitation to further litigation, the Court stated expressly that it had not reconsidered its reasoning in *Adkins* in deciding the case (604–5). The justices waited another year to revisit the issue in *West Coast Hotel*. In that case, the Court finally ruled that minimum wages for women did not violate the Constitution (*West Coast Hotel v. Parrish*, 300 U.S. 379 (1937)). Also on the federal level, one district court considered protective legislation for women, upholding Ohio's minimum wage in 1936; the court accepted the argument that the law was drawn carefully and reasonably enough to avoid the constitutional flaws of legislation struck down by the Supreme Court (*Walker v. Chapman*, 17 F. Supp. 308 (S.D. Ohio 1936)).

During these years, the courts struck down three protective measures that affected mostly male workers. The Bituminous Coal Restoration Act, which would have regulated several aspects of the coal-mining industry, including labor disputes, was invalidated in *Carter v. Carter Coal Co.* The Oregon federal district court struck down a statute that prohibited employers from requiring their employees to shop at a company store in *Owen v. West Lumber Co.* (22 F.2d 992 (D. Ore. 1927)). On the state level, the Georgia Supreme Court invalidated an ordinance regulating the hours of barbers and prohibiting blacks from serving as barbers to white boys (*Chaires v. City of Atlanta*, 164 Ga. 755 (1926)). On the state level, as mentioned earlier, the only decision to uphold protective legislation directed at both genders was *Stevenson v. St. Clair*, which upheld a minimum wage for children (161 Minn. 444 (1925)).

Minimum Wages and Liberty

In New York State we women now are free
To take our chance at wages with the men;
The courts uphold our right to misery.
The ancient right to starve is ours again.
A judge has pondered and has found a flaw:
"Unconstitutional," to fix our wage by law.

Congratulate us! Women now have leave
To work for any wages they can get.
Losing a living wage, we shall achieve
The right to cut our budgets, go in debt.
To bargain for existence we are free,
And though we fail, we die in liberty.

Give back the law! Let empty freedom end!
Give us the safeguards of the watchful state.
Children we have to rear, the sick to tend.
We must have food; the crying children wait.
And when the women's battle is fought through,
Extend the law! Protect our brothers too.

(Anonymous 1936)

This poem, written shortly after the Supreme Court announced its decision in *Morehead v. New York,* expressed the sentiments of women affiliated with the National Consumers' League and the National Women's Trade Union League about minimum wages and their limitations on liberty (Cushman 1936). Members of the National Woman's Party had different opinions about minimum wages; they saw them as violations of women's equality. Given the current level of sexism in the law, they argued, it would not be wise to "fight women's battle through" and only then to attempt to extend the laws to men (Smith 1937). These disagreements spilled over into the courts, coloring the arguments that attorneys made and influencing the ways that judges wrote their opinions. Nonetheless, the translation of these arguments was not completely faithful, as nonfeminist attorneys had different interests in constructing arguments using the concept of women's liberty than did feminist activists. The second decade of the century had seen the rise of a legal conception of women's liberty that differed from the implicitly male conception of liberty as autonomy and freedom from the state's intervention. Now this idea would be heavily debated both within and outside of the legal arena. This debate initially took place in gendered terms but increasingly appeared in gender-neutral language. The discussion of liberty in the years of gendered rebalancing contributed to the Court's decision largely to jettison the concept from constitutional analysis after 1937, at least in the context of contractual relations between employers and employees.

The Feminists' Battle over Liberty

In these years, feminists were in open and often bitter disagreement with one another concerning the nature of women's liberty. The splits that became public in the 1920s had existed before, but the disagreements over minimum wages provoked a rancorous debate that spilled over to the arena of litigation. Members of groups that advocated for protective measures for women were contemptuous of formalistic explanations of liberty of contract, claiming that this abstract legal right bore no relationship to women's vulnerabilities in the marketplace. In the previous period, the National Consumers' League and the National Women's Trade Union League had argued that protective legislation enhanced women's liberty of contract. During the years of gendered rebalancing, they redoubled their efforts to convince the legal community that this was in fact the case. Dealt a serious setback by the *Adkins* decision, they concentrated on minimum wages, seeking to connect a statutory living wage analytically to the freedom to bargain effectively with one's employer. Advocates for equality countered these arguments by claiming that those supporting legislation did not recognize the problematic implications of framing women's liberty as different from men's. The National Woman's Party and like-minded organizations were concerned about the differentiation between men and women brought about by protective measures that applied to women only; protection for women alone would ultimately harm their exercise of liberty by making them less able to compete effectively.

Bitter as the debate was, however, it was more a disagreement over essentialism and ultimately over tactics than a fight over the nature of relations between employees and employers. The feminists supporting legislation had an essentialist conception of women's liberty, arguing that women's particular vulnerabilities arose from their very existence as women and thus that these vulnerabilities could only be accommodated through the intervention of the state. In contrast, supporters of women's equality saw nothing natural or inherent in women's degraded position in the workplace. The emphasis of their arguments was on equality, and they believed that gendered protective measures injured women by encouraging paternalism toward them and making them less able to compete with men effectively. Despite these disagreements, however, supporters of equality largely rejected the laissez-faire model of the labor marketplace, occasionally arguing in favor of protection for all workers, both female and male. Despite their commitment to equality, these organizations had been active participants in the transformative battles for suffrage and conceived of the state as a potential ally, not a threat to women's freedom.

Activists promoting minimum wages spent much of their time strategizing about how to confront the precedent set in *Adkins*. For those who wanted to promote protective labor legislation for women, *Adkins* was a disastrous step backward. Pro-protection feminists developed deeply layered factual arguments to show that minimum wages were needed to enhance women's liberty. Feminists who opposed gendered minimum wages were quietly pleased with the reasoning in *Adkins* even though many on this side felt that the courts and legislatures eventually had to be convinced that gender-neutral protections were good for all workers. They saw nothing negative in the Supreme Court's assertions that women and men had the same political rights and that women's liberty was the same as men's.[2]

Women's groups favoring protective legislation pointed to the

---

2. Even among the feminists who supported minimum wages for women, not all statutes were acceptable. The laws needed to be carefully calibrated to the particular social circumstances and closely linked to the value of labor, since the point of the minimum wage was to enable women to strike fair bargains, thus enhancing their liberty. Josephine Goldmark, a longtime advocate for protective labor legislation, explained in her criticism of the law struck down in *Murphy v. Sardell* that the law was too broadly drawn, since it established a single wage for all female industrial workers: "the essential feature of all desirable minimum wage laws has been the establishment of separate wage boards for different industries, boards on which employers, employees and the general public have been represented and have deliberated together to fix minimum wages for their trade" (Goldmark 1925, 25). The Consumers' League assisted in the lengthy and detailed investigations to develop standards for minimum wages in many states that had minimum wages (Consumers' League of Connecticut 1931).

ways that minimum wages could strengthen liberty by improving access to information, as well as by encouraging women to cooperate with one another to ensure that the laws were being followed. Without protective measures, women had no firm basis on which to bargain, since they did not have the necessary knowledge about broader conditions in the labor market, nor did they have the stomach to use this information effectively. Josephine Goldmark explained in 1925 that female consumers and laborers needed to work together to ensure that minimum wages would be implemented and enforced, encouraging middle-class women to assist in monitoring corporations for compliance (Goldmark 1925). The wide dissemination of this information would enable women to bargain more effectively on the basis of knowledge, which would enhance workers' liberties by making them more substantively meaningful (Goldmark 1925).

Members of the National Woman's Party and like-minded groups disagreed with this analysis. The National Woman's Party spearheaded the opposition to minimum wages, claiming that their organization represented the true interests and desires of the working woman. They saw themselves as the champions of women's substantive liberty, thwarting the self-aggrandizing desires of meddling reformers (Smith 1932, 398). They believed that the measures would hurt women economically in the long run, ultimately limiting their freedom to work in their chosen fields. If employers had to pay women minimum wages, argued these feminists, they would not hire women but would rather hire men who would be able to work for less. This would limit women's liberty in an absolute sense by curtailing their options for securing paid employment. The National Woman's Party insisted that the solution to these problems was stronger trade unions for women or gender-neutral legislation that controlled working conditions for both men and women (National Woman's Party 1935). Such regulations, in these activists' views, would enhance liberty for everyone by providing fairer options in the labor marketplace for all employees and limiting employers' ability to strike coercive bargains.

These organizations disagreed not only about the fundamental nature of women's liberty, but about what kind of factual information was relevant to protecting this liberty. They thus presented arguments both about the abstract nature and quality of women's liberty and about the concrete impact of minimum wages on this liberty. As these discussions show, both sides were able to produce evidence to support their sides of the debate. Both sides also focused on women's particular liberty in relation to the liberty that men enjoyed but drew different conclusions from the comparison. Feminists promoting regulation maintained an essentialist analysis of women's trials in the workplace, attributing their lack of bargaining power to their femininity, while feminists committed to equality objected to the suggestion that inherent differences existed between women and men, assuming instead essential equality. Both sides actively sought to convince the legal community to rethink women's roles in the workplace and to calibrate the state's actions to account for these roles; on both sides, the fundamental question was how the legal system could best serve the real interests of working women. For these activists, while contention over the facts primarily played into their agenda for litigation, at bottom the fight over minimum wages was as much a fight over values as over strategies.

Conflicting Arguments and Motives concerning Minimum Wages

Attorneys arguing for and against minimum wages used similar types of claims to support their explanations of why such laws limited or did not limit liberty inappropriately. Their reasoning applied the kinds of evidence and arguments used by women's groups to the constitutionally significant issues, arguing for or against the permissibility of legislation in the public interest and pushing or denying parallels to other types of statutes held by the courts to be constitutionally valid. Nonetheless, they sometimes had different goals from the women's groups who supported their work. The arguments presented in *Adkins* and in *West Coast Hotel* are most illuminating, as the attorneys in these cases considered liberty thoroughly and largely grappled within the framework established to address women's legislation. Nonetheless, the briefs highlight the tension between emerging conceptions of liberty as the freedom to engage in meaningful bargaining and the older conceptions of male liberty based in autonomy and freedom from the state's intervention.

In the *Adkins* case, Francis Stephens and Felix Frankfurter prepared the lead brief with the assistance of Mary Dewson of the National Consumers' League. The authors framed the argument in gender-neutral terms (albeit with gendered pronouns), emphasizing the fictitious nature of freedom of contract when the employee was bargaining for a wage that did not meet her cost of living (Stephens, Frankfurter, and Dewson 1923, 412–13). In this analysis, the much-vaunted freedom was the liberty to choose between working for a substandard wage and starving. Such a choice was not a meaningful selection, nor was it acceptable as a merely private matter. Their argument used the same themes as those articulated by Goldmark and Frankfurter in their brief supporting Oregon's minimum wages and maximum hours for women at stake in *Stettler v. O'Hara*. The gender-neutral elements of the earlier argument were repeated here because they appeared to have been successful before the Court. The advocates also cited the large number of states (many of which had filed amicus briefs in the case) that had also concluded that minimum wages enhanced, rather than restricted, liberty (Stephens, Frankfurter, and Dewson 1923, 387). This reasoning did not depend upon women's differences from men except to the degree that women faced intensive competition for particular jobs.

In contrast, the State of Wisconsin's amicus brief presented a gendered argument for regulation, relying on women's special status to argue that their liberty would be enhanced rather than restricted by minimum wages. This reasoning compared to that of groups such as the National Consumers' League but presented women as largely incompetent to manage their own affairs. Citing the various limits on women's liberty arising from coverture and women's subsequent lack of experience in making contracts and managing their own affairs, attorneys for the State of Wisconsin argued that minimum wages gave women the freedom to act for themselves without risking injury (Ekern, Messerschmidt, and Wilcox 1923, 556). This argument portrayed women as a historically separate class who had never been free of the state's influence in the classical contractarian sense. More specifically, the advocates asserted that because of women's particular vulnerability to exploitation by their employers, women not covered by regulation had little liberty to lose (561). In their interpretation, minimum wages helped to create equality between female employees and their employers by compensating for women's inherent disabilities (561). The state's agenda was not necessarily feminist, however; rather than seeking empowerment for women by enhancing their bargaining power, officials of the state who supported protection for women did so to facilitate women's performance of their traditional responsibilities to home and family. In addition to contributing to better citizenship for children and potential children, this interest of the state was tied to granting working men fuller access to the rights and privileges of male citizenship, which included an orderly home (Stanley 1998).

Predictably, the opponents of the minimum wage relied on a broad conception of equal liberty to challenge the statute. In their analysis, they sought to shift the ground of analysis back from the publicly supported liberty now common in cases involving women to the private liberty endorsed with respect to men. Their arguments in part paralleled those of the National Woman's Party but had different implications. Paying lip service to feminism, they highlighted the connections between liberty and equality, claiming that limiting women who were not covered by the same rules as men could never achieve meaningful equality with men. Nonetheless, such attorneys did not recognize or acknowledge the implicit endorsement of male standards for liberty and equality. The attorney for the hospital claimed that the congressional statute was not at all beneficial to women's liberty interests: "I challenge the suggestion that the great body of women in this country, or any considerable number of them, prefer the fixing of wages for women while men are free to enjoy their liberty of contract" (Ellis 1923, 629). In his interpretation, the limitation on women's liberty of contract was insulting, implying that women were not competent adults (629). The background agenda, however, was lifting the burden of regulation from employers, not achieving meaningful equality for women.

By the time of *West Coast Hotel*, those who opposed regulations had settled on the mostly successful strategy of claiming that economic need, far from being related to liberty, was simply not an adequate counterbalance to liberty of contract. Nonetheless, the briefs in the case revealed the headway that the proposition that the state could legitimately promote liberty had made in the legal community. Lawyers in *West Coast Hotel* answered the amicus brief supporting the statute by claiming that if the wage had been more tied to the economic value of labor, it would have been more acceptable, but that as written, the law rested on necessity, not fair value (Roberts and Skeel 1937, 170). Not only did the law employ improper means of assistance, it did not in fact improve women's ability to achieve good bargains for themselves. Because these laws were based on economic need rather than on the value of services, they constituted an improper interference into the market and ultimately would not lead to increased liberty. These arguments sought to steer a middle course, suggesting that legislation seeking to correct for severe imbalances in the labor market might be permissible but that such interventions had to fit into a model of enhancing private bargaining power. Nonetheless, the writing was on the wall, indicating that the basic assumptions underlying the state's authority to intervene had shifted.

Superficially the attorneys' arguments about liberty continued along the same lines that had developed in the decade before 1920, though attorneys did not spend as much time working to articulate the precise and gendered nature of women's liberty. Nonetheless, litigation during the period of gendered rebalancing confirmed the analytical changes that had taken place. The fight over minimum wages took place with the underlying assumption that the state could appropriately regulate the conditions of labor in ways that would enhance liberty. During the period of laborer-centered analysis, the legal community had finally arrived at a consensus that limiting women's hours of labor was appropriate and acceptable, which undercut the laissez-faire model. By the end of the period of gendered rebalancing, specific discussions of liberty in briefs largely took place in gender-neutral terms, allowing analytical room for their transference to cases addressing men's position in the labor market as well. Furthermore, even opponents of protective legislation accepted the concept that liberty could be enhanced by the state. Nonactivist attorneys' reasoning sometimes distorted the insights of feminist activists and their counselors; nonfeminist advocates for minimum wages promoted a conception of women as incompetent, while their nonfeminist opponents sought to eliminate all types of protection, not simply to level the playing field.

The Courts' Analyses of Liberty and Its
Disappearance in *West Coast Hotel*

These tendencies continued to shape judges' reasoning about liberty. Some judges' broad endorsements of women's equality masked a belief that women were fundamentally different from men and were therefore subject to more regulation by the state; feminists devoted to equality vehemently opposed this position. Likewise, courts upholding protective measures implied that women were incapable of bargaining for a fair price for their labor; thus minimum wages enhanced their liberty. The disagreement over the nature and extent of women's liberty led the Supreme Court to determine that liberty was no longer an appropriate focus of the analysis. Throughout this period, the weight of analysis was shifting toward police power, and by the time of *West Coast Hotel*, police power and the proper relationship between the labor market and the state were at the center of the Court's reasoning, driving liberty out of the picture. Once laborer-centered analysis had become the norm and the ability to identify the state's interests with those of the worker had taken hold, the stage was set for the analytical decline of private liberty. As the legal community focused sharply on the meaning of gender, the period of gendered rebalancing saw liberty gradually retreating into the background, losing its effectiveness as a counterweight to police power and rendering the very concept of balancing one against the other less meaningful.

Ironically, this process began with *Adkins*, which partially revivified private liberty in relation to women and their labor. Over the next several years, judges moved to the position that liberty was not simply the absence of intervention by the state but rather was the ability to bargain with one's employer. In part this shift reflected the successful rhetorical manipulation of the extreme conditions of the Great Depression, which starkly highlighted the disingenuous nature of a model featuring an employer and employee bargaining over wages from an equal standpoint when the labor surplus was composed of defeated workers who would accept any wage to avoid starvation. The analytical basis for the shift, however, was the model of women's liberty and its relationship to the state developed in the century's second decade and applied by later judges to undercut the Court's ruling in *Adkins*.

In *Adkins*, the Court had analyzed liberty extensively, developing the claim that women's liberty of contract was the equivalent of men's (545–46). In doing so, it endorsed the idea that women held the same private right to bargain in the absence of the state's intervention as men did. The Court explained its disapproval of the statutory interference with women's liberty, asserting "we cannot accept the doctrine that women of mature age, *sui juris*, require or may be subjected to restrictions upon their liberty of contract which could not lawfully be imposed in the case of men under similar circumstances" (545–46). In the view of the majority, allowing such limitations would deny the emancipation of women, confirmed by the passage of the Nineteenth Amendment. Despite these sweeping pronouncements, however, the Court did not endorse the idea that women's liberty was the same as men's in its complete insulation from the state's interference. The justices reasoned that limits on women's liberty regarding hours of labor were different and permissible because of their clear relationship to health (554). The minimum wage, however, was a clear infringement on liberty not only because of its lack of relationship to women's health, but also because of its operation as a price-fixing statute. The question was thus not one of women's liberty being different from men's but rather one of the type of limit at stake and its relationship to the public interest. At the same time, the Court emphasized the legitimacy of viewing women as a class while reinforcing the unacceptability of viewing workers as a class. The Court would certainly not have been persuaded to uphold the statute had it applied to men as well as women, but the opinion rested upon the inequality of its operation and its portrayal of women as incapable of exercising liberty as wisely or effectively as men.

Later rulings of the Supreme Court initially read *Adkins* broadly, seeing it as barring almost any kind of law establishing a minimum wage and mandating support for women's liberty of contract with respect to the price of labor. In *Morehead* the Court explained this interpretation: "The decision and the reasoning upon which it rests clearly show that the State is without power by any form of legislation to prohibit, change or nullify contracts between employers and adult women workers as to the amount of wages to be paid" (*Morehead v. New York*, 611). Not all courts, though, read *Adkins* in this way, leaving the status of minimum wages ambiguous. For instance, in the same year that the Supreme Court ruled in *Morehead*, a district court in Ohio heard a challenge to Ohio's minimum wage for women. This court endorsed a distinction cited by attorneys who had argued against such measures in other cases: the Ohio law, in contrast to unconstitutional laws, set the minimum wage with reference to the value of the services rendered by the women the law covered. Because wages set in this way bore a clear relationship to the fair market value of labor, the regulation did not limit women's liberty in an inappropriate way (*Walker v. Chapman*, 310). The court explained that the Supreme Court had not absolutely barred the state from implementing minimum wages in its decision in *Adkins*; rather it had struck down the District of Columbia's statute because of specific problems in that statute. Because the focus of Ohio's law was on establishing the proper price for labor, the measure did not infringe on liberty; rather, it set wages at the level that they would be at under free and open competition. This ruling underlined the nature of liberty as a right that the state's intervention could enhance as well as limit, accepting the theory of market failure advanced by Goldmark and Frankfurter in the period of laborer-centered analysis.

In *West Coast Hotel*, the Court took up the inconsistency between rulings on minimum wages and other types of protective legislation for women, ruling that in both types of cases liberty was limited and that in both types of cases this limit was warranted (*West Coast Hotel v. Parrish*, 394–95). In the view of the Court, "The validity of the distinction made by the Court between a minimum wage and a maximum of hours in limiting liberty of contract was especially challenged. . . . That challenge persists and is without any satisfactory answer" (395). The Court also gave freer rein to the legislature in presuming that it had the proper motivation in passing the statute. The board created to establish minimum wages, the Court asserted, could be trusted to set wages based on the value of services rather than attempting to fix wages to advantage a particular class, and the propriety of its determinations could be assumed (396). In this reasoning the right to contract was not infringed as long as the wages earned bore a fair relationship to the value of the labor. More significantly, there was no question that the state's actions enhanced rather than curtailed individuals' bargaining authority. This finding closed and locked the door on arguments based in conceptions of liberty as freedom from the state's intervention in a private relationship between employer and employee.

These factors led the Court to validate Washington's minimum wage but also led to a repudiation of some of the key factors in *Adkins*. The Court avoided discussions about the extent to which minimum wages enhanced women's liberty, focusing instead almost exclusively on police power. No longer could courts simply assume that the legislature had an invalid purpose in mind when it changed the conditions of labor for women. Nor did judges have to analyze women's liberty carefully and separately from that of men in order to permit states to treat them differently in the labor market. Since the Court was reconceiving the relationship between police power and liberty, legislators and the legal community would no longer have to justify protective statutes by claiming that they enhanced, rather than restricted, liberty.

West Coast Hotel marked the end of extensive discussions of liberty for a while in the context of substantive due process, gendered or otherwise. The earlier debates over liberty among activists, attorneys, and judges had stabilized liberty conceptually. The central issue from a legal standpoint was the extent to which the state could articulate justifications for limiting liberty. These discussions took place in the broad context of police power, not liberty. While activists sought to convince the courts and the public either that protective measures enhanced or restricted liberty, the bulk of the analysis came down to the nature of the statutes involved and their impact on female laborers. *West Coast Hotel* merely confirmed that the feminists' disagreements over women's liberty were beside the point. With feminist consciousness at a low ebb in the general public, judges had little incentive to grapple with the larger questions of values that had driven the feminists' debate, and once women were no longer the center of analysis, the courts no longer had to address such questions even peripherally. The completion of gendered rebalancing in *West Coast Hotel* enabled the legal community to shift rapidly from analyzing women's relationship to the state back to centering male perspectives and interests. While the analysis of the 1920s and 1930s focused on women, the Court did not differentiate between men's and women's liberty—the days when such distinctions could have constitutional significance were over. The development of the nodes of conflict from the generalized balancing of liberty against police power after the passage of the Fourteenth Amendment to the specific rebalancing in gendered terms during the New Deal enabled the nearly complete elimination of liberty from the analysis by the beginning of the 1940s.

Justifications for Upholding Legislation

As in the second decade of the century, those supporting protective labor legislation continued to justify specific statutory exercises of police power. These explanations sometimes aimed to show that protective legislation was appropriate for women even if inappropriate for men; other framings of the arguments were more general, so as to apply to both women and men. As detailed in chapter 4, these justifications continued to address women's physical characteristics as well as their structural positions in the labor market. Ultimately these arguments would lead the legal community to endorse a different conception of the proper scope of public intervention in the labor market, supporting the idea that the state was a silent third party to all contracts between employers and employees. With respect to women, the factual

arguments over minimum wages centered around the appropriate
ways that the state could intervene to protect women because of their
particularly vulnerable natures.

These arguments were not new—as chapters 3 and 4 demonstrated, attorneys and judges had spent some time in the periods of specific balancing and laborer-centered analysis working out the ways that
women differed from men and the impacts those differences had on the
fate of protective labor legislation for women. By the end of the period
of laborer-centered analysis, however, some women's groups and
reform-minded attorneys had begun to frame these discussions
broadly enough to apply to male laborers as well as female laborers.
Furthermore, the discussion no longer focused so much on differentiating women from men, turning rather on the extent to which women's
particular circumstances warranted regulation. In the period of gendered rebalancing, women's groups and activist attorneys supporting
protective labor legislation put more effort into developing factual
records criticizing poor conditions in the workplace and delineating the
nature of women's weak bargaining power. Since the issue in these
cases was the minimum wage, on both sides women's organizations
and activist and nonactivist attorneys had to develop factual arguments about the extent to which low wages were damaging enough to
warrant interfering with the market's process of setting wages.

Feminist activists continued to argue over the extent to which
women were different from men and the implications of these differences for minimum wages. This disagreement, which influenced the
agendas for research by activist organizations, provided information
and arguments to attorneys. As with liberty, however, the legal community did not always translate these ideas uncritically into the legal
discourse. Particularly in arguments relating to women's health, attorneys often seemed to be arguing over whether women belonged in the
workplace at all. Gendered arguments about the structure of the marketplace also were not consistently feminist in their implications.

In this process, the earlier reasoning about women's differences
gradually came to support a structured analysis of laborers' deficiencies in the workplace that allowed for regulation of male labor. Gendered arguments based on women's physical differences gave way to
gender-neutral claims about the structure of the labor marketplace and
the harms of coercive bargains. This development grounded *West Coast
Hotel*'s reasoning that the states could regulate labor in the interest of

protecting workers from inequalities in bargaining power, regardless of the workers' genders.

Activists' Battles over Women's Capacities

As in the period of laborer-centered analysis, activists employed three lines of argument regarding women's capacities to participate equally in the workplace, addressing directly the node of conflict over police power's scope with respect to women. Their agenda for research and argument was indebted to the framework of the legal battles in which they were engaged, centering on developing facts that would enhance their interpretations of the legal categories of public interest and public harm. They argued over the significance of motherhood, over women's particular health risks, and over the economic and social risks that women faced in bargaining for wages. Feminists promoting protection advanced largely the same arguments regarding motherhood and women's health that they had promoted in the teens and early twenties but expanded their analysis of the labor marketplace. The big development was that they now had to deal with an organized feminist opposition, which countered their reasoning on nearly every point. The disagreements between these groups of feminists were fundamental and irreconcilable. By the mid-1920s, feminists promoting equality were rejecting not only maternalist strategies for achieving reform but also the basis for maternalism itself: a belief in women's different exercise of citizenship based in their roles as mothers and potential mothers.

During the years of gendered rebalancing, women's groups advocating for protective labor legislation focused more on health than on motherhood. They nonetheless did continue to refer to women's reproductive role as a valid reason to regulate their labor. As in the earlier years, the National Consumers' League and its companions argued that pregnancy and motherhood differentiated women from men substantially and continued to highlight women's double work shift in the labor market and at home (see, e.g., Hamilton 1924). They also maintained that women's health generally was more fragile than men's health, supporting these assertions with voluminous evidence (Perkins and Baker 1926, 529). Of increasing concern to such advocates was the threat that women would turn to illegal activities, particularly prostitution, to save their failing health (Consumers' League of Connecticut 1933). Their arguments generally assumed that women's differences from men were inherent and essential and thus that rectifying their ill effects would require the state's action. The advocates framed these claims specifically to justify the exercise of police power.

Supporters of equality disagreed both with the proposition that women's health risks from working were higher than those of men and with the idea that such differences, if they even existed, justified special protective legislation. As one would expect, they spent little time discussing motherhood, choosing instead to question the motives of those who supported protective labor legislation. Such advocates pointed out that women had always performed physically taxing work: "It was not until women entered the field of paid labor that there was concern for their welfare" (Mabie 1928, 4). They asserted that those who wanted to regulate women's work had their own selfish interests to fulfill—male trade union members wanted to protect their jobs from female competition, and sexist legislatures were only too eager to oblige them (Mabie 1928). Their focus was nonetheless on the extent to which women were the same as men, not on questioning the appropriateness of the male standard.

Believers in equal rights also claimed that women were not frail or subject to more injuries than men were. They argued that using these sexist assumptions as a basis for protection was ultimately dangerous to women and also that such notions were completely out of line with reality. An editorial in the National Woman's Party publication *Equal Rights* asserted: "The effete notion that a woman's existence is necessarily subject to recurring periods of illness which unfit her for free competition in the economic struggle is a spectre that should be laid to rest. . . . Womanhood is precisely as normal a condition of humanity as manhood" ("Unphysiological Physiology" 1924, 68). In this interpretation, women's fragility became an issue only when someone was seeking to deny women access to a paying job or other benefit. This reasoning combated the view of women as special and different from a universal male standard, though at this time the National Woman's Party was not devoting its resources to advocating for general protective labor legislation.

The third major justification relied upon by women's organizations and lawyers in promoting protective legislation for women was women's structural position in the workplace. While these arguments had arisen earlier, in the years of gendered rebalancing they achieved their potential. Advocates for protective labor legislation rebutted their opponents' belief that women could gain the same advances in the labor market as men through collective bargaining, articulating three reasons why unionization would not solve women's problems. First, they claimed, women were temporary employees, often working only between leaving school and getting married, which provided little incentive for them to commit to unions for long-run gains. Second, women were paid so poorly that union dues were a financial hardship. Finally, female workers were generally too youthful and naive to be able to appreciate the benefits of collective bargaining (Perkins and Baker 1926, 530). For the most part, such arguments focused on women as laborers and on the particular conditions that female workers faced. Further, these differences were assumed to be outgrowths of women's fundamental natures rather than learned or (to use an anachronistic term) socially constructed behavior. While male workers also had low wages, worked at a young age, and often experienced high turnover, the advocates used them as a foil to portray female workers as more vulnerable and thus as legitimate targets for regulation and protection. In this view, women's differences, while not genetic or immutable,[3] nevertheless posed real problems for women in the trade union movement.

The problems that advocates for women's legislation identified were not limited to women's unwillingness to join labor unions. Continuing to focus on women rather than on the labor they performed, the Consumers' League of New York argued that women failed to bargain collectively because they knew that the alternative to accepting low wages was to join the burgeoning ranks of the unemployed (Herrick 1933, 13–14). Because of the desperate circumstances engendered by the depression, marginalized female workers in particular were hard enough pressed to accept almost any wages, since they were having an even harder time than men in finding viable work. Advocates for protective labor legislation argued that women were even more likely than men to accept wages below the level at which they and their families could live because of their commitment to caring for their hungry children.

---

3. The dichotomy between mutable and immutable differences did not appear to be of great concern to any of the feminists writing at the time, though advocates and opponents of equality appeared to agree that differences in bargaining power could be remedied either through better organization or through state intervention. Women who argued for the constitutionality of protective legislation, however, often spoke as if women's roles as the nurturers of children and families were natural and perhaps immutable.

Both advocates for and detractors from protective labor legislation for women agreed that bargaining power was a crucial site at which equality was necessary for women. In a statement that could have been issued by the National Woman's Party, Ethel Smith, a member of the executive committee of the National Women's Trade Union League, argued, "The important conclusion . . . is this: That we keep our eyes on the relative bargaining power of women and men and let all efforts at equalization centre there" (Smith 1929, 797). The core of the disagreement was how this equality was to be achieved; underneath this battle was a fundamental split about the extent to which women and men differed fundamentally and essentially.

Addressing this issue, members of the National Woman's Party emphasized that the protective laws embraced by some feminists were written, enforced, and interpreted by men. They argued that the current legal structure had been created and administered by men since before the beginning of the Republic (National Woman's Party n.d.). Women would thus be better off if they worked on their own to achieve improved industrial standards. The National Woman's Party also uncovered embarrassing evidence about the call for regulation of night work by women during the depression, citing the testimony of an officer of New York's Federation of Labor. "'Unemployed men waiters are now walking the streets of this State,' said he at a legislative hearing on the amendment to give female restaurant workers the right to work on a night shift; 'if women are allowed to work at night, thousands of men will be thrown out of employment'" (Smith 1932, 396–97). If men were the ultimate beneficiaries of protective legislation, how could it be expected to serve women's interests consistently?

The disagreement was thus framed over the significance of women's differences from men with little recognition that men provided the standard. Activists on both sides disagreed over whether women were men's equals and sought to raise women to the level of men either legislatively or by advocating for increasing membership in trade unions. They nonetheless had some basic points of agreement: both sets of feminists wanted to see higher industrial standards for both men and women. In these arguments, they intentionally and inadvertently provided arguments and data to attorneys seeking to win victories on both sides of the question of minimum wages. For these contending feminists, acknowledgment of difference corresponded with support for protective legislation, and commitment to equality was linked to opposition to such laws. While advocates for and against minimum wages tailored their factual investigations to address the existing legal categories, the information they developed would ultimately assist in the reshaping of these categories. This reshaping, however, was not only in response to feminist pressures but also incorporated the agendas of nonfeminist supporters of the state's authority to regulate and of corporate actors who sought to escape regulation.

Attorneys' Arguments about Police Power and Difference

Attorneys did not address arguments about the male-centered nature of the law, instead maintaining the familiar disagreements over the various justifications advanced for minimum wages. In doing so, they continued the discussions that had been initiated in the period of laborer-centered analysis. As in the previous decade, the line between attorneys and activists sometimes blurred, and some attorneys argued on the behalf of feminist organizations. With the rise of full and open opposition by feminist advocates for women's equality, some cases included four perspectives: arguments from the National Consumers' League or other organizations promoting minimum wages to advance feminist goals, arguments from the state to promote its authority to regulate labor, arguments from the National Woman's Party to enhance women's equality, and arguments from the regulated industry to overturn the burdensome minimum wage. These crosscutting agendas necessarily complicated the production of doctrine, particularly when nonfeminist individuals or organizations drew on the factual arguments developed by feminist investigations to advance their agendas.

Those attorneys who supported minimum wages sometimes relied on differences between men and women to ground their arguments, but they also presented some of their arguments in general terms. They emphasized the same justifications as feminist organizations—women's roles as mothers and wives, the physical risks of the workplace, and women's bargaining power—but the image of women they invoked in their briefs was often subtly different from that presented by feminists who advocated for protective labor legislation. Nonfeminist supporters of minimum wages tended to rely more on arguments involving biological differences between women and men, reiterating the kinds of arguments that had worked to justify protective labor legislation for women in the previous period. As with the activists' arguments about difference, attorneys' discussions of motherhood and physical disability were similar to those made in the previous years. Attorneys began to broaden their analysis of the labor market at this time and also began developing more reasons to explain men's particular need for protection.

Both activist attorneys supporting minimum wages and representatives of the states sponsoring the legislation maintained their focus on women's roles as mothers, emphasizing both the state's direct interest in women's health and the health of their children and women's role as transmitters of American culture. They also continued to rely on the factual information developed by the National Consumers' League and the new Children's Bureau; as mentioned above, Mary Dewson, the secretary of the National Consumers' League, was the coauthor of one of the lead briefs in *Adkins* (Stephens, Frankfurter, and Dewson 1923). These arguments were no different from arguments made in the early twentieth century, except in the attorneys' ability to cite a great deal of factual evidence to support their propositions. The claims remained deeply gendered and focused on laborers.

During these years, however, nonfeminist attorneys began to exhibit more explicit concern with women's roles as the translators of culture to the next generation and to explain more fully the dangers of allowing women to be overly burdened by the economic system. For instance, the attorney defending California's minimum wage sought to show that women who overworked and received low pay would not have the proper attitudes to be fit mothers. Their daily struggles for subsistence would embitter them toward the world, and they would pass on this disillusionment to their children (Pillsbury 1925, 45–46). In fact, the brief went on to argue, such cynicism could lead to the decline of the state, and ultimately even to bolshevism. Women thus needed particular protection because of their greater vulnerability and because of the potential impact of the injuries they might suffer.

Recognizing the analytic significance of the differentiation between male and female workers, some lawyers opposing minimum wages for women argued that women were not the sole transmitters of health and social values to the next generation, framing their discussions more generally to apply to men. These corporate lawyers assumed that convincing the courts of women's equality with men would persuade the courts that regulation was inappropriate. After all, claimed an opponent of New York's statute, men more often tended to be the primary supporters of children; thus "the health and well-being of adult women and of children is just as injuriously affected when a man cannot earn a living wage or a reasonable wage for his family as when a woman cannot do so. The effect as to 'deterioration of race' is the same in either case" (Campbell 1936, 14). Cynical and embittered men could threaten society through the values they passed on to their children as easily as women could. If the state was nonetheless not permitted to protect men, why should it be permitted to protect women? The attorneys for the state maintained their framing of reproduction and raising of children as strictly women's work, not acknowledging the possibility of turning this argument into a defense of general protective legislation.

As in earlier years, the arguments made in favor of protective legislation by women's organizations differed from those made by nonfeminist attorneys. Both groups were certainly worried about the coming generation, but many nonfeminist attorneys focused on the damage that poor mothering could do. Rather than emphasizing the difficulties that responsible working mothers faced in trying raise their children successfully, such attorneys often related scenarios of mothers who did not Americanize their children sufficiently, mothers who let their children's health decline into weakness and decrepitude, and mothers who were unable to maintain households that inculcated morality in their families (Hamilton et al. 1937). Much of this difference could be attributed to the attorneys' need to emphasize the public's direct interest in women by identifying areas where the state would ultimately have to intervene if women failed in their roles as mothers. Without feminist sensibilities, attorneys found it easier to raise the specter of injury to the state through negligent mothering than to argue directly for the empowerment of women in the workplace as a good in and of itself.

Nonfeminist concerns with health appeared most clearly in the discussion of night work, an unsurprising development despite the earlier fairly radical conception of women's equality in New York's invalidation of a prohibition on night work in *Williams*. The New York court's endorsement of full substantive equality in *Williams* was anomalous both in its outcome and in its reasoning. In *Radice*, the attorney general of New York filed a factual brief based on the specific dangers of night work for women, focusing on perceived differences between women and men. While many of the dangers cited in the brief applied to men and women, the brief emphasized the ill effects on women specifically. Women, like men, suffered from lack of sleep, but women were further injured by having to take care of their households during the day after working all night (Sherman and Goldsmith 1923, 1). Another direct evil of night work was that it often occurred after a woman had worked all day through overtime; the attorneys authoring the brief argued that such work could cause permanent injury to women (114). Furthermore, it could lead to sexual impropriety and abuse of alcohol (224). These risks warranted prohibiting women from working at night altogether for the good of society. Most of these detriments were not limited to women, but the brief presented them in gendered terms.

Those who objected to protective legislation also addressed differences in women's health, using two basic lines of argument. They used the same types of reasoning that feminist supporters of equality promoted, but also argued against minimum wages more generally. In *Adkins,* attorneys challenging the law sought to show that, regardless of any real or perceived differences between men and women, the law itself did not protect health (Ellis, Folk, and Ellis 1923, 473). As far as minimum wages were concerned, they claimed, "Wage laws are not health laws at all. There is no direct or immediate relation between health, morality and general welfare, on the one hand, and wages on the other. High wages, and resulting extravagant living, may be as detrimental to health as low wages" (Ellis 1923, 644). This position, if adopted, would remove the legislation from the preserve of public health and subject it to more searching inquiry by the courts. In framing the law in this way, the attorneys encouraged the adoption of a hard separation between minimum wages and accepted types of protection on the ground that minimum wages were merely interferences with the market's process of setting wages. Interpreting minimum wages in this way placed them on the extreme end of a spectrum of state actions that worked to benefit a particular class of individuals based on their structural positions in the labor market rather than on particular vulnerabilities that they exhibited in the workplace. By presenting the issue in these stark terms, attorneys opposing regulation hoped to convince the courts that minimum wages constituted class warfare rather than protection for individual workers. In addressing the problem in this way, however, they unconsciously legitimated the concept that protecting workers was an appropriate aim for the state.

Laws addressing night work were not so vulnerable to claims that they constituted illegitimate incursions into the market's operation, as their advocates emphasized. Opponents thus reverted to the strategy of the era of specific balancing of showing that the particular work involved was not dangerous or unhealthful, claiming, "The work of women as waitresses in restaurants is easier than housework . . . and there is nothing in such employment or conditions surrounding waitresses or females employed in restaurants that is deleterious to their health" (Hill and Hill 1923, 27). This type of argument, however, was not winning adherents in any courts by this time, as laborer-centered analysis had foreclosed the analytical operation of such claims.

Nonactivist attorneys discussing the risks to women's health thus advanced arguments similar to those used by women's organizations, but these attorneys portrayed women differently than the women's organizations and their advocates did. Attorneys without feminist connections had no compunctions against arguing that women were weaker or less sensible than their male counterparts in order to justify protective legislation. This portrayal emphasized the state's need to monitor women's contracts carefully, since women were presumed to be more likely to negotiate contracts that threatened the state's interests. Further, attorneys concentrated on showing that women faced greater health risks than men, rather than focusing on health risks themselves as a reason for regulation. As those advocating for regulation promoted their claims with regard to the specific issue of the minimum wage, they focused on women's relationship to the process of negotiating contracts in the context of a competitive and harsh labor market, promoting a gendered rebalancing on the basis of women's inability to negotiate effectively. While this tactic followed the successful pattern of the years between 1911 and 1923 of maintaining the laborer as the center of analysis, arguments that could have been generalized remained mostly specific to women during these years. The focus on women was probably related to the sense of retrenchment brought about by the Supreme Court's ruling in *Adkins*, which left proregulation attorneys in a position of having to fight a battle they thought they had won in the years before 1920.

The final justification for protective legislation involved women's bargaining power. Advocates for protective labor legislation tried to show women's relative impotence at the bargaining table, while attorneys opposing such legislation countered such arguments. These arguments largely tracked the claims that feminists had made about women's bargaining power, though the implications differed in the analyses of nonfeminist attorneys. Following the example set by Goldmark and Frankfurter in the years before 1920, those supporting protective labor legislation argued principally that minimum wages made up for women's inherent lack of bargaining power. Those who opposed minimum wages for women argued that even if such inequality existed, trying to balance the scales through gender-specific legislation was inappropriate. Unlike the arguments regarding motherhood and health, discussions of bargaining power were more frequently presented in terms that could easily apply to all laborers. This argument, which was starting to emerge in the briefs before *Adkins,* played a much larger role in the battles during the later 1920s and 1930s than it had earlier. On both sides of this analysis, the concept of a completely private relationship between employer and employee was gone; the question was simply one of what kind of interventions were appropriate when serious imbalances in bargaining power could be demonstrated. This shift moved the locus of conflict to the question of what constituted an imbalance in bargaining power.

Attorneys for the State of Arkansas, arguing before the economic disruption of the depression, nonetheless framed their argument in general terms. They explained that a valid contract required a meeting of the minds, but coercion in the workplace could prevent the free and open bargaining necessary for such an agreement (Applegate et al. 1926, 31). They then applied this reasoning to women's work specifically, claiming that if women were forced into unfair bargains, the state had the authority to assist women to bargain from a stronger position. Likewise, the State of Wisconsin, filing an amicus brief in support of its minimum wage in *Adkins,* framed the argument in gender-neutral terms. These advocates for protective legislation asserted that the government was authorized to "stop the exploitation of those who are unable to protect themselves" despite the marginal effects upon women's liberty (Ekern, Messerschmidt, and Wilcox 1923, 561). They also made the now-familiar claim that state intervention on women's behalf granted more liberty to employees by giving them equal power with their employers (561). In this sense, protective legislation could be understood to extend additional liberty to female workers (and presumably male workers as well) rather than as a means of taking it away.

Arguments specific to women could be found as well. As detailed above, in the view of advocates for protective legislation, women's lack of labor organization contributed to their need for protective legislation. The factual brief filed in *Morehead* explained this discrepancy's effect in leading to lower wages and poor working conditions (Heffner and Crary 1936, 40). While individual employees were at a decided disadvantage, organized employees could bargain more equally with their employers. In this analysis, the state would in effect act as a labor union for women at the bargaining table. Further, the attorneys argued that "some form of wage fixing, whether it be through collective bargaining or some other device, is necessary to assure to the interested parties equality of bargaining power" (20). By likening bargaining through a labor union (the bargaining tool available to men) to minimum wage legislation (the bargaining tool available to women), the attorneys hoped to convince the Court that such regulation was permissible.

Ultimately, attorneys seeking validation of protective labor legislation cast it as an equalizer, objecting to its characterization as a limit on women's autonomy. The equalization was between women and men as well as between women and their employers. Thus, the ultimate goal of minimum wages in their view was "to create an equality where none existed to prevent employers from making an unfair use of their superior bargaining power" (Hamilton et al. 1923, 146). This equality, attorneys argued, would reinforce women's position in the workplace and enable them to drive bargains that were closer to those agreed upon by male workers and their employees. The state's assistance in bargaining was both efficient and legitimate, obviating the need for later action by the state to address the public problems that underpayment of women would cause. In this analysis, the state's intervention would be necessary at some point; the only questions were whether it would come early or late and whether the state could be permitted to assist women before they began to suffer the negative effects of their subordination in the labor market.

Advocates for employers challenged the regulations' supporters' use of gender-specific arguments, pointing out that unequal bargaining power was not a special condition known only to women. In response to the attorney general's brief in *Morehead*, the attorneys in favor of striking down the law argued that while "[t]he Attorney General of New York appears to think that inequality in bargaining power has developed since the decision in the *Adkins* case, . . . few bargains have ever been made between parties of exactly equal bargaining power, and undoubtedly that is especially true in . . . contracts of employment" (Miller et al. 1936, 23). This argument could easily have been turned around to support minimum wages for all workers, but the attorneys for Morehead trusted that the Court would not take such a radical step, continuing instead to support implicitly the differentiation between women and men. In framing their argument this way, they relied on the Court to endorse their conception of relationships between employers and employees as fundamentally private. If such relationships were fundamentally private, showing a factual equality between men and women would necessitate the finding that all such measures were invalid. They anticipated correctly that the Court was not ready to extend the concept that relationships concerning employment had public significance beyond regulations of women's hours of labor. They also trusted that the Court would not endorse the broad claim that the labor market itself was not a private and legitimate means of setting the price for labor.

For these conservative supporters of business, women could not rely on the state to equalize their bargaining power. This belief corresponded with the National Woman's Party's insistence that women needed to concentrate more heavily on organizing the industries in which they were prominent, rather than pressing for protective legislation that would differentiate them from men (National Woman's Party 1936). Again, though, few were inclined to question the male standard or the lack of regulation attached to it. Attorneys arguing on the behalf of businesses implicitly supported the lack of regulation that was the norm in cases involving general legislation, while the advocates for the National Woman's Party were implicitly seeking the regulation of all laborers, but the businesses had significantly more resources and influence than feminist organizations.

As this example shows, the arguments of attorneys representing businesses and women's organizations devoted to equality related well to each other and facilitated gendered rebalancing. Among opponents of minimum wages, both corporate attorneys and women's organizations worked to show that men's freedom of contract—their private liberty—was illusory in the same ways and for the same reasons that advocates for protective legislation argued about women. A similar relationship existed between nonfeminist attorneys supporting protective legislation and feminist supporters of such laws. If such attorneys could successfully portray women as the weak and unorganized victims of unscrupulous employers and show that women's liberty of contract was limited or nonexistent, they could defeat arguments that under the Constitution women were entitled to as much freedom as men. In both cases, the attorneys' arguments benefited from feminists' reasoning but did not always endorse a feminist vision of women's roles in the world. Further, gendered and gender-neutral arguments played out in contradictory ways: on the one hand, gender-neutral arguments were effective in negating the legitimacy of minimum wages, but ultimately such arguments grounded first the state courts' and then the federal courts' validation of minimum wages. This process was the key to nodal conflict, as it maintained and enhanced the ambiguities that the courts then had to address.

The Courts, Women's Differences, and Police Power

Arguments regarding bargaining power finally reappeared on the courts' agenda in a major way during these years and focused the debate over rebalancing the tension between liberty and police power. The federal courts drew on the attorneys' arguments but placed differing emphases on them than the attorneys had advocated. In this process, judges concentrated their analysis on the arguments relating to the labor marketplace. By the time of the Supreme Court's ruling in *West Coast Hotel,* the courts had settled that women were fundamentally different from men, but that difference no longer grounded opposing outcomes for protective measures. Instead, men had been shown to be similar enough to the new standard of the female laborer to warrant protection under the same principles. The doctrinal path thus simultaneously rejected and accepted equality. Judges drew on filtered feminist thinking and factual evidence but used this information differently from those who had compiled it.

The courts grappled with the evidence before them, which focused first on women as laborers and later on laborers more generally. In the battles over minimum wages, individual judges either explicitly or implicitly had to determine the proper relationship between the state and these laborers. The Supreme Court's ruling in *Adkins* reinvigorated the debate by referring frequently to women's liberty of contract, conceiving of it as a private right. Nonetheless, even the Court's opinion in

Adkins did not completely endorse the laissez-faire conception of the private nature of contracts concerning labor, since the opinion explicitly avoided overruling *Muller v. Oregon*. The fight over minimum wages in the courts was largely a fight over the public significance of women's work and of their conditions of labor. By 1923, no one in the legal community was denying that women themselves were legitimate subjects of public regulation in their roles as mothers. The conflict was rather over whether women's special conditions justified intervention into the process for setting wages.

While attorneys still argued to some degree about the legal consequences of women's motherhood and potential motherhood, the Supreme Court spent very little time discussing it. In *Adkins,* maternity was not really a factor, as the Court ruled that the minimum wage in question did not address public interest properly construed. Reversing *Adkins* in *West Coast Hotel,* however, the Court cited *Muller v. Oregon* and that case's endorsement of protection for women because of their maternal roles (*West Coast Hotel v. Parrish,* 394). In this view, motherhood was a sufficiently important state interest to warrant the intervention of the state; the Court, however, had nothing substantive to add to what had been said on this matter in 1908.

Likewise, the Court spent little time analyzing women's physical risks in the workplace even in cases in which it upheld protective legislation. The *Radice* Court explained that the legislature's finding of particular health risks to women from night work was a sufficient grounding for regulation, but did not detail these risks (*Radice,* 294). *Adkins* was largely decided based on the Court's finding that the minimum wage did not address women's health risks (554). In citing *Muller, West Coast Hotel* also mentioned but did not analyze the risks to the health of women involved in paid labor (*West Coast Hotel v. Parrish,* 394). The Court thus embraced again a strong understanding of the public interest in women connected to their health (398). The Court also endorsed the idea that women's differences from men justified regulation but did not engage in lengthy explanations. In this sense, *West Coast Hotel* was backward looking: it could be read as a return to earlier reasoning about women's differences and the impact of these differences on their regulation in the workplace.

Nonetheless, the case had forward-looking aspects as well. The Court finally embraced the arguments regarding bargaining power presented in attorneys' briefs and in the state courts during the previous several years. The *Adkins* Court had flatly refused to consider such arguments, asserting, "The necessities of the employee are alone considered and these arise outside of the employment and are as great in one occupation as in another" (558). In this view, such concerns as inequality of bargaining power either between men and women or between women and their employers could not be a basis for regulation. *West Coast Hotel* looked in the opposite direction.

The Court relied on a mixture of gendered and nongendered arguments, citing both *Holden v. Hardy* and *Muller* for support (*West Coast Hotel v. Parrish*, 394). At first, the Court seemed to be focusing principally on the dangers that women faced in the marketplace, explaining that women particularly needed protection from industrial exploitation and reiterating that women's protection was clearly in the public interest. In this reasoning, women appeared weak, pathetic, and needful of the state's strong hand. The justices explained, "The . . . State was clearly entitled to consider the situation of women in employment, the fact that they are in the class receiving the least pay, that their bargaining power is relatively weak, and that they are the ready victims of those who would take advantage of their necessitous circumstances" (394). Because women were at a deep disadvantage in the struggle for adequate wages, the legislature could legitimately enhance their condition (394).

Such arguments, however, quickly segued into general arguments. The Court went on to explain that the legislature had the authority to prevent the exploitation of workers who were earning wages below the cost of living, a class of workers who clearly were not solely female (*West Coast Hotel v. Parrish*, 394). Without legislation, warned the Court, the state might have to support such laborers, warranting the state's intervention beyond gendered concerns into the labor market in the public interest (394). This justification confirmed the public significance of bargains over wages as well as over the conditions of labor. In perhaps the most telling statement in the case, the Court declared, "The argument that the legislation in question constitutes an arbitrary discrimination, because it does not extend to men, is unavailing. This Court has frequently held that the legislative authority . . . is not bound to extend its regulation to all cases which it might possibly reach" (400). This statement was the writing on the wall foretelling the demise of *Lochner* and its principle of judicial intervention against protective labor legislation for both women and men.

West Coast Hotel thus marked the repudiation of the model of the relationship between employer and employee as basically private. The state had an interest in relationships of employment because of the laborer's connection to the state. The initial focus on women as particularly vulnerable workers had enabled the logical extension of the argument that the state could intervene in any relationship of employment because all such relationships had potential impacts on the state. Once the legal system had acknowledged inequalities in bargaining power as potentially burdensome for the state, the only logical and factual connection remaining to be made was the argument that such inequalities indeed existed. Given the legal system's rejection of rigid formalism by the 1940s and the widespread influence of sociological jurisprudence and legal realism, these arguments were readily forthcoming in a milieu that was receptive to them.

The reasoning in *West Coast Hotel*, like many other landmark rulings by the Supreme Court, had notable precursors in the state courts. Like the nine justices, judges in the state courts of this period also oscillated between framing their discussions in gender-specific ways and doing so in general terms. They also focused more on inequalities in bargaining power than on the arguments common in the earlier cases regarding physical risks. The New York trial court that upheld the minimum wage at issue in *Morehead* based its acceptance of the statute on specific arguments, finding that the minimum wage for women "ameliorate[s] human distress by affording a measure of security to women who, by reason of unprecedented adverse conditions existing at the time, were unable to adequately protect themselves in an industrial life in which, as compared with men, they were at a disadvantage" (*People v. Morehead*, 581 (1935)). The court went on to find that the situation in this case differed sufficiently from *Adkins* because of the desperate conditions of the depression, which had placed unprecedented pressure on all workers, but on women in particular (581). Similarly in this case, a dissenting justice on the New York Court of Appeals argued that the courts should take into consideration the public's interest in not having to support women whose health had been damaged by their artificially depressed wages (*People v. Morehead*, 805 (1936) (Justice Lehman, dissenting)).

In *West Coast Hotel*, the Supreme Court's acceptance of general arguments had some basis in the state court ruling it validated. The Washington Supreme Court proclaimed, "The underlying principle in all such cases is the state's right, the state's duty, to interfere in the terms of a contract between private parties when there is an inequality in bargaining power" (*Parrish v. West Coast Hotel*, 1089). The inequality troubling the court in this statement was not between men and women, but between employer and employee. This ability to bargain, a gender-neutral power, depended upon the state's ability to intervene on the behalf of exploited workers, protecting them from the vicissitudes of a depressed and cutthroat labor market (1089). This reasoning would support regulation on behalf of all workers, not just for women.

The legal community thus continued along the path established during the years of laborer-centered analysis. During the earlier years, the arguments that had the most impact on the courts were those that relied on physical risks of the workplace and women's roles as mothers. While these arguments continued to carry weight between 1923 and 1937, the more significant points were those regarding bargaining power and the labor market, issues that were only introduced in the briefs in the earlier cases. By and large, the courts followed the lead of nonfeminist attorneys, using the information developed by feminists for their own purposes, which did not always correspond to the purposes of feminist researchers. At the same time, the legal community struggled over the tension between phrasing arguments to relate specifically to female laborers and expressing them in general terms that would address both women and men in the workplace. By 1937, the Supreme Court had finally endorsed both versions, though its principal reasoning in *West Coast Hotel* was gendered. In this ruling, the Court confirmed the developments that had taken place earlier on the state level in response to *Adkins*.

The courts were also pushed to address the arguments from all sides regarding women's equality. An early determination that women were equal would have cut against protective measures for women, since it would have led the analysis toward the default position of unconstitutionality for protective laws addressing male labor. The period of specific balancing had resulted in the determination that men's work could only be limited through showing that the work itself was dangerous, so if women were equal to men, the same showing would presumably be necessary for women's labor. By the end of this period, the implications of equality were less clear. Women's cases had become central enough that the analytical devices designed to address cases involving women's protective legislation now became prominent in all cases involving regulation of the conditions of employment. Laws protecting men could be validated to the extent that men could be compared to women.

The courts maintained a narrow perspective on equality, not attempting to resolve any of the more complicated theoretical debates about its meaning. The *Adkins* Court embraced equality in some respects. Justice Sutherland explained that a main reason for striking down the gendered minimum wage was that women were no longer politically unequal to men and thus subject to special protection by the state. Using the Nineteenth Amendment as evidence, he remarked, "In view of the great . . . changes which have taken place . . . in the contractual, political and civil status of women, culminating in the Nineteenth Amendment, it is not unreasonable to say that these differences have now come almost, if not quite, to the vanishing point" (*Adkins*, 553). Ironically in this interpretation, because women now had the ability to vote, they could no longer be protected through the legislative process. In Sutherland's view, their political equality with men had rendered them subject to the same deprivations; if they were sufficiently powerful to persuade the nation to grant them the vote, individually they could negotiate effectively in the same way that male laborers did with their employers.

Sutherland's analysis of equality did not match the full-scale equality for which the National Woman's Party advocated, however. Even in light of this ringing endorsement of women's political equality, the Court still claimed that "the physical differences [between women and men] must be recognized in appropriate cases, and legislation fixing hours or conditions of work may properly take them into account" (*Adkins*, 553). Thus it was that Justice Sutherland also wrote the majority opinion in *Radice* the next year, upholding New York's limit on night work for women on the basis that it addressed real physical inequalities between the sexes (*Radice*, 295).

The Supreme Court's opinion in *West Coast Hotel* did not address equality extensively, relying on reasoning already summarized to rule that the legislature had the authority to establish minimum wages for women. In this, it followed the pattern that had developed in the state courts; neither the New York Court of Appeals nor the Washington Supreme Court had analyzed equality extensively (*People v. Morehead* (1936); *Parrish v. West Coast Hotel*). In *West Coast Hotel*, the Supreme Court's references to *Muller* showed a reliance on physical, social, and economic inequality as one basis for the ruling (*West Coast Hotel v. Parrish*, 394–95). Justice Sutherland, author of the majority opinion in *Adkins*, objected bitterly to these new/old characterizations of women's capabilities and their relation to men's position in society, complaining that the Washington statute and others like it limited only adult women's wages, leaving adult men free to bargain with their employers: "Women today stand upon a legal and political equality with men. ... [T]hey should [not] be put in different classes in respect of their legal right to make contracts; nor should they be denied ... the right to compete with men for work paying lower wages (*West Coast Hotel v. Parrish*, 412–13 (Sutherland, J., dissenting)). The day for these statements of broad equality, though, had passed. It was now up to the state legislatures to determine what kinds of regulations would be permitted, and the gendered nature of these regulations would not be open to question again for several more decades.

For the courts, equality was only one factor in invalidating laws, not the centrally significant issue that it was for feminists. Both federal and state courts upholding statutes believed that if concrete differences between men and women could be demonstrated, regulation of women alone was justified. This attitude elided the more nuanced discussions of equality and its effects developed through debates within the women's movement at this time. Most judges simply endorsed simple essentialist conceptions of women's differences from men and left it at that. By the end of this period, factual determinations about equality, like liberty, could no longer drive the development of doctrine. *West Coast Hotel* had confirmed the shift in emphasis born of the struggles in the 1920s and early 1930s, rebalancing the tension between liberty and police power effectively to cut liberty out of the analysis. The post–*West Coast Hotel* conflicts would no longer center on liberty; the burning issue on the agenda was now determining exactly how far the ruling would extend.

The Impact of West Coast Hotel v. Parrish

While *West Coast Hotel* settled a number of important issues, most particularly the question of the constitutionality of minimum wages for women, its reasoning did not definitively finalize the Court's position on the constitutionality of general regulations of labor for all workers. On the one hand, the reasoning in *West Coast Hotel* was readily generalizable, as the Court spoke of the legislature's authority to regulate (*West Coast Hotel v. Parrish*, 400) and the broad disruptions in the labor market affecting all workers (399). Nonetheless, the Court had explicitly over-ruled *Adkins*, not *Lochner* (400). It had also based much of its reasoning on *Muller v. Oregon*, a case decided only three years after *Lochner* that explicitly did not affect *Lochner*'s status regarding legislation limiting men's hours of labor. Nonetheless, the aftermath of the ruling demonstrated that the legal community had finally resolved the question of how to analyze the validity of protective labor legislation, implementing the framework for analysis that had been developed in response to cases involving protective statutes directed at women. In that sense, *West Coast Hotel* was a watershed moment, although the debate over minimum wages had thoroughly prefigured its reasoning and approach. After this ruling, feminist arguments over the nature of labor and laborers no longer played a role in the development of doctrine.

Activists promoting protective labor legislation, as well as broader segments of the population, had been enraged by the outcome in *Morehead v. New York*, viewing it as the last straw from a Supreme Court that had clearly lost touch with the realities of life ("Technicalities" 1936). In prior years, the Court had struck down minimum wages for women (*Adkins; Murphy v. Sardell; Donham v. West Nelson Mfg.*), comprehensive congressional regulation of child labor (*Hammer v. Dagenhart*, 247 U.S. 251 (1918); *Bailey v. Drexel Furniture Co.*, 259 U.S. 20 (1922)), the National Recovery Act (*Schechter Poultry*), and the Bituminous Coal Conservation Act (*Carter v. Carter Coal*). All of these regulations had been strongly supported by a number of reformers, including the National Consumers' League, and a drive was under way to amend the Constitution to permit the congressional regulation of child labor (Wood 1968). The outcome in *Morehead* ignited a firestorm of criticism and condemnation both within and outside of feminist reform circles.

In the wake of the *Morehead* ruling, members of the National Consumers' League decided that such an amendment (which had already lost a good deal of momentum in the state legislatures) would not be enough. At the NCL's thirty-seventh annual meeting, held in December 1936, the addresses focused on the need to amend the Constitution to provide broad powers to the states and Congress to intervene in industrial relations and labor matters generally (National Consumers' League 1936). A national committee was established to consider the possibilities and issued an invitation to reformers to attend a meeting in

March 1937 to discuss the need to restructure radically the federal
courts' role in the national system (National Committee on Clarifying
the Constitution by Amendment 1937). This conference was postponed
in the wake of President Roosevelt's announcement of his so-called
court-packing plan in early 1937 (Murphy, Fleming, and Harris 1992,
234–37), but the strong sentiment of anger against the Court generated
by the decision in *Morehead* remained.

Activists pushing for protective labor legislation were thus quite
pleased with the ruling in *West Coast Hotel*. It went as far as the most
optimistic had hoped, strongly supporting regulation for female workers and hinting at applications beyond this scope to general regulations
covering men as well. Further, the reasoning appeared to ground a
wider scope for congressional action as well as regulatory legislation
on the state level. Advocates for protection adopted the most expansive
reading of the case, which legitimated various attempts to regulate
labor on all levels. The Department of Labor began investigating the
parameters for legislation and in October 1938 issued a recommenda-
tion that "specific labor laws such as hours, workmen's compensation
and child labor should cover all workers, and that coverage should be
extended as rapidly as possible" (U.S. Department of Labor 1938).

The next major issue on the horizon was the constitutionality of the
Fair Labor Standards Act, which had been passed in the wake of the
Court's ruling in *West Coast Hotel*. The act comprehensively regulated
the terms and conditions of labor, establishing minimum wages and
maximum hours for any employees who engaged in the production of
goods to be shipped in interstate commerce (*U.S. v. Darby*, 312 U.S. 100,
108–9 (1941)). In order to circumvent one of the objections to earlier
provisions limiting hours, Congress allowed employees to work more
than the maximum number of hours if their employers compensated
them additionally with overtime pay (108–9). The act thus challenged
the Court's earlier limitations on the government's ability to regulate
men's labor (*Lochner*) and on Congress's authority to legislate under the
commerce clause (*Hammer v. Dagenhart; Carter v. Carter Coal*). The outcome of the case would clearly turn on the breadth with which the
Court was willing to read *West Coast Hotel* both with respect to gender
and with respect to federal authority. The case's subject matter—minimum wages for women established on the state level—gave reason for
hope that the reach of the ruling might be limited.

Attorneys challenging the statute's validity sought to limit the impact of *West Coast Hotel*. In doing so, they relied on the fact that *West Coast Hotel* addressed a statute mandating a minimum wage for women and minors: "Adult men did not come within its scope. Contrastingly, the *Fair Labor Standards Act* is a bold and unparalleled piece of legislation of the most sweeping and drastic character" (Lovett et al. 1940, 88). They argued that the outcomes in Supreme Court cases demonstrated the Court's commitment to differentiating between men and women; while minimum wages had been approved for women, only in *Wilson v. New* had such a provision been approved for men (Lovett et al. 1940, 88). Because *Wilson v. New* had dealt with the railway industry in the wake of mass disruptions and strikes, the attorneys argued, that case did not govern the fate of the FLSA. Echoing arguments made by advocates for protective labor legislation in past years, the attorneys seeking its invalidation cited the pattern among state legislatures to regulate women's but not men's labor, claiming that such choices were based on women's lack of bargaining power (Lovett et al. 1940, 89). Their position thus mirrored that of advocates for gendered minimum wages. They endorsed the framework used by attorneys arguing in the late 1930s for Washington's minimum wage for women: because industrial disruptions particularly affected women and their ability to drive a fair bargain in the marketplace, women's labor could be regulated in ways that men's could not. They struggled to preserve the laissez-faire model, albeit on a limited basis.

The government's arguments in favor of the FLSA rested on a reading of *West Coast Hotel* that understood the decision to have fundamentally altered the framework for analyzing protective legislation. Summarizing earlier results, the brief claimed that the Court's precedents clearly indicated the constitutionality of the statute. The United States explained, "This Court has sustained legislation fixing maximum hours for both men and women, and minimum wages for women generally and for men under certain circumstances. The only remaining question, that of a statute providing for minimum wages for men generally, is clearly governed by the other decisions" (Biddle et al. 1940, 17). The brief assumed that public intervention in labor contracts was presumptively legitimate; the only question was the extent of this intervention. Earlier understandings of protective labor legislation had differentiated between cases involving regulations for women and cases involving general limitations; in the cases involving general legislation, the courts had largely embraced the notion that the contract between employers and employees was not subject to regulation without special justification. As detailed earlier, the proponents of such legislation then had to show that the statute addressed a particular type of labor in need of regulation. The government's brief claimed that *West Coast Hotel* had shifted the analysis to the standard framework for women's legislation. Rather than treating the challenged legislation as presumptively questionable, the courts would look to the conditions facing the laborers in the workplace and justify regulations on that basis, endorsing the idea that the relationship between employers and employees had public as well as private significance. All aspects of the labor market affected individuals' interactions with the state, and the market did not necessarily produce neutral or fair results. Regulation was thus no longer an illegitimate attempt by one economic class to secure the state's assistance in its struggles against another economic class; rather it was the state's prerogative to protect itself by preventing laborers from making bargains so bad that they would require the state's assistance later.

The government's brief then analyzed the case within the framework established to address women's protective labor legislation. The attorneys argued, "Facts of common knowledge, together with technical and statistical studies in great volume, all show that the health and welfare of both the worker and the nation depend upon the elimination of substandard conditions" (Biddle et al. 1940, 17). They did not present detailed evidence regarding the harms facing male workers but instead included a footnote reference to "some part of the voluminous source material which demonstrates in detail that low wages and long hours are harmful to the health and well-being of employees and their families" (104). Like the arguments favoring regulation in the cases involving minimum wages for women, their argument emphasized the disparities in bargaining power between employers and employees and the public significance of these disparities. They had adopted Goldmark and Frankfurter's assertion in their brief in *Stettler v. O'Hara* that substandard wages constituted an illegitimate subsidy to unscrupulous employers, the employees of whom would have to depend upon the state for assistance (103).

Biddle and his fellow attorneys explained that *West Coast Hotel*'s references to *Muller* and its emphasis on women's circumstances in the labor market merely reflected the fact that the statute in question addressed female laborers. The attorneys simply adapted the analysis developed with respect to women to address the male laborer rather than the female worker. They reasoned, "Since the Washington statute involved in that case was concerned only with women, the Court's opinion does, of course, emphasize the importance of safeguarding the health of women. But in every respect its reasoning applies equally as well to men" (Biddle et al. 1940, 105–6). Noting the Court's explanation that the law was not invalid because it did not reach every situation in which it might apply, they argued that the Court had clearly contemplated the extension of the ruling to male laborers. Like male workers in Washington, the workers covered by the FLSA faced precisely the same kinds of disruptions in the labor market as women, even if the disruptions were not as traumatic to male laborers.

To be on the safe side, the government's brief also sought to link general regulations to the protection of women. This analytical move demonstrated the extent to which consideration of women's health and roles with regard to children had led to the development of a new framework to address questions concerning the constitutionality of protective labor legislation. The attorneys claimed that maintaining men's health and wages would help the men to protect the health of the women and children in their families; thus paying higher wages to men would have the permissible effect of improving women's health and quality of life (Biddle et al. 1940, 106). Further, if providing minimum wages for women would address women's concerns for their children, protecting men's wages would serve this goal even better, since men were more frequently the sole wage earners in their families (106). Thus, in effect male workers could be protected because regulation of their labor advanced the accepted public purpose of protecting women and children.

The Supreme Court dealt with the question of the statute's validity under the Fifth Amendment's due process clause quite summarily. The Court explained "Since our decision in *West Coast Hotel* . . . it is no longer open to question that the fixing of a minimum wage is within the legislative power and that the bare fact of its exercise is not a denial of due process under the Fifth more than under the Fourteenth Amendment" (*U.S. v. Darby*, 125). The Court also approved the establishment of maximum hours, citing *Muller* and *Holden v. Hardy* (125). The only mention of gender by the Court was its denial that the statute was subject to invalidation because it "applied alike to both men and women" (125). The Court's entire discussion of due process encompassed only a paragraph in the opinion and generated no new analysis of the topic.

The tone of the discussion emphasized that challenges to protective measures on the basis that they interfered with workers' rights to liberty of contract or equal protection would no longer be acknowledged.

This brief discussion confirmed the growing trend to read *West Coast Hotel* as establishing the public significance of contracts between employers and employees and their consequent subjection to regulation. Between 1937 and 1950, forty-three Supreme Court and state cases cited *West Coast Hotel* in addressing protective legislation; between the Court's ruling in 1937 and 1950, the Supreme Court did not strike down any such statutes, and none of the thirty-five state court rulings citing *West Coast Hotel* struck down any laws of this nature between 1944 and 1950.[4] A number of state court judges began looking to *West Coast Hotel* as authority for the states' power to limit hours and establish minimum wages for all workers. For instance, only one year after *West Coast Hotel*, the Montana Supreme Court ruled in favor of a statute limiting work in retail sales to forty-eight hours per week, claiming that the earlier case supported its reasoning with regard to maximum hours (*State v. Safeway Stores*, 76 P.2d 81, 85–86 (Montana 1938)). Others used *West Coast Hotel* as an opportunity to reinstate minimum wages for women and children, laws that had sometimes gone unenforced since the Supreme Court's decision in *Adkins* (*Tepel v. Sima*, 7 N.W.2d 532, 534 (Minn. 1942); *Strain v. Southerton*, 62 N.E.2d 633, 634 (Ohio Court of Appeals 1945)).

State court judges also largely interpreted the Supreme Court's ruling in *West Coast Hotel* as endorsing the application of the framework for analyzing women's legislation to cases involving general restrictions on labor conditions, relying on concerns about the health of laborers to uphold statutes. For most of these judges, the question of balancing private liberty against public interest was no longer salient, as the state's clear interest in protecting workers displaced the idea of a private labor market. For instance, the Oklahoma high court extended

---

4. In the period between 1937 and 1943, eight state courts struck down protective legislation. Five of the statutes struck down involved limitations by the states on prices and/or hours for barber shops (*Ex parte Kazas*, 70 P.2d 962 (Cal. 1937); *Oklahoma City v. Johnson*, 82 P.2d (Okla. 1938); *State v. Greeson*, 124 S.W.2d 253 (Tenn. 1939); *Noble v. Davis*, 161 S.W.2d 189 (Ark. 1942); *City of Cincinnati v. Correll*, 49 N.E.2d 412 (Ohio 1943)), the sixth was a twelve-hour-per-day limit on laborers in mercantile and manufacturing establishments in South Carolina (*Gasque, Inc. v. Nates*, 2 S.E.2d 36 (S.C. 1939)), the seventh sought to limit the dry cleaning industry (*Smith Brothers Cleaners & Dyers v. People*, 119 P.2d 623 (Colo. 1941), and the eighth was a Massachusetts provision that would have prevented most married women from working as public employees (*In re Opinion of the Justices*, 22 N.E.2d 49 (Mass. 1939)).

the interest in health to men as well as to women in *Associated Industries v. Industrial Welfare Commission*, declaring a minimum wage to be constitutional (90 P.2d 899 (Okla. 1939)). The court reasoned that men's liberty was no more sacred than that of women and that men's general health and morals were no less a fit subject for regulation than women's health and morals (911). Thus, with little fanfare the state courts simply began implementing the extension of protective labor legislation to men that activist organizations had fruitlessly sought for nearly a half-century. This reasoning also demonstrated the analytical reversal that had taken place. In the years after 1910, judges had struggled to work out the rules for women's protective labor legislation by thinking about how women's situation compared to men's; now that the most recent interpretive energy had been focused on the women's cases, judges reasoned by considering the ways that men's situations could be analogized to those of women.

Minimum Wages and Equality

The final years of the period of negotiation leading up to *West Coast Hotel* were characterized by the narrowing of the discourse. Rather than discussing broad-ranging questions about the scope of police power and the role of public interest as it related to general legislation and affected women's lives, all parties focused more directly on the significance of equality and difference with regard to women's protective labor legislation. Drawing on and transforming the arguments of feminists, the legal community grappled with the problem of minimum wages. The focus on the constitutionality and meaning of women's minimum wages in the period of gendered rebalancing came out of the Court's ruling in *Adkins*, but the shape of this debate in the legal community depended on earlier developments. This focus ultimately gave rise to the reasoning in *West Coast Hotel*, which adopted the approaches that state courts had devised to get around *Adkins*. Some of the arguments used in favor of minimum wages for women in the 1920s and 1930s could be used later to support more general protective labor legislation. The post-1937 developments in the courts confirmed this trend.

　　West Coast Hotel marked the Supreme Court's endorsement of the legal community's growing consensus to reject a simple split between public and private with relationships between employers and employees on the private side of the line. Even in *Adkins*, the Court suggested that the framework of balancing private liberty against public interest was not entirely applicable to women's protective labor legislation, since women's relationships with their employers had inherent public significance. As members of the legal community contended over minimum wages, however, arguments about women's degraded position in the marketplace for labor gradually gave way to arguments that could be generalized to include male laborers. Nonetheless, even as the arguments became broader in scope, most members of the legal community retained an essentialist conception of the differences between men and women and the significance of these differences. While the legal community rebalanced the scales in favor of regulatory authority, very few members were interested in considering the balance of power between women and men.

Some feminist reformers advocating for equality pushed the courts to evaluate generalized protective legislation both in terms of the dangers of overwork to the health of all workers and in terms of the dramatic changes in the American economy since the early cases striking down such legislation were decided. They argued that the state had an interest in the welfare of all workers, not just women or particular classes of men. Other reformers instead emphasized what they perceived as women's differences and sought to persuade those within and outside of the legal system that women needed special protection. These arguments nonetheless largely accepted men as the implicit standard. Further, the conflict over women's minimum wages, while it was the only legally available conflict, precluded a larger legal debate over the status of the working class generally. This period saw open division among feminists over the question of equality and ended with the gradual fading of active and visible feminism; it likewise saw the rise to legitimacy of a labor movement that had been stripped of its radical elements.

Attorneys focused on the minimum wage, the flash point for debates about the legitimacy of substantive due process; in part they supported feminist interests, but not always. Their arguments too were narrower than in previous periods. *Adkins v. Children's Hospital* overshadowed the period of gendered rebalancing, influencing the framing of legal debates to a greater degree than either *Lochner* or *Muller* had done in the years between 1897 and 1923. The briefs attorneys filed on minimum wages addressed women's roles in society and the significance of motherhood, drawing on the factual records developed by organizations interested in promoting reform, but they also considered women's position in the labor market and their vulnerability to the economic disruptions of the Great Depression. Attorneys representing feminist interests and arguing for minimum wages relied on arguments intended to improve women's position in a difficult labor market, while some nonfeminist attorneys general portrayed women primarily as mothers and only secondarily, if at all, as workers.

Courts struggled with the question of minimum wages' legitimacy, often desiring to uphold them but not being able to develop a response to *Adkins* and its progeny. Finally, some courts began to rebel, relying on the desperate conditions created by the Great Depression and upon arguments about the special need to protect women. They often framed the constitutional question simply as a question of whether women were equal to or different from men, relying on the general resonance of essentialist conceptions of women's status and roles to support their reasoning. In contrast to earlier discussions of protective legislation during the years of laborer-centered analysis, courts on both the federal and state levels fully considered arguments about the labor market and its negative effects on workers. These discussions were often gendered, focusing on women's particular difficulties in competing with male workers, but sometimes courts phrased their discussions in gender-neutral terms. Such gender-neutral language could cut against protective measures, as some courts asserted that the evils of the labor market that justified limiting women's work also affected men's work. They could also, as in *West Coast Hotel* and its predecessors, establish the first hints that the legal community would eventually embrace regulation for all workers, since the harms that legitimately justified protective measures for women also existed for male laborers.

After the Supreme Court's ruling in *West Coast Hotel*, two questions remained. The main question was whether the Court had really meant what it had said about the broader and gender-neutral aspects of the reasoning it had endorsed in cases involving women's labor. Members of the legal community also needed to know whether a ruling endorsing the states' authority to regulate would apply to federal efforts as well. By the mid-1940s, the answers to both questions were emphatic yeses. These developments did not, however, undermine the gendered nature of considerations of laws affecting women. While the litigation in women's cases had established a new generic standard, women once again became special cases under this standard, a situation that would persist for years to come.

Asking whether the minimum wage was good or bad for women is perhaps beside the point. Certainly if some women had been able to obtain a minimum wage during the depression, their lives would have been easier. The debate over the minimum wage focused on women's situation in the marketplace, and thus many of the legal principles that affected the fate of such legislation generally were articulated with respect to women's work. As this chapter has shown, many of the arguments that activists and attorneys were making about the minimum wage certainly would have applied to men. With the concept of the family wage so dominant in the society of the time, advocates could easily have argued that the desperate economic conditions of the depression destroyed men's ability to support their families and thus to produce a healthy and educated citizenry in the next generation.

Part of the problem with this framing was that the family wage forced women's advocates into a trap. Yes, they wanted women to earn enough to support themselves and their families, and they relied on the rhetoric of motherhood to achieve this goal. They did not, however, want women to be forced out of the marketplace entirely—one of the fundamental principles of the family wage. Maternalist rhetoric, however, was not the sole province of reformers, and the implications could be damaging to women's interests. Some attorneys and judges had different agendas than the advocates, as they sought to enhance men's positions in the workplace, disapproving of women's activities outside of the home. Those who advocated for equality escaped this conundrum by simply refusing to support a gendered minimum wage.

If one accepts that any kind of support, however minimal, would have been helpful for women, though, the position of advocates for equality is too simple. The more difficult question is whether there was any way for feminist advocates to push for a minimum wage that would not have entailed relying on damaging stereotypes about women and their capabilities and liberty as workers. Such an approach would have emphasized women's disempowerment as workers primarily rather than resting so heavily upon the disabilities that mothers and potential mothers faced in their forays into the labor market. If such an approach existed, then one can claim that the approaches of both sets of feminist advocates were fundamentally misguided.

In 1912 Pauline Newman urged individual working women to combine and demand their own terms in the labor market (Newman 1912a; see chap. 4). She argued that female workers would see significant advancement in employment only when they were able to begin taking responsibility for enforcing the policies and rules established to protect them (Newman 1912b, 7). She spurned protective labor legislation, viewing it as a distraction from the more pressing task of unionization (Newman 1912a, 7). She pushed working women to assert their own voices and desires, rather than leaving the construction of women's roles and capabilities to female middle-class and upper-class reformers.

Newman was probably naive in her belief that the answer to the problem was simply to ensure that all women join active labor unions that would represent their interests. As several reformers observed, many of the working women they sought to protect were young and easily cowed by employers' authority and the pressures of supporting their families (whether the family was their parents and siblings or their own children). Further, women were socialized to accept the middle-class ideal that the married woman was first a mother and homemaker and only secondarily, if at all, a worker. Newman's analysis was probably too challenging because it pushed women to think of themselves as laborers rather than women first and to put their collective rights before their immediate individual economic and social needs. Given the dominance of maternalist thinking and its obvious advantages in achieving success, it was probably unrealistic for reformers to link women's needs primarily and principally to their positions as members of the working class.

Still, perhaps if the reformers had spent less time engaging in the destructive debate over equality and difference and more time on projects such as the Bryn Mawr summer school, which brought working-class and middle-class women together, the situation would have been better (McGarry 1931).[5] Further, reformers could have worked in their arguments to the courts to explain the structural reasons for women's weaker position in the marketplace. Such arguments would have required focusing on sex segregation in the workplace, women's lack of unionization, and the fact that women in the workplace had socially

---

5. The Bryn Mawr summer school was a project that selected promising young working-class women and funded their participation in a summer institute that educated them and encouraged them to participate in labor organizing.

constructed rather than biological needs to put their children (both real and potential) above their own interests. The implications of such an approach would have included a deeper rebalancing on the basis of gender, not only between liberty and the state's authority to regulate or between women's needs and fears of intervention in the labor market, but also between women's roles as workers and their maternal roles. This plan, however, would have required dropping what appeared to be the strongest arguments for supporting women's protective labor legislation—those depending on the state's desire to reinforce and protect women's roles as mothers.

In the years of gendered rebalancing, the legal community in its consideration of due process focused heavily on women's cases. As the post-1937 analysis shows, the frameworks established in these cases provided the standards for future analyses under the due process clause. Contrary to dominant interpretations of the era, the legal community was not consumed in disagreement over *Lochner* and men's rights to exercise liberty of contract, but rather over *Adkins* and the authority of the state to protect women. It was the battle over women, and specifically over minimum wages for women, that provided the framework under which the reforms of the New Deal, and ultimately the legislative foundations of the modern welfare state, found their constitutional validation. While *West Coast Hotel* finally permitted the state to protect the interests of the working class in their bargains with employers, it did so on the basis of an analytical structure created to differentiate between and divide workers, not to unite them.

Chapter 6

Reflecting on Gender, Due Process, and Constitutional Development

At the beginning of the twenty-first century, we stand on a threshold, looking back into a collective past, seeking to imbue it with meaning. Many who consider themselves to be liberal see the recent past as the shredding of the legacy of the Warren Court and embrace the tattered remnants of a lost tradition of struggle. Many who consider themselves to be conservative view recent history as an effort to reassemble the solid objective bricks that were scattered by the whirlwind of the 1950s, 1960s, and 1970s. Regardless of our political and jurisprudential standpoints, we are all nonetheless the inhabitants of a post–*West Coast Hotel* world, living in a modern interventionist state. If we wish to confront seriously the assertion that the birth date of the modern Constitution was the Court's 1937 ruling on a hotel chambermaid's claim for back wages, we must address the developmental forces that contributed to the conception of this modern Constitution. This book has shown that this confrontation leads to a new analysis of the central role that women's protective labor legislation played in the process of constitutional development.

In light of this analysis, several insights should be clear. First and most obviously, gender had a large impact on the discussion that gave rise to the constitutional foundations of the welfare state. Those seeking to promote protective legislation in both the legislative and judicial arena found themselves arguing almost as much over gender and the attributes of women and men as over the laws themselves. Scholars as diverse as Skocpol, Mink, Lipschultz, and Gordon have focused attention on maternalism as a political phenomenon during the Progressive and New Deal years, but this analysis seeks to present the full ambiguities of maternalism and feminists' use of it in the legal sphere.

Second, the rise of women's labor legislation to the central place in the analysis was an inadvertent outcome, not a conscious strategy for litigation on the part of particular members of the legal community. It was a result of the interplay among activists, lawyers, and the courts, none of whom had complete control over the evolution of doctrine. As Epp and McCann have shown in other contexts, focusing too intently on the activities of judges blinds the observer to the interactive and dynamic ways in which lawyers and interested lay communities actively participate in the creation of law through the judicial process. It should be emphasized as well, however, that this dynamic mode of doctrinal production only became possible after the rise of legal realism, which simultaneously changed the grounding for legal argumentation and enabled the entry of multiple knowledgeable interpreters. In contrast to analyses that present judges as having significant autonomy and control in the production of doctrine, this reading suggests that in a postrealist world, even when judges actively try to shape the future course of constitutional litigation, they are limited in their ability to manage the process.

Finally, *West Coast Hotel* and thus the basic legal framework for the modern welfare state had deep roots in a conversation that had been going on since the 1870s; the outcome and reasoning in the case were not merely the result of the justices' fears that the Supreme Court as an institution was threatened by political hostility in the 1930s. While many scholars have acknowledged and explored the impact of the dichotomy between liberty and police power, the dichotomies between male and female workers and between labor and laborers also influenced constitutional development in significant ways. This understanding of *West Coast Hotel* and of the process of constitutional development generally marks a sharp break with Ackerman's vision of constitutional moments. In Ackerman's reading of the New Deal crisis, the Court's shift marked a fundamental change as the justices acknowledged the existence of a moment of successful higher lawmaking by abruptly reversing course and striking out in a new jurisprudential direction. While the observer of nodes of conflicts acknowledges that *West Coast Hotel* was an important case, she or he recognizes the reasoning and analysis of the Court as continuing a discussion within preestablished frameworks.

The move toward rethinking the *Lochner* era and its meaning is a worthwhile endeavor, because new historical analyses have countered simplistic political explanations of the era and its impact. By refusing to accept the ruling in *West Coast Hotel* only as a response to a political or even a constitutional crisis, such thinkers as Howard Gillman, William Forbath, and Barry Cushman have cleared a space in which it is possible to consider seriously the jurisprudential developments of the Progressive and New Deal years and the broader social and political milieu without assuming a mechanical causal relationship between the two. Simultaneously, feminist inquiries into the historical legacy of maternalism as a political and politicized ideology have raised our consciousness about the importance of the concept not only for women, but also for the Progressive agenda more generally. These dual developments ground the foregoing centering of the battle over women's protective labor legislation in the story of the rise of the modern welfare state.

Nodes of Conflict and the Centrality of Women's Protective Labor Legislation

This book has sought to answer the question of how the legal community came to place women's protective labor legislation at the center of their discussions regarding the legitimacy of statutes addressing the terms and conditions of bargains between employers and employees. Now that the doctrinal story has been told in detail, we can trace the circuitous path through which considerations of legislation aimed at protecting women came to drive the development of general doctrine regarding the relationship between liberty and police power under substantive due process. In line with the observations of Charles Epp and Michael McCann in other contexts, this development did not take place because any of the players in the process—the activists, the attorneys, or the courts—had the ability to control it. Rather, the interaction among different actors with varying agendas contributed to focusing attention on the status of women as marginal laborers with only partial access to the constitutional guarantee of liberty. This shift in focus produced the reasoning in *West Coast Hotel v. Parrish* that would ultimately ground the extension of federal power to previously unthinkable degrees.

Initially, discussions of protective labor legislation took place within a framework designed to address the broad question of whether laws limiting the terms and conditions of labor could be permitted under the Fourteenth Amendment. The framework was adapted from earlier understandings of due process rooted in the concept of due process as a boundary for legitimate governmental action (Ely 1999). The first period, that of generalized balancing, saw the development of this framework. Discussions in the 1870s and 1880s refined the question a bit, focusing attention on the validity of statutes under the due process and equal protection clauses of the Fourteenth Amendment as well as under parallel state provisions. The gendered division that would ultimately drive the evolution of doctrine was an artifact of the next period. During these years, cases involving women's protective measures were adjudicated under the same standards as cases involving general protective measures; the courts did not recognize any analytical distinction.

In the period of specific balancing between 1898 and 1910, the legal community worked further to define the relationship between these constitutional guarantees and the state's authority through police power to regulate employment, developing general standards to address these cases. In this view, the implicit subject of the due process clause's guarantee of liberty was a male worker who could bargain freely with his employer and did not need the state's meddling in his private affairs. The general standards largely directed that regulation was impermissible unless it affected a particular type of labor or a particular type of laborer. In these years, the legal community gradually came to see women as a separate class of laborers and to address statutes limiting women's work as constituting their own category of regulations.

In the period of laborer-centered analysis between 1911 and 1923, the center of gravity of constitutional interpretation shifted. State and federal laws protecting women in the workplace were litigated more frequently, and these cases came to drive the development of doctrine with regard to general protective labor legislation. During these years, the legal community continued to struggle over regulating labor and laborers, but ultimately began to focus more interpretive energy on laborers, in line with the framework that was emerging to address women's protective labor legislation. While members of the legal community addressing legislation for women between 1898 and 1910 had focused on women's differences from men, later analyses centered more on women's specific hardships in the labor market, leaving difference as a less emphasized element in their reasoning. In these years, the belief that women could exercise the liberty guaranteed by the due process clause more effectively with the help of the state came to dominate analyses of women's protections under constitutional provisions. Toward the end of these years, some members of the legal community began to frame their arguments broadly enough to incorporate male laborers as well as women within their compass. Following the lead of Brandeis and Goldmark, lawyers who were also progressive reformers increasingly played a role in this process, consciously framing their arguments toward a larger political agenda. In supporting Oregon's limit on hours for both male and female workers, activists Goldmark and Frankfurter applied general versions of the arguments that had developed to justify women's protective measures, achieving a tie vote in the Supreme Court.

Finally, in the time of gendered rebalancing the battle over *Adkins v. Children's Hospital* highlighted growing differences among feminists and between feminists and the nonfeminist lawyers who were using their arguments and data in court. The Court's ruling in *Adkins* was a great blow to the advocates for protective legislation and provoked an intensive struggle over minimum wages for women. The Court seemed to be rejecting the entire carefully constructed framework for addressing protections for women that was the fruit of litigation in the first two decades of the twentieth century. Advocates for protective labor legislation sought to continue their work within it, struggling to convince the courts that female laborers needed protection. Shifting their arguments somewhat, advocates focused increasingly on the extent to which labor legislation could be a liberating force in the constrained market and sought to show that industrial conditions were so poor for women that they had no liberty without protection. Attorneys also worked to develop general arguments as well, but focused their attention on portraying women as victims of industrial disruption in need of the state's protection. Feminists and others resisting gender-specific protective labor legislation emphasized equality, relying on the Court's statement in *Adkins* that women were now men's political equals and arguing that protective labor legislation aimed at women alone was both demeaning and harmful. While the arguments of both feminists and nonfeminist attorneys opposing minimum wages were similar, the implications that these groups drew from these arguments were quite different: lay feminists and their attorneys largely sought regulation across the board, but many corporate opponents of women's minimum wages wanted no regulation for men or women. *West Coast Hotel* settled the issue, determining that protective legislation was permissible and largely applying the framework articulated with respect to laws protecting women. Later rulings confirmed that this shift was indeed permanent even with regard to legislation affecting male workers and further extended the reach of *West Coast Hotel* to allow deference to federal legislative decisions as well as to those of the states. The constitutional shift that legitimated a high degree of intervention by the state was rooted in fights over the meaning of women's protective legislation, not in a judicial reconsideration of the theoretical underpinnings of *Lochner v. New York*. While Ackerman rightly emphasizes the growing hostility both within and outside of the legal community to the jurisprudence of *Lochner*, he and others who focus exclusively on *Lochner*'s analysis of the balance between private right and public authority overlook the gendered grounding of the alternative that replaced it.

Nodes of Conflict and the Development of Doctrine

This entire process of conflict and development was the fruit of the judicial community's complex and multivocal response to the framing attempts and interaction among lay activists and attorneys. In relation to and in competition with each other both within and without their respective communities, the judges were active in creating the analytical shifts described above. However, no individual judge or court, not even the Supreme Court, controlled this process. The Constitution is a product of reasoning sedimented over time, as Friedman notes; as Kahn explains, the sediments themselves depend on judges' ability to mediate a relationship between constitutional principles and social facts. In the wake of the realist revolution, both of these processes have relied on the intervention of activists and attorneys to identify and shape the social facts and legal constructs that ground constitutional doctrine.

    In the nineteenth century, activists within the feminist community were interested in questions relating to protective labor legislation. Nonetheless, their work did not have a great impact on litigation before the twentieth century, when the rise of legal realism provided a comprehensive justification for linking specific factual constructs to doctrine. At around the turn of the century, however, as the courts engaged in generalized balancing, veterans of the settlement house movement, trade union organizers, and middle-class reformers began to promote legislative reform. By this time, the corporate community had already discovered the value of the courts as a forum in which coordinated activity could produce satisfactory outcomes. Statutes protecting both male and female laborers were facing difficulty in the courts, though those limiting women's work were faring better. While some activists promoted such laws as a means of eventually convincing the courts to endorse provisions protecting men as well, others believed that women would always need special protections over and above those that men required.

In the period of specific balancing immediately after the turn of the century, activists intervened directly in the process of litigation. Many reforming organizations, most notably the National Consumers' League and the National Women's Trade Union League, began working to support protective labor legislation in the courts, focusing on such legislation for female workers. As Skocpol, Stanley, and Hart have recognized in different ways, maternalism provided a powerful political justification for regulating women's labor. Using maternalist conceptions of women's proper role in the polity, reformers compiled extensive evidence about the dangers to employees in various industries and the risks to women from universal conditions such as overwork and low pay. Progressive organizations were now tailoring their agendas for research to the legal categories of public interest and public health that had emerged as the keys to legitimating protective measures. The most notable achievement from this process was the brief that Josephine Goldmark and Louis Brandeis submitted in *Muller v. Oregon,* which the Supreme Court cited as presenting a compelling basis for its ruling that women's differences from men warranted their protection even in the face of *Lochner.* Consumers' leagues in various states duplicated this strategy, developing extensive factual records about women's experiences in the workplace and using this information to promote protection for women. Recognizing that a narrow focus on women had a higher probability of success than broad claims addressing all workers, advocates for protective labor legislation framed their statements and research to address the need for legislation limiting only women's work. This pattern persisted, yielding many legislative and judicial victories through the focus on labor-centered analysis in the second decade of the twentieth century.

This success, however, could not mask growing dissension within the feminist community over the advisability of protective labor legislation for women. After suffrage had been achieved, the National Woman's Party announced a major new initiative supporting the passage of an equal rights amendment to the Constitution. Such an amendment would almost certainly render unconstitutional any protective labor legislation aimed only at women. Feminists now found themselves fighting openly with other feminists during the period of gendered rebalancing as divisions within the movement quickly became public and hostile. Each side identified protective labor legislation as the main issue in the campaign for equal rights; the National Consumers' League and its associates sought to show that women needed protective measures, while the National Woman's Party argued that such statutes had a negative impact on women's search for meaningful equality. As the debate grew increasingly heated, the Supreme Court's decision in *Adkins* was announced, creating a sense of crisis among the feminists favoring protection for women. Throughout the 1920s and 1930s, feminists argued publicly about the benefits of gender-specific regulations and sought to influence the outcome of litigation in both directions. Ultimately, their disagreements over women and equality found their way into the legal community as women's organizations sponsored or filed briefs on opposing sides of major cases.

As Epp and McCann have shown, attorneys also had a major role in driving the development of doctrine. Seeking to translate their clients' wishes into legal terms, they helped to generate the nodes of conflict that shaped and transformed the lengthy struggle over the validity of protective labor legislation. Attorneys initiated this process prior to the turn of the century in the period of generalized balancing by debating the question of how the Fourteenth Amendment could be used to address protective labor legislation. Initially, some attorneys sought to use the privileges or immunities clause as a theoretical home for protections for substantive rights under the Constitution, but the *Slaughter-House Cases* and subsequent affirmations of the principles established in them closed off this route, which no one attempted seriously to reopen. Attorneys then turned to the equal protection and due process clauses, relying on past uses of due process to limit states' regulatory authority in identifying these portions of the Fourteenth Amendment as major interpretive foci during the years between 1873 and 1897. In doing so, those supporting protective statutes sought to convince the courts that these statutes were valid exercises of the states' police power. Those opposing the laws claimed that the constitutional guarantees barred such interventions into the newly re-articulated and popularized freedom of contract. During these years, both legal realism and sociological jurisprudence were beginning to make significant inroads in the legal community, and toward the end of the period, these philosophical approaches to law began to influence the production of legal arguments. Nonetheless, at this point most of the attorneys were not seeking to reform state or national policy through litigation; to the extent that any attorneys had a stake in litigation, it was the businesses' attorneys, who were connected personally and professionally to the corporate interests they represented.

Attorneys continued to develop such themes in the period of specific balancing, though the analysis became more focused and limited. Soon after the turn of the century, lawyers opposing protective labor legislation recognized that they could not win their cases simply by claiming that the states had no authority to regulate the terms and conditions of labor. On both sides, discussions increasingly focused on the particular authority that police power encompassed: the power to regulate on the behalf of the health, morals, or in the public interest of the community at large. As the theoretical frame in which cases were adjudicated became increasingly set and as legal realism and sociological jurisprudence expanded their influence, emphasis turned to the facts of the particular cases. The historical moment was ripe for the emergence of nodes of conflict; they could not fully emerge as described here without attorneys' having the opportunity to weave new jurisprudential narratives dense with facts. This turn to facts was in part due to the courts' greater willingness to hear deeply factual claims as a result of intellectual developments but also was a result of the development and movement of the nodes. Attorneys thus sought to show that particular regulations either served or did not serve the required public purpose, analyzing the relationship between the questioned regulation and the community at large. As these factors increasingly came to dominate the analysis, a new pattern emerged. As laws involving women's work found favor in the courts, attorneys developed a separate analytical framework to address such cases. In these cases, attorneys arguing in favor of the constitutionality of protective labor legislation began to produce briefs that relied on detailed factual analyses of the impact of industrial conditions upon workers. This tactic became increasingly popular among those supporting such legislation after the Supreme Court publicly acknowledged the persuasive power of the facts reported in Goldmark and Brandeis's brief in *Muller v. Oregon.*

In the succeeding years, direct connections between attorneys and activists became increasingly common, as members of the National Consumers' League assisted in the research of the massive briefs popularized by the *Muller* case. Both activist and nonactivist attorneys in the period of labor-centered analysis found themselves increasingly involved in filing briefs addressing women's protective labor legislation and focused their arguments accordingly. The initial analyses of attorneys arguing for women's protective labor legislation had focused on showing precisely how women differed from men, while later briefs emphasized the nature of women's deprivations in the marketplace, presenting a picture of women as victimized workers in need of the state's intervention. Attorneys representing manufacturing interests challenged this largely factual characterization, seeking to convince the courts that women had liberties equal to men's and that the guarantee of due process should operate for women as it did for men. Subtle differences began to emerge between feminist activists' and their attorneys' arguments and those generated by states' attorneys favoring protective laws; while prolegislation activists often portrayed women as competent but exploited and physically at risk, state-supporting attorneys often painted women primarily as mothers, emphasizing their status as marginal and expendable workers who needed the state's intervention to protect their publicly valued reproductive capacities.

This tendency continued in the years of gendered rebalancing, though during these years feminist organizations increasingly filed their own briefs on both sides of the issue. In these years, attorneys, like the activist community, focused principally on the legitimacy of minimum wages. Those promoting such statutes sought to distinguish various minimum wage provisions from the congressional statute struck down in *Adkins,* arguing that the later provisions bore a closer relationship to the permissible constitutional goal of promoting liberty for women. They also claimed that the necessity of addressing the massive economic disruption of the Great Depression warranted extreme measures with regard to women, whom they portrayed as particularly vulnerable. Those opposing protective legislation praised the Court's ruling in *Adkins* and relied upon the argument that men and women were equal for all practical legal purposes. In this interpretation, such laws, regardless of how carefully they were crafted, limited women's liberty substantially and insulted women by classing them with children. Attorneys on both sides presented arguments specific to women's situation and broader arguments about the impact of poor economic conditions on workers generally, but most attorneys continued to differentiate women from men at least implicitly. As mentioned above, for nonfeminist attorneys, the implications of these arguments differed greatly from the activists' vision. After the ruling in *West Coast Hotel*, attorneys opposing protective measures could claim only that the decision was limited to female workers, a route that the Supreme Court quickly closed off in *U.S. v. Darby* (312 U.S. 100, 125 (1941)).

During the period of generalized balancing at the end of the nineteenth century, the courts struggled to articulate an appropriate role for the Fourteenth Amendment and parallel state provisions, drawing on older interpretations of due process as a significant limit on the state's power. Early on, the Supreme Court foreclosed consideration of the privileges or immunities clause as a basis for substantive rights, but due process quickly emerged as an alternative home for such claims. In the early years, courts began to work out the relationship between the constitutional guarantees and the states' claims to be able to regulate the terms and conditions of labor through the appropriate use of their police power. In their initial considerations of protective measures, the courts spent much energy articulating the relationship between liberty and property and establishing the nature of the right to contract freely with one's employer. This right gradually came to dominate the discourse in the later years of the period of generalized balancing, though some courts were willing to acknowledge particular countervailing public interests with respect to notably dangerous industries such as mining. With regard to cases involving women's protective labor legislation, the courts mostly upheld such measures but did not use any particularized reasoning to address them. In Massachusetts and Illinois, state supreme courts ruled in opposite directions regarding limits on women's hours of labor, but neither court made gender a central feature in its analysis (*Commonwealth v. Hamilton Mfg. Co.*, 120 Mass. 383 (1876); *Ritchie v. People*, 155 Ill. 98 (1895)).

The courts continued to grapple with the proper relationship between liberty on the one hand and police power on the other as the legal community moved to specific balancing. In these years, a tentative consensus emerged around a framework used to adjudicate cases involving general protective labor legislation. The courts largely focused on liberty's nature and extent, assuming a male subject of the guarantee of liberty. Most judges then interpreted police power somewhat narrowly, allowing the state to intervene only upon definitive showings by the legislature that the type of labor being regulated warranted public intervention due to its particular characteristics. The application of this framework led to a general consensus that the states could regulate the contracts of miners and public employees but also led to the outcome in *Lochner* striking down the regulation of New York's baking industry. In addressing protective measures for women, the courts gradually began to classify them in a separate category, treating such statutes with the same kind of deference they were extending to laws protecting child laborers. In both cases, the emerging consensus was that the laborers themselves were the proper focus for analysis, and because of these laborers' special natures, regulations concerning them were more justifiable. In both types of cases, intensive focus on the facts was an increasingly significant factor in the legal analyses.

In the era of laborer-centered analysis, the courts reported more cases involving women's protective labor legislation than cases addressing general legislation. In keeping with this shift in focus, they brought their interpretive energies to bear on analyzing women's protective measures; presumably the articulation of a suitable framework would stem the tide of appellate litigation over these issues. In their struggles over the constitutionality of such laws, they focused their interpretations on women as workers and as subjects both of the guarantee of liberty and of the state's interest in future citizens. The courts debated the validity of three justifications for statutes protecting women: female workers' competing roles as mothers, the physical risks they faced in the workplace, and the exploitative nature of contracts between them and their employers. In judges' published decisions, most of which upheld protective measures on these grounds, the courts produced a gendered reading of substantive due process, justifying protection on the basis of women's special status. While the Oregon high court used the same arguments to uphold a statute protecting male laborers on the same grounds, most other judges analyzed these cases in specifically gendered and heavily fact-sensitive terms, resting their reasoning on motherhood, women's particular physical fragility, and women's vulnerability to exploitation by their employers.

Ultimately the courts had to reconcile the tension between framings that focused on women's position in the workplace and the earlier modes of analysis that had applied to cases involving general measures. This reconciliation took place during the period of gendered rebalancing, reaching its climax in the Supreme Court's ruling in *West Coast Hotel*. In 1923, the Supreme Court lobbed a hand grenade at the carefully established framework addressing the constitutionality of protective labor legislation, ruling in *Adkins* that women's minimum wages were no longer unquestionably constitutional. Initially, the state courts accepted this ruling and dutifully struck down minimum wages on the ground that they improperly interfered with women's liberty of contract. These rulings endorsed the *Adkins* Court's finding that in the wake of the Nineteenth Amendment's passage women were now men's political equals and could negotiate successfully on their own behalf. Later, however, the state courts and one federal district court returned to the justifications that had successfully validated protective measures in the previous years, relying principally on the dangers raised by women's exploitation in the labor market as a result of the Great Depression. Ultimately the Supreme Court accepted this analysis, ruling in *West Coast Hotel* that women's circumstances in the market and the public's interest in their protection warranted the overturning of *Adkins* and the acceptance of a minimum wage for female workers. Both federal and state courts quickly extended this analysis to cover male workers as well, while the Supreme Court emphasized that the principle of deference to legislative expertise would carry over to congressional legislation.

Focusing on nodes of conflict shows that the process of constitutional development took place only partially within the legal community. At the turn of the century, legal realism and sociological jurisprudence began to supplant formalism as a means of interpreting the law and promoting legal change. This shift provided an opening for lay activists who sought to use litigation to advance policies. Activists promoted particular legal and factual arguments solely for instrumental purposes; attorneys transformed these positions into legal discourse, but these legal framings did not always have the implications that activists would have embraced. The courts determined outcomes in particular cases but were ultimately not in control of the process of doctrinal change. This process, rather than the particular intentions of any of these actors, resulted in the centering of gender in the significant constitutional questions of the day. Reading *West Coast Hotel* as the watershed moment for several nodes of conflict focuses attention away from highly abstracted legal concepts such as police power and due process and toward their contextual manifestations within the legal community over time. Analysis of the various nodes that gave rise to the justices' reasoning exposes the case's gendered roots and provides a more satisfying explanation for the development of the Court's new framework for adjudicating due process claims.

The benefits of studying nodes of conflict should now be evident when compared with approaches such as Ackerman's. By engaging with a fuller range of historical development through an institutional focus on multiple actors with different roles, the constitutional historian can read the process of development as hesitant, complex, multivocal, and contingent. Ackerman's work, on the other hand, can be characterized as monumental history. This type of historical analysis focuses on singular moments in which constitutional interpretation can be understood to have undergone a profound change. Monumental historians such as Ackerman consider particular moments in history to show how these moments shaped subsequent litigation in their doctrinal areas and possibly in other areas of law. Monumental history can grant significant agency to the actors in the drama; for Ackerman, members of Congress in the Reconstruction era and President Roosevelt in the New Deal era were the architects of constitutional change (Ackerman 1997). Nonetheless, in Ackerman's vision, these actors are fundamentally subordinate to the moment itself and its genesis through the process of higher lawmaking. Ackerman's monumental history of the struggles over New Deal reveals his background assumption that individuals gain power and authority through their institutional roles, but he portrays the fight as the gradual recognition and endorsement of a triumphal and nearly inevitable march toward an administrative state with broad regulatory powers.

The analyst of nodes of conflict does not highlight the impact of major cases or constitutional moments. Instead, she or he looks at the ways that major cases failed to resolve questions as judged by their reception within the legal interpretive community. If monumental history is the history of singular moments, the analysis of nodes of conflict is a history of fissures, discontinuities, conflicts, and ruptures. The goal is to explain how the legal interpretive community has struggled to produce meaning through the collective enterprise of constitutional interpretation as a dynamic and conflict-laden process. Through this type of analysis, we finally see that feminists' contentious struggles over the use of maternalism as a political tool played a significant part in shaping the discursive framework through which the modern welfare state was legally legitimized. We also see why this insight is important.

Distinctions between Labor and Laborers and the Significance of Gender

Examining nodes of conflict highlights the process through which two significant distinctions emerged in the doctrine largely in the context of litigation over women's protective labor legislation. The first was the difference between focusing on the regulated labor on the one hand, and the regulated laborer on the other; the second was the use of gender-specific versus generally applicable arguments in reasoning about the validity of particular justifications for protective measures. Both of these distinctions had major impacts upon the legal community's thinking regarding liberty and police power, and both were products of a complex series of negotiations among the various actors. The significance of these distinctions in the development of constitutional principles confirms the feminist insight that political and legal struggles over women's status and roles in the Progressive and New Deal years were crucial, rather than a mere sideline, in the emergence of the modern administrative state.

Early reasoning of the legal community about the validity of protective measures focused on the type of labor being performed. In the era of general balancing, advocates for and against protective statutes centered their reasoning on the relationship between the statutes in question and the type of labor they were regulating. This focus was largely the product of attorneys' analysis of *Holden v. Hardy;* many read the case as establishing the principle that mining could be regulated because it was a particularly dangerous type of labor. As attorneys struggled to convince courts to uphold general legislation and courts largely resisted such efforts, a small category of successful statutes began to emerge. Reformers emphasized that these statutes had sought to regulate types of labor that were readily distinguishable from the typical forms of wage labor. Statutes regulating public labor succeeded as attorneys advocating for these laws largely convinced the courts that in these cases, the state stood in the shoes of the employer and had the right to determine the terms and conditions of labor through legislation. The other major class was labor that could be presented as particularly risky or harmful to the employee; mining was the paradigmatic example. The New York legislature clearly had *Holden v. Hardy* in mind when it passed the limit on hours at issue in *Lochner*; it produced extensive documentation showing that the labor involved was dangerous both to the employee and to the general public (*People v. Lochner*, 177 N.Y. 145, 162–63 (1904)).

However, just as the focus on labor came to dominate the analysis, another way of construing the problem was emerging, creating ambiguity about the appropriate means of analysis. Those advocating for statutes limiting the employment contracts of women and children were beginning to claim that such laborers constituted a special class worthy of consideration outside of the emerging paradigms addressing general legislation. In this view, women were different enough from men to constitute a separate class for analysis under the due process clause. This tactic, which had originated simply to evade invalidation on equal protection grounds, developed quickly into a powerful tool for convincing the courts to uphold protective measures for women. Attorneys arguing for such statutes focused on the particular characteristics of female laborers, and activists who favored protection for women readily provided them with reams of information analyzing women's position in the workplace generally. Both state and federal courts adopted the practice of looking at women as laborers rather than considering primarily the labor they were performing, focusing on women's situation in the workplace and emphasizing the state's authority to regulate women as workers rather than its ability to limit the labor they performed. As cases involving women's protective labor legislation came to dominate the legal landscape, this mode of analysis increasingly influenced the development of doctrine, culminating in *West Coast Hotel*.

The second distinction was between specifically gendered arguments and those that applied at least facially to all workers. In the early years, discussions about both general and women's protective labor legislation took place in nongendered, general terms. While cases involving women's protective labor legislation tended to validate the challenged law, the reasoning was largely that which applied to general legislation. In the period of specific balancing straddling the turn of the century, separate modes of discourse developed with regard to general legislation and legislation limited to women. While discussions of gender-neutral legislation took place in facially gender-neutral terms, the clear subject of these discussions was increasingly male. Analyses of liberty assumed a male laborer, even as both the legal community and feminist activists were coming to understand women's statutes as constituting a separate body of regulations for purposes of Fourteenth Amendment review.

With regard to women's protective labor legislation, as the weight of the analysis fell increasingly on the particular characteristics of the female laborer, those promoting protective measures in the legal community toward the end of the period of specific balancing articulated explicitly gendered justifications for such laws. During these years, advocates for women's protection focused on women's roles as mothers and as the raisers of children, ignoring men's roles in family life. Likewise, when such advocates discussed the physical risks of the workplace, they cited information showing that women faced particular danger due to their reproductive capacities and their weaker physical frames. Women were also portrayed as more subject to nervous exhaustion and other ailments associated with overwork. The third justification, women's vulnerability to exploitation, was also expressed in specific terms. Advocates for protection, whether they were feminist activists, state attorneys general, or judges, discussed women's inability to negotiate fair bargains for themselves due to their feminine psychological capacities or lack of unionization. Such advocates also noted the gendered moral risks that exploited women faced, addressing particularly the threat that underpaid women would turn to prostitution. As noted above, the framings and implications of these factual arguments often differed subtly depending on whether feminist activists and attorneys or nonfeminist attorneys were offering them.

Ultimately this development led to complex and crosscutting arguments articulated most fully in the period of gendered rebalancing but emerging from the Oregon cases late in the second decade of the century addressing minimum wages and maximum hours. Advocates for women's minimum wages continued to make gendered arguments, focusing heavily on the particular exploitation of women in the labor marketplace and emphasizing the need for public intervention. In their analysis, female workers suffered deprivations that were qualitatively different from, and worse than, those faced by men. They linked women's exploitation in the marketplace to their roles as mothers, claiming that the maternal instinct drove women to accept lower wages and poorer working conditions than men. At the same time, however, some advocates discussed justifications for legislation in terms that could apply to male laborers as well. These advocates noted that men also faced physical risks in the workplace, and that the severe economic disruption created by the Great Depression could also lead men to enter into bargains for substandard wages, ultimately rendering them dependent upon the state.

Arguments that the proposed justifications applied equally to both men and women, however, were largely the province of those opposing the constitutionality of minimum wages for women in the post-*Adkins* era. Representatives of manufacturing interests and advocates for women's equality challenged minimum wages for women on the grounds that men also faced physical risks in the workplace, that men also suffered from great disparities in bargaining power with their employers, and that men also had responsibilities to their families and children. While the arguments that both sets of advocates made were similar, the implications differed significantly: attorneys representing business interests maintained as their primary goal the elimination of protective measures across the board. They clearly sought to convince the courts to shift considerations of protective labor legislation back to the framework that had developed with respect to general legislation early on—a framework that had led to the invalidation of a great many protective measures. The Supreme Court in *West Coast Hotel* used several specifically gendered arguments, relying on *Muller v. Oregon* for some of its conclusions. Nonetheless, the justices also employed general discussions of the negative effects of the labor market. The later applications of the case were general, as its reasoning was extended to uphold numerous types of protective statutes addressing men's labor in the 1940s. In these interpretations, the impact of the case was limited neither by the gendered nature of the statute at issue in *West Coast Hotel* nor by the fact that the case involved a state's law rather than federal policy.

The distinctions between labor and laborers and between gendered and gender-neutral arguments defined the periods described in the book. As different ways of framing the problem of due process rose to ascendancy, the analysis shifted around the fulcrum of gender, further contributing to the lack of efficacy of economic class as a legally meaningful category. Activists promoting regulation gradually began orienting their work toward addressing the female laborer's particular issues in their attempts to validate protective measures. They did so in response to the legal community's framing of the central question as one about the gendered nature of laborers. While this gendered framework ultimately gave rise to successful arguments on the behalf of male workers, it simultaneously grounded in legal and social history the belief that women were marginal and problematic workers. This tension highlights the problematic legacy of maternalism: as Skocpol has noted, it provided a powerful political justification for policies that benefited women, but as Mink cautions, it contributed to women's separate incorporation into the welfare state and their subordination within it. Only by understanding the process through which the legal community came to focus on specifically gendered arguments about labor can we make sense of arguments about the balance between liberty and police power during these years. Further, only through perceiving the significance of these tensions can we explain the Court's grounding of the broad expansion of state authority in the 1940s and the ambiguous effects of this expansion for women.

The Tension between Liberty and Police Power
in Context

The doctrinal battles during these years centered around the tension between two legal concepts, liberty and police power. Throughout the entire period of negotiation, the legal community struggled over the appropriate balance between the two, developing increasingly finer-grained analyses of both. The center of debate regarding both also shifted as the legal community turned increasingly to cases involving women's protective labor legislation. For liberty, this meant a focus on the subject of the guarantee of liberty rather than on liberty itself, and for police power, this meant a sharp concentration of interpretive energy on the concepts of health and the public good.

Work by Gillman, Cushman, Forbath, Orren, and others on the *Lochner* era has shown that the doctrinal questions at the heart of the conflict between individuals' liberty and the state's authority to regulate were far more than mere political posturing. Instead, they revealed the growing tensions in the judiciary's shared understanding of the structural economic and political landscape in a state of courts and parties. The key institutional question pursued by Gillman, Orren, Skocpol, and other social scientists is how this shared understanding fragmented in the face of rapid changes both in the underlying eco-

nomic structure and in the courts' institutional engagement with political issues of development. Surveying the period of negotiation from
beginning to end through the lens of gender suggests that the struggles
over the balance between liberty and police power turned on shifting
contextual conceptions of both, not on purely political preferences of
the judges or on a stubborn commitment to laissez-faire.

After the false start of privileges or immunities, the concept of liberty took the center stage in considerations of protective labor legislation. Both state and federal courts took the constitutional guarantee of
liberty seriously, expending a great deal of interpretive effort to trace
out its content and contours. In the early period of general balancing,
the courts interpreted liberty as a broad guarantee of freedom from
state intervention except in certain narrow circumstances. In doing so,
some members of the community promoted a rigid separation between
public and private and interpreted the relationship between employer
and employee as fundamentally private, reading governmental influence on the relationship as a violation of liberty. During these years and
in the following decade, the legal community also struggled with the
right to contract, conceiving of it as a combination of the guarantees of
property and liberty under the due process clause. The right to contract
gradually came to take center stage in the development of reasoning
regarding general protective labor legislation. As the legal community
argued increasingly over this right and its scope with regard to general
protective labor legislation, its members spent little time investigating
the subject of the guarantee of due process. Through this failure to
question the identity of the subject exercising the right, the subject came
to be an implicitly male holder of the guarantee. In the period of specific balancing, the legal community gradually settled on the idea that
for many male laborers, limiting their liberty in order to protect them
from abuses in the labor marketplace would be an affront to their
authority to manage their own lives and an insult to their manliness.

The legal community initially did not question women's specific
exercises of liberty, instead analyzing women's cases within the same
framework as the general cases. After the turn of the century, however,
interpretations in women's cases began to diverge. By the time that the
Supreme Court had decided *Muller* in 1908, cases involving women's
legislation constituted their own category, and, as explained above, the
legal community was focused on the laborers involved in these cases.
This pattern led to the emergence of a distinct analysis of liberty for

women. The period of laborer-specific analysis saw the legal community confirming and solidifying this pattern. Rather than considering liberty and its scope generally, members of the legal community, regardless of their positions on the issue, focused on women as the subjects of the due process guarantee. In doing so, they engaged in disagreements different from those taking place with respect to general legislation. In the general cases, the legal community argued over the scope of the guarantee of liberty, but with respect to women's cases, the legal community increasingly addressed women's exercise of liberty, focusing on women's ability to make contracts freely for themselves.

Advocates on both sides thus had to wrestle with women's relationship to the guarantee of liberty. In doing so, they confronted maternalism as a tempting but problematic frame for arguments in favor of protection. Those supporting protective labor legislation emphasized women's differences from men—their lack of unionization, their greater concern for children, their temperamental deficiencies—all of which contributed to women's inability to drive adequate bargains for themselves without the state's assistance. For supporters, protective labor legislation for women enhanced their liberty by enabling them to negotiate on a more equal basis with their employers and to achieve the fairer bargains that men could accomplish without the state's assistance. They relied on essentialist conceptions of women's natures and extrapolated from these notions to argue for protection. Women's liberty thus differed from men's in that it was not fundamentally private in the sense of existing independently of the state's intervention; this reasoning repudiated the laissez-faire model that applied to men's contracts for labor. It also laid the groundwork for the open exposing of the weaknesses of the laissez-faire ontology with respect to men. Those opposing protective labor legislation insisted that such limitations harmed women by perpetuating the myth that they could not act independently for themselves. Worse, construing women's exercise of liberty in this way classed them with children and incompetents, further hindering the long-term goal of achieving equality with men. Practically, opponents claimed that limiting women's liberty would ultimately contribute to women's lessened ability to compete effectively in the marketplace. Opponents finally argued that women should also be viewed as independent holders of the guarantee of liberty and that they should be left to negotiate their employment contracts on the same terms as men.

The focus on how workers exercised liberty spilled over to influence the analysis of general legislation in the period of gendered rebalancing, in some respects echoing the narrower reasoning of the Supreme Court in *Holden v. Hardy,* in which the justices had noted the bargaining disparities in the mining industry. During the 1930s, however, reformers and some members of the legal community argued that protective labor legislation would appropriately enhance the bargaining power and thus the liberty of all workers. The Court's ruling in *West Coast Hotel* addressed women's particular benefits from legislation that enabled them to negotiate more favorable contracts, but much of the reasoning was expressed in terms that suggested that men, too, would benefit from such interventions. Nonetheless, the Court emphasized that it was no longer necessary to claim that a protective measure enhanced a worker's liberty; addressing the older view that protective labor legislation limited liberty, the Court ruled that such limitations were perfectly permissible. In framing the ruling in this way, the justices possibly averted another decade of litigation in the state courts over whether particular statutes enhanced or limited liberty.

Interpretations of police power, too, changed dramatically over the decades. At first, discussions of police power were broad, drawing on established definitions from the antebellum era to explain the concept. In the period of generalized balancing, the legal community settled on the explanation that the state's police power encompassed the authority to regulate concerning issues affecting the public health, peace or order, morals, or general welfare of the community. This grant of authority then balanced against the due process clause's guarantee of liberty. In considering general legislation, many courts initially read police power as narrowly as they read liberty broadly, but in time more sophisticated interpretations developed that went beyond merely weighing one concept against the other.

Toward the end of the nineteenth century and at the beginning of the twentieth century, the legal community began to focus on particular aspects of police power. Two central elements quickly emerged: the power to regulate in the interest of public health, and the authority to regulate generally in the public interest. Considerations of general legislation turned on these elements. Reformers and state legislatures began to concentrate their efforts on regulating particular types of labor that were linked to public health and public interest, promoting the creation of areas that would stand as havens of regulation within the unregulated expanse of paid labor. The paradigmatic example of this strategy was the regulation of the mining industry, which was construed as requiring dangerous and unhealthy work. States' and the federal government's attempts to limit the hours of public employees also began to make headway in the courts as members of the legal community were able to connect the element of public interest to such regulations. Battles broke out over the extent to which the health risks in particular industries were sufficient to warrant the exercise of police power.

As the legal community turned to specific balancing at the turn of the century, it worked to articulate the relationship between women's work and appropriate exercises of police power. With respect to women's protective legislation, public health and the public's interest in women's reproductive roles quickly became the center of analysis. As described above, the focus on women's health differed from the concerns with men's health. In addressing women's health, reformers and the legal community emphasized women's particular biological differences from men that allegedly made them more vulnerable to workplace injury and exploitation, while analyses of men's health focused more directly on the risks connected to particular industries. The brief filed by Goldmark and Brandeis in *Muller v. Oregon* confirmed this tendency, providing detailed citations and information about studies in the United States and abroad addressing women's general physical condition and the injuries that women suffered from excessive fatigue. These briefs notably neglected to analyze women's work in laundries specifically, which was the issue that the statute in question had addressed. The failure to analyze the particular industry soon became a trend, as future attorneys focused much more on women, their physiques, and their natures than upon the specific risks inherent in particular regulated industries.

Focus on women's roles as mothers and the public implications of this function continued as women's cases began to dominate the legal landscape in the period of laborer-centered analysis. Activists, attorneys, and judges debated the significance of women's responsibility for raising the next generation of citizens, often concluding that acknowledging this responsibility justified restricting women's labor. Throughout this debate, most of the discussants presented reproduction and child rearing as having public aspects and accepted unquestioningly women's near identification with both. Late in the second decade of the

century some feminists and members of the legal community began to
address men's relationship to the family as a reason for regulating their
labor, but for the most part, this argument remained focused on women
throughout the 1920s and 1930s. In the 1920s and 1930s, discussions of
women's health linked up with analyses of women's precarious situation in the labor market, and those promoting regulation claimed that
the public's interest in healthy children required the payment of a minimum wage to women. Those opposing minimum wages for women
claimed that the same public interests existed with regard to male
workers. Manufacturers maintained that in neither case did these interests warrant governmental intervention, while feminists advocating for
women's equality claimed that if these interests warranted intervention
on women's behalf, they justified interventions on men's behalf as well.

The balance between police power and liberty and the political
content of these concepts have traditionally been the focus of constitutional historians of the *Lochner* era. This book has shown that a consideration of the abstract doctrinal arguments regarding these concepts
does not reveal the nature of their evolution during the early twentieth
century. Only by incorporating a study of the role gender played and
by looking beyond the actions of judges can we see how the Court ultimately arrived at its ruling in *West Coast Hotel* and why that ruling
applied as broadly as it did. As Carol Nackenoff has observed,
although women were not incorporated into the formal deliberative
bodies, women's activism under the banner of maternalism generated
a new narrative space for redefining a reciprocal network of obligation
between citizens and the state (Nackenoff 1999). This narrative space
intersected with legal doctrine to promote the gendered reconceptualization of labor, laborers, and the state's appropriate role.

The Implications of the Research

The primary empirical goal of this book has been to reframe understandings of the development of substantive due process with respect
to protective labor legislation by centering gender in the analysis. In
doing so, I have expanded the temporal frame of analysis beyond the
Lochner era, which is generally considered to begin with the Court's
decision in 1905 and end with *West Coast Hotel* in 1937, in order to incorporate the genesis of the nodes of conflict described above. In centering
gender, the analysis reflects the legal community's own shift in inter-

pretation as cases involving women's protective labor legislation ultimately came to drive the development of doctrine. The pages above have shown how this shift, combined with considerations of nodes of conflict, has led to a fundamentally different understanding of the period of negotiation, and therefore to a rethinking of the doctrinal antecedents for the modern welfare state.

The book also presents four central insights that have implications beyond the scope of the research into the fate of protective labor legislation at the hands of late-nineteenth- and early-twentieth-century judges. First is the approach of analyzing nodes of conflict as a means of understanding the development of constitutional doctrine. This means of analysis provides certain revelations that are unavailable from more conventional approaches and helps the historian to understand better the political nature of courts as institutions. The next two insights concern the nature of liberty under the due process clause and the framing of the state's authority to legislate in ways that limit liberty. Understanding both of these concepts requires a closer analysis of the individual subject of the guarantee of liberty, who always exists either in the background or the foreground of the interpretive problems raised by collisions of liberty and the state's authority to regulate.

The final insight is that reformers need to be careful to ensure that the paths they choose to initiate reform do not ultimately create negative results. The study has shown that even though legal actors cannot fully control events, they can choose strategies for reform that will not obviously lead to dangerous results. Reformers need to think carefully about the legal categories they create and how the next set of factual arguments down the road will transform these categories. While no one can predict accurately or completely manage the turns and twists that doctrinal and constitutional arguments will take, some paths bear more risks of co-optation by hostile actors than others.

With regard to nodes of conflict, this study has shown that thinking about doctrinal development without considering judges' struggles to frame particular key issues substantially limits the story that can be told. Certainly the role of individual judges in shaping the development of constitutional doctrine should not be diminished; their words are the very stuff of doctrine. As such legal scholars as Ackerman and Sunstein have shown, judges play important and sometimes dangerous roles in mediating between the political process and the system's commitment to constitutional principle. Nonetheless, judges are not the sole actors in the process through which doctrine emerges. This study has focused on a period in American history during which intensive public conflicts over the propriety of measures purporting to shield workers from exploitation and abuse at the hands of their employers ended up affecting the development of a significant area in constitutional law. The lay reformers of the late nineteenth and early twentieth century had no direct interest in influencing interpretations of the relationship between liberty and police power; they simply wanted to find a way to convince the courts not to invalidate their hard-won victories in the state legislatures. Similarly, those political actors opposing regulation had no direct stake in technical jurisprudential issues; they were perfectly happy to use the Fourteenth Amendment to support business interests if it could be helpful. In fact, manufacturing interests in the post–*West Coast Hotel* era dutifully cited that case with great approval to support corporate-backed statutes preventing the establishment of union-only workplaces (*American Federation of Labor v. American Sash & Door Co.*, 189 P.2d 914 (Ariz. 1948); *McKay v. Retail Automobile Salesmen's Labor Union*, 90 P.2d 113 (Cal. 1939)). Nonetheless, their efforts had a significant impact on the development of constitutional principles.

In general, constitutional scholars can broaden their understandings of how certain doctrinal points of law become particularly contested by seeking in judges' opinions the origins of these struggles in the public's interest in controversial policies or practices. Charles Epp's suggestion that we consider the related efforts of organizations for advocacy and the government's own role as an advocate is helpful, but one must not lose sight of Barry Friedman's and Ronald Kahn's admonitions that the creation of constitutional law is a complex historical process of interpretation and reinterpretation. Epp's analysis of the growth of rights in a cross-national context is insightful, but at times his narrative is more monocausal than historically interpretive. The study of nodes of conflict shows both that this process is historically contingent and that it extends beyond the formal boundaries of the law.

One of the most significant developments in American law during the early twentieth century was the growing role that scientific evidence came to play in determining the outcome of cases. Without this development, the nodes of conflict described in the book could not have played out in the ways that they did. While the distinction between law and fact was a long-standing feature of Anglo-American law, during the early twentieth century masses of factual evidence from expert sources not directly connected to the litigating parties began to influence both the outcomes in individual cases and also the development of judicial reasoning. The changes in constitutional doctrine were largely due to the research efforts of attorneys assisted by lay activists and transformed the role that attorneys played by enabling them to promote agendas for policy effectively through litigation. That these changes took place in the doctrinal area of women's protective labor legislation is testimony to the power of combining maternalist ideology with a legal realist commitment on the part of much of the legal community to addressing concrete factual circumstances through constitutional doctrine. This process is not limited to the struggles over protective labor legislation; one need only look to the ever-increasing use of amicus briefs to detail factual information that would otherwise be unavailable to the courts in a bewildering array of doctrinal areas. Nonetheless, the use of social science research conducted within a maternalist framework was particularly potent in the historical context of the Progressive and post-Progressive years. Studying nodes of conflict reminds the observer that attorneys often originated and principally articulated particular framings of the issues at stake in the struggle over protective labor legislation. This primary function of attorneys addressing developing legal areas is all too often overlooked.

As mentioned above, none of this is intended to diminish the role of the courts, but judges do not have the degree of control over doctrine that some theories suggest. Judges adjudicate cases in particular areas and may have the authority to approve or disapprove particular framings of legal issues; through this process, the due process clause came to house the substantive rights that the privileges or immunities clause could not. Nonetheless, the developments detailed above were not solely the result of judicial activity. Students of the Constitution can benefit by considering the role that judges play in framing the parameters of debates rather than simply looking to outcomes or rules. Studying nodes of conflict encourages questions about the kinds of issues that courts leave open or ambiguous either intentionally or unintentionally and how these lacunae in the doctrine become ripe for use by the other actors in the process of interpretation.

A second significant outcome of this reading of history addresses substantive due process specifically. As Rowe's review essay suggests, we cannot begin to assess the liberative potential for the doctrine without breaking away from a crabbed interpretation of its genesis in a

political commitment to laissez-faire economics that renders liberty as
a suspect and infinitely interpretable category. Liberty had specific and
bounded meanings throughout the period of negotiation, and the
struggle over liberty ultimately became a struggle over how problematic citizens such as women could be integrated into the nation-state.
Liberty provided justifications early on for striking down general protective measures. Later the concept encouraged the legal community to
focus on women as workers and was itself questioned in its relationship to female employees. The juxtaposition between analyses of male
liberty on the one hand and female workers' exercise of liberty on the
other thus had a significant impact on the doctrinal story told in the
book. If *West Coast Hotel* had indeed been the last word on substantive
due process, the story might be of purely historical interest. However,
as numerous commentators ranging from Conkle to Sunstein have
observed, the Court's action in 1937 was in no way a stake in the heart
of the concept that protection of individuals' rights to liberty can justify
invalidating state statutes under the due process clause (Conkle 1987;
Sunstein 1987). Recent judicial discussions of substantive due process
in the context of abortion, gay rights, and assisted suicide as only a few
examples confirm this observation.

This research suggests that in considering due process' protection
for liberty, the constitutional interpreter must be careful to look at the
subject of the guarantee of liberty. This advice arises most directly from
the experience of women with protective labor legislation. As demonstrated here, almost as soon as the legal community began considering
them as the subjects of the guarantee of liberty, the interpretations of
liberty the community advanced began to shift. Advocates for protective labor legislation could claim that the state's restrictions enhanced
the liberty of female subjects who deviated from the male norm by facing different situations in the workplace and exercising additional
responsibilities outside of it. While opponents of protective labor legislation challenged this interpretation of liberty, they could not dismiss it
out of hand and maintained the focus on women as the subjects of the
liberty guarantee. Modern constitutional scholars can find parallels in
other instances in which discussions of liberty focus on subjects who
are problematic in some way because they deviate from the unstated
norm. In such instances, the constitutional scholar can seek to understand the ways in which the nonnormative subject may bear a different
relationship to the guarantee of liberty, analyzing the implications of

this difference, if it exists, and the harms that a separate analysis may entail for that nonnormative subject.

Focusing on the subject of the guarantee of liberty can also be helpful even when the subject is not the center of the analysis. By considering the implicit subjects of the right to contract as it applied in cases involving general protective labor legislation, this work has shown the connection between liberty and a particular conception of manliness that encompassed men's ability to negotiate labor contracts for themselves in the absence of particular countervailing circumstances. This conception of liberty was undoubtedly damaging to sweated male workers before and after the turn of the century. It resulted in many courts' decisions to trade off men's concrete statutory rights to reasonable hours of labor and wages that reached the subsistence level for the more abstract right to bargain freely with their employers, which was rendered largely meaningless by major disparities in bargaining power in many industries. Modern interpretations of due process thus must consider the connection between the subject of the guarantee and the allegedly protected liberty: what kind of liberty is claimed, and what kind of subject is asserted or assumed as the holder of the claimed liberty?

This research also suggests the value of paying more attention to interpretations of the state's authority in cases in which claims of liberty clash with the state's desire to regulate. Here too, looking at the subject of the state's regulatory impulse can reveal undercurrents in interpretation that previously remained hidden. The state's regulatory authority, referred to as police power, was initially understood to be quite narrow, expanding only in response to carefully crafted legal arguments attempting to justify regulations on the basis of connections between the state's interests and the regulated individuals. This connection, often overshadowed in modern equal protection analysis by attention to the relationship between the state's interests and the means chosen to achieve those interests, is worthy of deeper analysis in many contexts.

With respect to women's protective labor legislation, the state's interest in protection related principally to women's roles as the bearers and raisers of the next generation of citizens. Because women served this public function, the state could protect them from the ravages of the marketplace to a greater extent than it could protect men. This protection was nonetheless a double-edged sword; some women undoubtedly lost desired positions because of regulations, and some statutes, like those barring night work by women, were not crafted primarily to serve the interests of female workers. Repeatedly, many members of the legal community revealed in their analyses that their main concerns were not with enhancing women's position in the workplace but rather were with reinforcing the belief that women's primary function was to bear and raise children who would become suitable citizens. The focus on women as the subjects of the state's regulatory interests revealed the differences between the agendas pushed by feminist reformers, many of whom sincerely wanted to improve conditions for female laborers, and the agendas of some proregulation attorneys general and judges, who sought to validate statutes that reinforced traditional gender roles. Likewise, modern constitutional interpreters might consider the interests that the state seeks to achieve through regulation and question the extent to which these interests match up with the interests of the subjects of regulation.

Regulation of men's labor on a large scale could not be achieved until the legal community could envision men as subjects in need of protection. The early history of litigation over protective labor legislation reveals that courts endorsed the belief that state intervention on men's behalf would be an insulting affront. This belief rested on an idealized conception of male workers' capacity to negotiate with their employers. Modern interpreters would do well to examine underlying beliefs about subjects for whom the courts largely refuse to allow state intervention. The history of protective labor legislation teaches that protection of liberty can be as much a mask for coercive practices as a guarantee of desired freedoms.

Nonetheless, such examinations have liberating possibilities as well. Understanding the legal community's implicit or explicit beliefs about the subjects of regulation can unveil disjunctures between reformers' interests and legal framings of these interests. Such understandings can also provide a way to challenge inappropriate assumptions of inequality between subjects and to implement regulations more fairly across the board. While such understandings may not change the outcomes in individual cases, in the appropriate hands, they can lead to the recognition and remedy of underlying inequities.

Feminist reformers struggled throughout the period of negotiation to bridge the tension between achieving positive outcomes for female workers and grounding these achievements on dangerous endorsements of difference. In the course of this struggle, bitter splits emerged within the feminist community over both tactics and fundamental philosophy. As Mink, Nackenoff, and Baer among others have recognized, the problem then as today arises from the difficulty of developing an approach that recognizes the social inequality of women without turning this recognition into a trap. For the feminists of the early twentieth century, the source of the bind was interest in supporting protective measures, which encouraged many activists to accept current social understandings of liberty rather than trying to change them. Even though feminists disagreed about the proper approach, they agreed on the ultimate goal of their activities: to secure a more equitable and safe workplace for all workers, male and female. What appeared to be the easiest way to achieve protection for women, however, entailed some feminists' embrace of potentially crippling conceptions of women and their capacities as workers. In practice, this contributed to women's double entrapment. Protection was won at the expense of the recognition of women's full citizenship and furthermore cost women the opportunity to organize effectively as members of the working class.

Feminists supporting protective labor legislation had laudable goals, but the arguments they used were easily co-opted and used by agents of the dominant culture to deny women's rights. Many feminists in favor of protective legislation sought protection for all workers and believed that obtaining protective legislation for women would help them to achieve this goal. In a way, they were right: the New Deal swept away many of the barriers that had previously blocked protective legislation for all workers. Further, protective legislation probably did some good for women, particularly at first. Since women did not have the same bargaining power through membership in labor unions, demanding equal treatment in the law would not have led to equal treatment in the workplace. Rather, across-the-board equal treatment would simply have confirmed women's lower wages and longer work hours.

Other feminists had advocated for equal treatment. These people saw the dangers inherent in relying too heavily on women's roles as mothers at the expense of emphasizing women's roles as workers. Their ideal solution would have been to push for equal treatment of women in employment and other contexts through the implementation of general laws, but they were willing to accept the invalidation of laws for women rather than endorse inequality in legislative outcomes. In doing so, they advocated for protective legislation for all workers immediately rather than focusing on women first. The feminists who promoted equal treatment countered the difference approach because they feared that it would reinforce social beliefs in women's difference from men and provide the ground to protect women beyond the scope imagined by feminist advocates for women's protective legislation. They also warned that gender-specific protective legislation would ultimately protect women out of better-paying and higher-status work. If the elimination of all protective legislation was the only way to achieve equality, they preferred this outcome to continued reinforcement of negative conceptions of women and their capabilities through the law.

This interpretation correctly identified the costs associated with gender-based protection. The courts, as Judith Baer points out, were willing to accept the concept of difference but on the dominant societal terms rather than as the feminists focusing on difference had intended it (Baer 1978). Rather than seeing the difference between women and men as a result of long-term discrimination by employers and labor unions, members of the legal community often framed difference as natural and immutable. Some proregulation feminist rhetoric certainly gave grounds for these conclusions. Ultimately, this concept of difference allowed states to uphold protective labor legislation long after it was a valuable tool for women. Cases such as *Goesaert v. Cleary* revealed that in the era after World War II, protective legislation had become more of a burden than a help to women.[1] Not until Title VII and the Pregnancy Discrimination Act became law did many of the statutes and policies spawned by social and political beliefs in differences that limited women against their wills pass into deserved oblivion.

Some feminist researchers such as Theda Skocpol have heralded the heavy influence that women reformers had during the Progressive Era as showing their ability to effect social change through manipulating the prevalent maternalist ideology of the time. In this view, women developed a certain public power that men lacked through their capacity to use socially constructed themes to advance their agenda of protection. Other thinkers such as Alice Kessler-Harris, Wendy Mink, and Carol Nackenoff, however, have demonstrated that this method of influencing public policy was by no means unproblematic. I have sought to steer a related course, using nodes of conflict to analyze the

---

1. This case, a direct descendant of the early cases like *In re Considine,* upheld the long-unquestioned principle that states could bar women from working as servers of alcoholic beverages (*Goesaert v. Cleary,* 335 U.S. 464 (1948)).

influence of the women's movement on the development of doctrine and vice versa. This work explains the processes through which women's organizations saw their political advocacy transformed into legal language and highlights the risks that this transformative process entails. This, then, is the lasting legacy and lesson of the six decades of struggle over protective labor legislation in the new industrial order.

Appendix on Data
and Methods

My research materials consist of judicial opinions, briefs, historical sources, and materials cited by briefs to provide empirical evidence for the arguments advanced in court. I reviewed documents discussing the cases or protective legislation that were published by organizations involved in litigation over the legal regulation of women in the workplace. I also reviewed a broad array of background historical evidence, both primary and secondary, on the relevant time period.

I reviewed all published judicial opinions in the United States regarding the legal regulation of employees in the workplace from the late nineteenth century (starting in 1873) and going through the Court's decision in *West Coast Hotel* in 1937. I located approximately two hundred cases. While other cases addressed the debate over the scope of the state's regulatory authority, this selection of cases enabled me to show in depth how the relevant doctrinal questions developed over time, leading ultimately to *West Coast Hotel*. The selection of cases included all reported decisions on the state and federal level regarding the constitutionality of protective legislation for women decided between 1873 and 1937, plus all other reported decisions involving constitutional challenges to protective legislation. Protective labor legislation included any statutory provision on the state or federal level that sought to alter the terms or conditions of employment, directly limiting the authority of employee and employer to negotiate concerning the labor contract. This could include setting maximum hours for work or minimum wages, controlling conditions in certain kinds of work, protecting labor union members in various ways, or protecting some classes of laborers (often by occupation). I also analyzed a selection of cases regarding related issues, including understandings of the scope of liberty under the Fourteenth Amendment and other considerations of protective legislation. To locate these cases, I used electronic and digest sources, as well as tracking down cases cited in other cases or in briefs.

My research included a review of the work that feminist historians have done regarding this time period. I principally relied upon feminist accounts of women in the labor force in the early twentieth century, but I also used other historical work on the time period.

Finally, I also analyzed discussions of litigation over protective legislation and other limits on women's work taking place in journals of advocacy organizations and other sources of public commentary. Feminists were involved on both sides of the issue and discussed their standpoints in women's magazines, trade journals, and other public forums.

Bibliography

The bibliography is divided into three sections. Legal briefs are listed first, followed by materials from the women's movement and other contemporary sources, then by secondary sources.

LEGAL BRIEFS

Applegate, H. W., Brooks Hays, J. S. Utley, and William T. Hammock. 1926. *Donham v. West Nelson Mfg. Co.* Brief for Appellants. Filed May 18.

Arnold H. B., and W. Wilson Carlile. 1914. *Jeffrey v. Blagg Mfg. Co.* Brief for Plaintiff in Error. Filed November 13.

Arnold, H. B., and W. Wilson Carlile. 1914. *Jeffrey v. Blagg Mfg. Co.* Reply Brief for Plaintiff in Error. Filed November 30.

Beck, James M., Solicitor General, and Robert P. Reeder. 1922. *Bailey v. Drexel Furniture Co.* Brief for Appellants and Plaintiffs in Error. Filed March 1.

Bennett, John J., Jr., and Henry Epstein. 1936. *Morehead v. New York.* Petition for Writ of Certiorari and Motion to Advance. Filed March 16.

Bennett, John J., Jr., Henry Epstein, and Henry S. Manley. 1934. *Nebbia v. New York.* Brief for Appellee. In *Landmark Briefs and Arguments of the Supreme Court of the United States: Constitutional Law.* Vol. 27. Washington, D.C.: University Publications of America, 1975. 695–762.

Bennett, John J., Jr., Henry Epstein, John F. X. McGohey, Benjamin Heffner, and John C. Crary Jr. 1936. *Morehead v. New York.* Appellant's Brief on the Law. Filed April 22.

Biddle, Francis, Thurman Arnold, Robert Stern, Hugh Cox, and Warner Gardner. 1940. *U.S. v. Darby.* Brief for the United States. Filed September.

Brandeis, Louis D. 1908. *Muller v. Oregon.* Brief for the Defendant in Error. In *Landmark Briefs and Arguments of the Supreme Court of the United States: Constitutional Law.* Vol. 16. Washington, D.C.: University Publications of America, 1975. 63–178.

Brandeis, Louis D., counsel for sheriff and Labor Commissioner of the State of California, and Josephine Goldmark, Publication Secretary, National Consumers' League. 1915. *Miller v. Wilson.* Brief for defendant Wilson and Appellees. Filed January 2.

Bricker, John W. 1934. *Nebbia v. New York.* Brief of the Attorney General of Ohio as *Amicus Curiae.* In *Landmark Briefs and Arguments of the Supreme Court of the*

United States: Constitutional Law. Vol. 27. Washington, D.C.: University Publications of America, 1975. 795–819.

Bricker, John W., Attorney General of Ohio, William S. Evatt, Isadore Topper, John K. Evans, and Marvin C. Harrison. 1936. *Morehead v. New York.* Motion for Leave to File Brief as *Amicus Curiae* and Brief in Support Thereof. Filed March 27.

Brizzolara, James, Henry L. Fitzhugh, and William F. Kirby, Attorney General. 1908. *McLean v. Arkansas.* Brief and Argument for Defendant in Error. Filed April 7.

Brown, George M., Attorney General, and J. O Bailey. 1916. *Bunting v. Oregon.* Brief for Defendant in Error. Filed April 8.

Brown, L. L., William A. Lancaster, and Milton D. Purdy. 1912. *Central Lumber Co. v. South Dakota.* Brief for Plaintiff in Error. Filed March 2.

Bulkley, Gray & More. 1913. *Sturges & Burn Mfg. Co. v. Beauchamp.* Brief and Argument for Plaintiff in Error. Filed October 17.

Bynum, William P. 1922. *Bailey v. Drexel Furniture Co.* Abstract of Oral Argument for the Defendant in Error. Filed March 1.

Campbell, Charles J., Campbell & Boland. 1936. *Morehead v. New York.* Brief of New York State Hotel Association as *Amicus Curiae.* Filed April 27.

Carpenter, Matthew H. 1871. *Bradwell v. Illinois.* Argument for Plaintiff in Error.

Chase, Nathan H., and M. H. Boutelle. 1931. *Hardware Dealers Mutual Fire Ins. Co. v. Glidden Co.* Appellant's Brief. Filed April 18.

Clarke, Albert E. 1899. *Petit v. Minnesota.* Brief for Plaintiff in Error. Filed December 27.

Coghlan, Henry D., and Joseph A. O'Donnell. 1901. *Connolly v. Union Sewer Pipe Co.* Brief and Argument of Plaintiffs in Error. Filed April 1.

Coleman, C. C., Attorney General, and N. H. Loomis. 1903. *Atkin v. Kansas.* Brief for Defendant in Error. Filed April 28.

Colston, Edward, and George Hoadly Jr. 1895. *Hennington v. Georgia.* Brief for Plaintiff in Error. Filed November 8.

Conner, C. B., and Sam M. Driver. 1937. *West Coast Hotel v. Parrish.* Brief of Appellee. In *Landmark Briefs and Arguments of the Supreme Court of the United States: Constitutional Law.* Vol. 33. Washington, D.C.: University Publications of America, 1975. 125–29.

Davis, John W., W. L. Frierson, and Robert Szold. 1918. *Hammer v. Dagenhart.* Brief for Appellant. In *Landmark Briefs and Arguments of the Supreme Court of the United States: Constitutional Law.* Vol. 18. Washington, D.C.: University Publications of America, 1975. 831–920.

Dawson, John S., Attorney General of Kansas, J. S. Sheppard. 1914. *Coppage v. Kansas.* Brief and Argument for Defendant in Error. Filed June 12.

Dever, Paul A., and James J. Ronan. 1936. *Morehead v. New York.* Statement, on Behalf of the Commonwealth of Massachusetts, *Amicus Curiae,* in Support of the Petition for Rehearing. Filed October 5.

Dillon, John R., Winslow S. Pierce, and David D. Duncan. 1901. *Texas & Pacific Ry. Co. v. Humble.* Brief for Plaintiffs in Error. Filed March 7.

Douglas, W. B., Attorney General, and C. W. Somerby. 1900. *Petit v. Minnesota.* Brief for Defendant in Error. Filed March 12.

Dunlap, Robert, Terry, Cavin & Mills, and Gardiner Lathrop (of counsel). 1914. *Smith v. Texas.* Brief for Plaintiff in Error. Filed January 22.

Egan, John G. 1923. *Adkins v. Children's Hospital.* Brief of the State of Kansas as *Amicus Curiae.* In *Landmark Briefs and Arguments of the Supreme Court of the United States: Constitutional Law.* Vol. 21. Washington, D.C.: University Publications of America, 1975. 609–14.

Ekern, Herman L., J. E. Messerschmidt, and Fred M. Wilcox. 1923. *Adkins v. Children's Hospital.* Supplemental Brief of *Amici Curiae.* In *Landmark Briefs and Arguments of the Supreme Court of the United States: Constitutional Law.* Vol. 21. Washington, D.C.: University Publications of America, 1975. 553–66.

Ellis, Challen B., Joseph W. Folk, and Wade H. Ellis. 1923. *Adkins v. Children's Hospital.* Brief for Appellees. In *Landmark Briefs and Arguments of the Supreme Court of the United States: Constitutional Law.* Vol. 21. Washington, D.C.: University Publications of America, 1975. 435–521.

Ellis, Wade H. 1923. *Adkins v. Children's Hospital.* Oral Argument, March 14, 1923, on behalf of the Appellees. In *Landmark Briefs and Arguments of the Supreme Court of the United States: Constitutional Law.* Vol. 21. Washington, D.C.: University Publications of America, 1975. 627–64.

Fenton, William D., and Henry H. Gilfry. 1908. *Muller v. Oregon.* Brief for Plaintiff in Error. In *Landmark Briefs and Arguments of the Supreme Court of the United States: Constitutional Law.* Vol. 16. Washington, D.C.: University Publications of America, 1975. 3–35.

Field, Frank Harvey. 1905. *Lochner v. New York.* Brief for the Plaintiff in Error. In *Landmark Briefs and Arguments of the Supreme Court of the United States: Constitutional Law.* Vol. 14. Washington, D.C.: University Publications of America, 1975. 653–717.

Flint, Frank P., and Henry S. Van Dyke. 1914. *Miller v. Wilson.* Brief for Plaintiff Miller in Error. Filed June 1.

Frankfurter, Felix, of counsel for the State of Oregon, and Josephine Goldmark, Publication Secretary, National Consumers' League. 1916. *Bunting v. Oregon.* Brief for Defendant in Error. Filed March 3.

Frankfurter, Felix, Counsel for the Industrial Welfare Commission, and Josephine Goldmark, Publication Secretary, National Consumers' League. N.d. *Stettler v. O'Hara* and *Simpson v. O'Hara.* Brief for Defendants in Error upon Re-Argument.

Friend, Harvey M. 1918. *Dominion Hotel v. Arizona.* Brief for Plaintiff in Error. Filed October 2.

Fulton, C. W., and W. Lair Thompson. 1916. *Bunting v. Oregon.* Brief for the Plaintiff in Error. Filed January 31.

Galen, Albert J., Attorney General of Montana, and W. H. Poorman. 1911. *Quong Wing v. Kirkendall.* Brief of Defendant in Error. Filed December 6.

Godard, A. A., Attorney General, and B. H. Tracy. 1899. *Cotting v. Kansas.* Statement, Brief, and Argument for Attorney General. Filed October.

Gorman, George E., and John M. Pollock. 1913. *Sturges & Burn Mfg. Co. v. Beauchamp*. Brief and Argument for Defendant in Error. Filed October 17.

Goudy, W. C. 1876. *Munn v. Illinois*. Brief for the plaintiff in error. In *Landmark Briefs and Arguments of the Supreme Court of the United States: Constitutional Law*. Vol. 7. Washington, D.C.: University Publications of America, 1975. 457–534.

Griffith, Charles B., Attorney General of Kansas, John G. Egan, and Randal C. Harvey, Chester I. Long and Austin M. Cowan, of counsel. 1923. *Wolff Packing Co. v. Industrial Court*. Brief on Behalf of Defendant in Error. Filed April 21.

Guthrie, William D., Albert H. Horton, and B. P. Waggener. 1899. *Cotting v. Kansas*. Brief in Reply to the Argument of Attorney General of Kansas. Filed November 9.

———. 1901. *Cotting v. Kansas*. Brief for Appellants on Reargument. Filed January 11.

Hagerman, Frank. 1917. *Wilson v. New*. Summary of Appellant's Arguments. Filed January 8.

Hall, Matthew A., Raymond G. Young, and Carroll S. Montgomery. 1923. *Burns Baking Co. v. Bryan*. Supplemental and Reply Brief for Plaintiffs in Error. Filed October 11.

Hamilton, G. W., W. A. Toner, Geo. G. Hannan, and Temple of Justice. 1937. *West Coast Hotel v. Parrish*. Brief of *Amici Curiae*. In *Landmark Briefs and Arguments of the Supreme Court of the United States: Constitutional Law*. Vol. 33. Washington, D.C.: University Publications of America, 1975. 137–55.

Hamlin, Herbert, and Edwin Walker. 1901. *Connolly v. Union Sewer Pipe Co.* Motion to Dismiss Writs of Error and Brief and Argument for Defendant in Error. Filed April 8.

Hardy, Leslie C., and Alexander Britton. 1924. *Murphy v. Sardell*. Brief of Appellee. Filed December 12.

Heffner, Benjamin, and John C. Crary (on the brief), Henry Epstein, and John F. X. McGohey (counsel). 1936. *Morehead v. New York*. Factual Brief for Appellant. Filed April 22.

Herrick, John J., and Chester M. Dawes. 1910a. *Chicago, Burlington & Quincy R.R. Co. v. McGuire*. Brief and Argument for Plaintiffs in Error.

———. 1910b. *Chicago, Burlington & Quincy R.R. Co. v. McGuire*. Reply for Plaintiffs in Error. Filed December 17.

Hill, Henry W., and Dean R. Hill. 1923. *Radice v. New York*. Brief for Plaintiff in Error. Filed October 18.

Hogan, Timothy S., Attorney General, and James I. Boulger. 1914. *Jeffrey v. Blagg Mfg. Co.* Brief of Defendant in Error. Filed November 27.

Holmes, Daniel B. 1908. *McLean v. Arkansas*. Revised Brief for Plaintiff in Error. Filed November 23.

Hovey, Charles E. 1876. *U.S. v. Martin*. Brief for Appellee.

Howell & Elgin and A. J. Baker. 1910. *Chicago, Burlington & Quincy R.R. Co. v. McGuire*. Brief and Argument of Defendant in Error.

Idsall, James K., Attorney General. 1876. *Munn v. Illinois.* Brief for Defendants in Error. In *Landmark Briefs and Arguments of the Supreme Court of the United States: Constitutional Law.* Vol. 7. Washington, D.C.: University Publications of America, 1975. 599–660.

Irvine, R. T., and Bullitt & Chalkley. 1914a. *Keokee Coke Co. v. Taylor.* Brief for Plaintiff in Error. Filed April 20.

———. 1914b. *Keokee Coke Co. v. Taylor.* Additional and Reply Brief for Plaintiff-in-Error. Filed May 18.

Jacobson & Murray and William Lemke. 1932. *Advance-Rumely Thresher Co. v. Jackson.* Appellee's Brief. Filed October 28.

Jennings, Andrew J., and Israel Brayton. 1914. *Riley v. Massachusetts.* Brief of Plaintiff in Error. Filed February 13.

Jewett, Jno. N. 1876a. *Munn v. Illinois.* Brief for the Plaintiffs in Error. In *Landmark Briefs and Arguments of the Supreme Court of the United States: Constitutional Law.* Vol. 7. Washington, D.C.: University Publications of America, 1975. 535–72.

Jewett, Jno. N. 1876b. *Munn v. Illinois.* Further Brief for the Plaintiffs in Error. In *Landmark Briefs and Arguments of the Supreme Court of the United States: Constitutional Law.* Vol. 7. Washington, D.C.: University Publications of America, 1975. 573–98.

Johnson, John G., Arthur Miller, and Walker D. Hines. 1917. *Wilson v. New.* Brief for Appellees. Filed January 8.

Johnson, Royal C., Attorney General, Samuel W. Clark, and James M. Brown. 1911. *Central Lumber Co. v. South Dakota.* Brief for Defendant in Error. Filed May 9.

Jones, Wiley E., Attorney General. 1919. *Dominion Hotel v. Arizona.* Brief for the State of Arizona. Filed February 20.

Krum, John M., John B. Henderson, and Francis Minor. 1875. *Minor v. Happersett.* Brief for Plaintiff in Error. In *Landmark Briefs and Arguments of the Supreme Court of the United States: Constitutional Law.* Vol. 7. Washington, D.C.: University Publications of America, 1975. 209–49.

Lindsley, Henry A., Halstead L. Ritter, and Charles R. Brock. 1903. *Cronin v. Adams.* Brief for Defendants in Error. Filed December 1.

Lockwood, Belva. 1894. Affidavit of Belva Lockwood, Sworn to Edward A. Paul Sr., Notary Public. Filed April 23.

Lockwood, Belva. N.d. Petition to Justices from Belva Lockwood.

Looney, B. F., Attorney General, and Luther Nickels. 1914. *Smith v. Texas.* Brief for the Defendant in Error. Filed February 24.

Lovett, Archibald B., R. Basil Morris, Robert M. Hitch Jr., and Malberry Smith, Jr. 1940. *U.S. v. Darby.* Brief for Appellee.

MacVeagh, Wayne. 1887. *Powell v. Pennsylvania.* Brief of Argument for Defendant in Error *sur* Motion to Dismiss or Affirm. Filed March 21.

Manning, John, A. M. Crawford, B. E. Haney, and Louis D. Brandeis. 1908. *Muller v. Oregon.* Brief for the State of Oregon. In *Landmark Briefs and Argu-*

ments of the Supreme Court of the United States: Constitutional Law. Vol. 16. Washington, D.C.: University Publications of America, 1975. 37–61.

Matthews, Burnita Shelton, and Rebekah Scandrett Greathouse. 1936. *Morehead v. New York.* Brief as *Amici Curiae* on behalf of the National Woman's Party, National Association of Women Lawyers, Bindery Women's Union, Local No. 66 of the International Brotherhood of Bookbinders, Brooklyn-Manhattan Transit Women's League, Business Women's Legislative Council of California, and Women's Equal Opportunity League of New York. Filed April 27.

Mayer, Julius M. 1905. *Lochner v. New York.* Brief for the Defendants in Error. In *Landmark Briefs and Arguments of the Supreme Court of the United States: Constitutional Law.* Vol. 14. Washington, D.C.: University Publications of America, 1975. 715–47.

McConnell, George A. 1927. *Donham v. West Nelson Mfg. Co.* Abstract and Brief for Appellee. Filed January 10.

Miller, Nathan, Arthur Levitt, Harold Allen Gates, and Challen B. Ellis. 1936. *Morehead v. New York.* Brief for Respondent. Filed April 27.

Murphy, Matthew W., Howard G. Fuller, and Joseph M. Powers. 1932. *Advance-Rumely Thresher Co., v. Jackson.* Appellant's Brief. Filed September 13.

Nelson, Arthur E., Eugene M. O'Neill, Edward L. Boyle, and H. C. Fulton. 1931. *Hardware Dealers Mutual Fire Ins. Co. v. Glidden Co.* Appellees' Brief. Filed April 27.

Noel, J. C., and Duncan & Cridlin. 1914. *Keokee Coke Co. v. Taylor.* Brief for Defendants in Error. Filed May 4.

O'Brien, Morgan J., Clement Manly, W. P. Bynum, Junius Parker, and W. M. Hendren. 1918. *Hammer v. Dagenhart.* Brief for Appellees. In *Landmark Briefs and Arguments of the Supreme Court of the United States: Constitutional Law.* Vol. 18. Washington, D.C.: University Publications of America, 1975. 921–86.

Pence, Charles J., and John H. Murphy. 1897. *Holden v. Hardy.* Brief for Defendant in Error.

Pillsbury, Warren H. 1925. *Murphy v. Sardell.* Brief of *Amicus Curiae* on Behalf of Industrial Welfare Commission of the State of California. Filed May 25.

Pollock, T. A. 1903. *Atkin v. Kansas.* Brief of Plaintiff in Error. Filed April.

Roberts, John W., and E. L. Skeel. 1937. *West Coast Hotel v. Parrish.* Appellant's Answer to Brief of *Amici Curiae.* In *Landmark Briefs and Arguments of the Supreme Court of the United States: Constitutional Law.* Vol. 33. Washington, D.C.: University Publications of America, 1975. 161–80.

Saunders, John R., Attorney General, and J. D. Hank Jr. 1920. *Royster Guano Co. v. Virginia.* Brief on Behalf of the Commonwealth of Virginia. Filed March 11.

Scott, Oscar D. 1901. *Texas & Pacific Ry. Co. v. Humble.* Brief for Defendant in Error. Filed January 30.

Searle, A. C. 1884. *Barbier v. Connolly.* Brief for Plaintiff. Filed November 10.

Sherman, Carl, Attorney General of the State of New York, and Irving I. Goldsmith. 1923. *Radice v. New York*. Brief for the Defendant in Error. Filed December 28.

Smith, Edwin B., Asst. Attorney General, and John S. Blair. 1876. *U.S. v. Martin*. Brief for Appellants.

Smith, Milton. 1903. *Cronin v. Adams*. Brief of Plaintiff in Error. Filed November 7.

Stephens, Francis H., and Felix Frankfurter, assisted by Mary Dewson. 1923. *Adkins v. Children's Hospital*. Brief for Appellants. In *Landmark Briefs and Arguments of the Supreme Court of the United States: Constitutional Law*. Vol. 21. Washington, D.C.: University Publications of America, 1975. 359–431.

Sutherland, Arthur E. 1934. *Nebbia v. New York*. Brief for Appellant. In *Landmark Briefs and Arguments of the Supreme Court of the United States: Constitutional Law*. Vol. 27. Washington, D.C.: University Publications of America, 1975. 663–94.

Swift, James M. 1914. *Riley v. Massachusetts*. Brief of Defendant in Error. Filed February 24.

Terrell, J. M. 1896. *Hennington v. Georgia*. Brief and Argument for Defendant in Error. Filed March 9.

Thompson, W. Lair. 1916. *Bunting v. Oregon*. Reply Brief for Plaintiff in Error. Filed April 10.

Todd, G. Carroll, E. Marvin Underwood, and Frank Hagerman. 1917. *Wilson v. New*. Brief for the United States. Filed January 8.

Van Arsdale, John A., Attorney for Defendant in Error, and Walter F. Hofheins. 1923. *Radice v. New York*. Brief for Defendant in Error. Filed November 19.

VanWinkle, Isaac H., Joseph N. Teal, and William L. Brewster. 1923. *Adkins v. Children's Hospital*. Brief of Industrial Welfare Commission of the State of Oregon as *Amicus Curiae*. In *Landmark Briefs and Arguments of the Supreme Court of the United States: Constitutional Law*. Vol. 21. Washington, D.C.: University Publications of America, 1975. 581–607.

Vermilion, R. R., and W. F. Evans. 1914. *Coppage v. Kansas*. Brief and Argument of Plaintiff in Error. Filed January 19.

Waggener, B. P., and Albert H. Horton. 1899. *Cotting v. Kansas*. Statement of Case, Brief, and Argument for Appellants. Filed October 7.

Webb, U. S., Attorney General for the State of California, William Denman, and G. S. Arnold, Attorneys for Defendant in Error and Appellees. 1914. *Miller v. Wilson* and *Bosley v. McLaughlin*. Brief on Behalf of Defendant in Error and Appellees. Filed December 3.

Weiss & Gilbert, W. B. Rodgers, and D. T. Watson. 1887. *Powell v. Pennsylvania*. Brief of Plaintiff in Error. Filed December 29.

Weiss & Gilbert and D. T. Watson. 1887. *Powell v. Pennsylvania*. Brief for Plaintiff in Error *sur* Motion to Dismiss or Affirm. Filed April 23.

Wheeler, Charles S., and John F. Bowie. 1914. *Bosley v. McLaughlin*. Brief for Appellant Bosley. Filed June 1.

Wight, Ira T., and Charles E. Pew. 1911. *Quong Wing v. Kirkendall*. Brief of Plaintiff in Error. Filed November 4.

Wilson, Jeremiah M. 1897. *Holden v. Hardy.* Brief for Plaintiff in Error. Filed August 20.

Wilson, John N., Clement Manly, William M. Hendren, William P. Bynum, and Junius Parker. 1922. *Bailey v. Drexel Furniture Co.* Brief for Defendant in Error. Filed March 4.

Wintersteen, A. H., and Wayne MacVeagh. 1887. *Powell v. Pennsylvania.* Brief of Defendant in Error.

Wood, Frederick H., and William D. Whitney. 1936. *Carter v. Carter Coal Co.* Brief for the Petitioner. In *Landmark Briefs and Arguments of the Supreme Court of the United States: Constitutional Law.* Vol. 32. Washington, D.C.: University Publications of America, 1975. 29–342.

MATERIALS FROM THE WOMEN'S MOVEMENT AND OTHER CONTEMPORARY SOURCES

American Federation of Labor. 1919. *American Federation of Labor Reconstruction Program.* January 22.

Angell, Alexis, and Thomas Cooley. 1890. *A Treatise on the Constitutional Limitations Which Rest upon the Legislative Power of the States of the American Union.* 6th ed. Boston: Little, Brown & Co.

Anonymous. 1936. "Minimum Wage." Elinore Morehouse Herrick Collection, Schlesinger Library, Radcliffe College.

Beyer, Clara M. 1928. "History of Labor Legislation for Women in Three States." *Bulletin of the Women's Bureau* 66, no. 1.

———. 1929. "Minimum Wage Laws in the United States." *Painter and Decorator* 43, no. 6 (June): 7–9.

Bittermann, Helen Robbins. N.d. *Protective Legislation and the Equal Rights Amendment.*

Blatch, Harriet Stanton, and Clara Mortenson Beyer. 1923. "Do Women Want Protection? A Debate." *Nation* 116 (January 31): 115–16.

Boyle, C. Nina. 1924. Letter to the Editor, *Equal Rights* 11, no. 9 (April 12): 67.

Bromley, Dorothy Dunbar. 1927. "Feminist—New Style." *Harper's,* October, 552–60.

———. 1929. "This Maternal Instinct." *Harper's,* October, 423–33.

Brooks, John Graham. N.d. *The Consumers' League.* National Consumers' League.

———. N.d. *New Aspects of Employers' Welfare Work.* American Social Science Association, Department of Jurisprudence.

Carrington, Walter, and Thomas Cooley. 1927. *A Treatise on the Constitutional Limitations Which Rest upon the Legislative Power of the States of the American Union.* 8th ed. Vol. 2. Boston: Little, Brown & Co.

Children's Bureau. 1923. "Mother's Employment and Infant Mortality." Press release, March 15.

Committee on Home Economics. 1902. "Announcement of the Mary Lowell Stone Prize Essay." Women's Educational and Industrial Union.

Consumers' League of Connecticut. 1916. *The Department Store Girl and Her Employer*. March.

———. 1919. *The Work of the Consumers' League of Connecticut*. July.

———. 1922. *Should Women Factory Workers Be Employed Ten Hours a Day in Connecticut?* January.

———. 1923. *Women in Industry*. January.

———. 1923. *Can Output Be Maintained on Shorter Hours?* February.

———. 1931. *Bulletin* 1, no. 1, May.

———. 1932. *Bulletin* 1, no. 5, June.

———. 1933. *Purchasing Power?*

Consumers' League of Massachusetts. 1908. *Catechism*. June.

———. 1924. *The Minimum Wage Law in Massachusetts*. Bulletin no. 24, January.

"Convention of the National Women's Trade Union League." 1908. *Union Labor Advocate*. December, 21–46.

Cooley, Thomas. 1868. *A Treatise on the Constitutional Limitations Which Rest upon the Legislative Power of the States of the American Union*. Boston: Little, Brown & Co.

———. 1874. *A Treatise on the Constitutional Limitations Which Rest upon the Legislative Power of the States of the American Union*. 3d ed. Boston: Little, Brown.

Council on Women and Children in Industry. 1924. *News Letter on Women and Children in Industry*. February.

Cushman, Robert E. 1936. "Must the Constitution Be Amended?" In *Clarifying the Constitution By Amendment: Addresses made at the Thirty-Seventh Annual Meeting of the National Consumers' League*. December 15.

de Lima, Agnes. N.d. *Night-Working Mothers in Textile Mills*. New Jersey Consumers' League.

Ely, Richard. 1898. *What is Our Social Ideal?* Women's Educational and Industrial Union.

Goldmark, Josephine. 1912. *Fatigue and Efficiency*. Russell Sage Foundation.

———. 1925. "Women Workers' Wages." Reprint. *The Woman Citizen*, December, 25, 38.

Goldmark, Pauline. Ca. 1910. *Do Children Work in the Canneries?* National Consumers' League.

Gompers, Samuel. 1915. *The Significance of the Labor Sections of the Clayton Act*. National Women's Trade Union League.

Hamilton, Alice. 1952. Letter to Florence L. C. Kitchell. May 13. Alice Hamilton Collection, Schlesinger Library, Radcliffe College.

———. 1924. "Protection for Working Women." Reprint. *The Woman Citizen*.

Herrick, Elinore. 1933. *Brief in Support of Minimum Wage Legislation*. Consumers' League of New York.

Holmes, Oliver Wendell. 1897. "The Path of the Law." *Harvard Law Review* 10: 457–78.

Industrial Commission. 1913–14. *First Biennial Report of the Industrial Commission*. Washington, D.C.: Industrial Commission.

"The International Charter of Labor." 1919. *Survey*, March 15, 857.

Kelley, Florence. 1923. *Progress of Labor Legislation for Women.* National Consumers' League. May.

———. 1924. "The Equal Rights Amendment: Why Other Women's Groups Oppose It." *Good Housekeeping,* March, 19, 162–65.

———. 1929. "Current Mergers in Business and Social Fields." Consumers' League Luncheon press release, National Consumers' League, November 1.

———. N.d. "Judge-Made Ignorance in Pennsylvania." Address. Florence Kelley Collection, Schlesinger Library, Radcliffe College.

Kelley, Florence. N.d. "The Right to Leisure." Address. Florence Kelley Collection, Schlesinger Library, Radcliffe College.

Lane, Victor, and Thomas Cooley. 1903. *A Treatise on the Constitutional Limitations Which Rest upon the Legislative Power of the States of the American Union.* 7th ed. Vol. 2. Boston: Little, Brown & Co.

Lowell, Joan. 1932. "Joan's Expose Stirs Up Probers: Sweatshops Visited by College Girls." *Daily Record* (Boston), January 30, 3, 10.

Lutz, Alma. 1930. *Shall Woman's Work Be Regulated by Law?* National Woman's Party.

Mabie, Janet. 1928. "Absolute Equality is Goal of Woman's Party—Rejects Even Favorable Discrimination in Laws." *Christian Science Monitor,* October 17, 2, 4.

Malkiel, Theresa Serber. N.d. *Woman and Freedom.* Socialist Literature Co.

Manufacturers' and Merchants' Association of Oregon. 1923. *U.S. Supreme Court Decision and Its Effect on Minimum Wage.* Child Labor Law, Manufacturers and Merchants Association of Oregon, May 19.

Manufacturers' Association of Connecticut and Connecticut Retail Merchants' Association. N.d. "Memorandum for Manufacturers' Association of Connecticut, Inc. and Connecticut Retail Merchants' Association Relative to the Several Bills Proposing a Reduction in the Legal Hours of Labor for Women in Manufacturing and Mechanical Establishments."

McGarry, Anne. 1931. *The Report on the Summer Practicum in Industrial Relations.* Summer Practicum in Industrial Relations.

Mussey, Henry Raymond. 1928. "Law and a Living for Women." Reprint. *Survey Graphic,* November.

National Committee on Clarifying the Constitution by Amendment. 1937. "Announcement of Upcoming Conference: National Conference on Constitutional Amendment." March 18–20.

National Congress of Mothers. 1915. *Report of Committee on the Maintenance of the Christian Standard of Marriage.*

National Consumers' League. 1922. *The Blanket Equality Bill Proposed by the National Woman's Party for State Legislatures: Why It Should Not Pass.*

———. 1932. *The Conference on the Breakdown of Industrial Standards.* New York: National Consumers' League, December 12.

———. 1935. "The Conference on Labor Law Administration." New York: National Consumers' League, December 9.

———. 1936. *Clarifying the Constitution By Amendment: Addresses Made at the Thirty-Seventh Annual Meeting of the NCL.* December 15.

National Garment Label Campaign Headquarters. Ca. 1933. *What the Garment Label Means to Women.*

National Woman's Party. 1926. Press release, November 30.

———. 1935. *The National Woman's Party—What Is it? Who Belongs to It? What Does It Do? What Should It Mean to You?* November.

———. 1936. *A Few Facts about the National Woman's Party.*

———. N.d. *Special Privileges for Women.*

National Women's Trade Union League. 1922. *Protective Legislation in Danger: Trade Union Women Oppose Blanket Amendment.* November.

———. 1923. *Why Labor Laws for Women? Because They Are Necessary.* January.

Newman, Pauline M. 1912a. "The Workers of the World." *Progressive Woman* 5, no. 59 (April): 7.

———. 1912b. "The Workers of the World." *Progressive Woman* 5, no. 60 (May): 7.

———. 1916. "Insuring Motherhood." *American Hebrew,* September 15, 590.

———. 1922. "Difficulties with Sister." *Labor Age* 11, no. 4 (April): 18–19.

———. 1933. "First Minimum Wage Law Goes Into Effect." *American Labor World,* November, 17.

———. N.d. *What Is the League for Equal Opportunities—and Who Is Behind It?* Report. National Women's Trade Union League.

News Service of National Consumers' League. 1921. "'Living-in' System in Hotels Condemned by National Consumers' League. Responsible for Low Wages, Long Hours, Extra Shifts and Seven Day Week." Press release, National Consumers' League, December 10.

Nock, Albert Jay. 1918. "What American Labor Does Not See." *Nation* 107 (August 24): 194–95.

Parton, Mabel. 1905. *Women's Work in Rubber Factories: Its Effect on Health.* Joint Committee on Sanitary and Industrial Conditions of the Massachusetts State Federation of Women's Clubs and the Women's Educational and Industrial Union.

Perkins, Frances, and Elizabeth Faulkner Baker. 1926. "Do Women In Industry Need Special Protection?" *Survey,* February 15, 529–31, 582–85.

"Protective Legislation vs. 'Equal Rights,' 1923. " *Nation* 117 (August 8): 128–29.

"Recognition for Labor." 1917. *New Republic,* November 24, 85–88.

Robins, Mrs. Raymond. Ca. 1920. *The Progress of Industry: Standards Raised through Legislation.* National Women's Trade Union League.

Sinclair, Upton. 1906. *The Jungle.* New York: Grosset and Dunlap.

Smith, Ethel. 1924. "Shall Child Labor Be Tolerated in the United States?" Statement, National Women's Trade Union League, October 13.

———. 1929. "Equal Opportunity for Women Wage Earners." *Current History,* February, 793–97.

Smith, Jane Norman. 1932. "Hours Legislation for Women Only." *Equal Rights* 17, no. 50 (January 16): 396–98.

———. 1937. Editorial. *Independent Woman.*

———. 1933. "Wage Laws Result in Unemployment." *Equal Rights* 19, no. 1 (February 4): 5–6.

Special Commission on the Hours of Labor. 1919. *The Hours of Labor Problem.*

Swarts, Maud. 1924. "Why We Should Have Labor Laws for Working Women." Statement, National Women's Trade Union League, January 4.

"Technicalities as Raw as a Washwoman's Hands." 1936. Editorial. *New York Post,* June 16, 8.

Union News Items. 1912. "What the Union Has Done For College Women." *Women's Educational and Industrial Union* 18 (June 13): 22–25.

———. 1913. "Tribute to Women Journalists." *Women's Educational and Industrial Union* 2, no. 3 (January): 9.

U.S. Department of Labor. 1938. *Report of the Secretary of Labor's Committee on the Extension of Labor Law Protection to All Workers.* Washington, D.C.: Department of Labor, October 31.

"Unphysiological Physiology." 1924. Editorial. *Equal Rights* 11, no. 9 (April 12): 68.

"A Woman's League Worth Joining." 1923. *Springfield Union,* April 9.

"Women Workers' Platform." 1919. *Survey,* March 15.

Women's Educational and Industrial Union. 1912. Union News Items: "Review of Fatigue and Efficiency." *Women's Educational and Industrial Union* 19 (July 3): 13.1.

———. 1913a. Union News Items: "Legislative Work of the Union." *Women's Educational and Industrial Union* 2, no. 5 (March): 4–5.

———. 1913b. Union News Items: "The Minimum Wage and Morals." *Women's Educational and Industrial Union* 2, no. 3 (January): 7.

Women's Trade Union League of Chicago. 1919. *Bulletin on the Eight Hour Day.* February 12.

Woodbury, Robert Morse. 1925. *Causal Factors in Infant Mortality.* Children's Bureau.

SECONDARY SOURCES

Ackerman, Bruce. 1991. *We the People: Foundations.* Cambridge: Belknap Press of Harvard University Press.

———. 1998. *We the People: Transformations.* Cambridge: Belknap Press of Harvard University Press.

Allen, Anita. 1998. *Uneasy Access: Privacy for Women in a Free Society.* Totowa, N.J.: Rowman and Littlefield.

Baer, Judith. 1978. *The Chains of Protection: The Judicial Response to Women's Labor Legislation.* Westport, Conn.: Greenwood Press.

Balkin, J. M. 1986. "Ideology and Counter-Ideology from *Lochner* to *Garcia.*" *UMKC Law Review* 54:175–214.

Barrett, James. 1990. "Women's Work, Family Economy, and Labor Militancy: The Case of Chicago's Packing-House Workers, 1900–1922." In *Labor*

Divided: Race and Ethnicity in United States Labor Struggles, 1835–1960, ed. Robert Asher and Charles Stephenson. New York: State University of New York Press.

Bewig, Matthew. 1994. "Lochner v. The Journeyman Bakers of New York: The Journeyman Bakers, Their Hours of Labor, and the Constitution." *American Journal of Legal History* 38:413–51.

Boris, Eileen. 1991. "Reconstructing the 'Family': Women, Progressive Reform, and the Problem of Social Control." In *Gender, Class, Race, and Reform in the Progressive Era*, ed. Noralee Frankel and Nancy Dye. Lexington: University of Kentucky Press.

———. 1992. "The Regulation of Homework and the Devolution of the Postwar Labor Standards Regime: Beyond Dichotomy." In *Labor Law in America*, ed. Christopher L. Tomlins and Andrew J. King. Baltimore: Johns Hopkins University Press.

Brigham, John. 1999. "The Constitution of the Supreme Court." In *The Supreme Court in American Politics: New Institutionalist Interpretations*, ed. Howard Gillman and Cornell Clayton. Lawrence: University Press of Kansas.

Brown, Wendy. 1983. "Reproductive Freedom and the Right to Privacy: A Paradox for Feminists." In *Families, Politics, and Public Policy: A Feminist Dialogue on Women and the State*, ed. Irene Diamond. New York: Longman Press.

Burgess, Susan. 1993. "Beyond Instrumental Politics: The New Institutionalism, Legal Rhetoric, and Judicial Supremacy." *Polity* 25:445–59.

Bussiere, Elizabeth. 1999. "The Supreme Court and the Development of the Welfare State: Judicial Liberalism and the Problem of Welfare Rights." In *Supreme Court Decision-Making: New Institutionalist Approaches*, ed. Cornell Clayton and Howard Gillman. Chicago: University of Chicago Press.

Clayton, Cornell. 1999. "The Supreme Court and Political Jurisprudence: New and Old Institutionalisms." In *Supreme Court Decision-Making: New Institutionalist Approaches*, ed. Cornell Clayton and Howard Gillman. Chicago: University of Chicago Press.

Cohen, Jean, and Andrew Arato. 1992. *Civil Society and Political Theory.* Cambridge: MIT Press.

Conkle, Daniel. 1987. "The Second Death of Substantive Due Process." *Indiana Law Journal* 62:215–42.

Cover, Robert. 1983. "Nomos and Narrative." *Harvard Law Review* 97:4–68.

———. 1986. "Violence and the Word." *Yale Law Journal* 95:1601–67.

———. 1992. *Narrative, Violence, and the Law: The Essays of Robert Cover.* Ed. Martha Minow, Michael Ryan, and Austin Sarat. Ann Arbor: University of Michigan Press.

Cumbler, John. 1990. "Immigration, Ethnicity, and the American Working-Class Community: Fall River, 1850–1900." In *Labor Divided: Race and Ethnicity in United States Labor Struggles, 1835–1960*, ed. Robert Asher and Charles Stephenson. New York: State University of New York Press.

Cushman, Barry. 1994. "Rethinking the New Deal Court." *Virginia Law Review* 80:201–61.

———. 1998. *Rethinking the New Deal Court: The Structure of a Constitutional Revolution.* New York: Oxford University Press.

Dailey, Ann. 1996. "*Lochner* for Women." *Texas Law Review* 74:1217–21.

Dworkin, Ronald. 1982. "Law as Interpretation." *Texas Law Review* 60:645–701.

———. 1986. *Law's Empire.* Cambridge: Belknap Press of Harvard University Press.

Ducat, Craig. 1996. *Constitutional Interpretation: Powers of Government.* 6th ed. St. Paul: West Publishing.

Dye, Nancy. 1991. Introduction to *Gender, Class, Race, and Reform in the Progressive Era,* ed. Noralee Frankel and Nancy Dye. Lexington: University of Kentucky Press.

Elshtain, Jean Bethke. 1981. *Public Man, Private Woman: Women in Social and Political Thought.* Princeton, N.J.: Princeton University Press.

Ely, James. 1999. "The Oxymoron Reconsidered: Myth and Reality in the Origins of Substantive Due Process." *Constitutional Commentary* 16:315–45.

Epp, Charles. 1998. *The Rights Revolution: Lawyers, Activists, and Supreme Courts in Comparative Perspective.* Chicago: University of Chicago Press.

———. 1999. "External Pressure and the Supreme Court's Agenda." In *Supreme Court Decision-Making: New Institutionalist Approaches,* ed. Cornell Clayton and Howard Gillman. Chicago: University of Chicago Press.

Erickson, Nancy. 1989. "*Muller v. Oregon* Reconsidered: The Origins of a Sex-Based Doctrine of Liberty of Contract." *Labor History* 30:228–50.

Ethington, Philip, and Eileen McDonagh. 1995. "The Common Space of Social Science Inquiry." *Polity* 28:84–90.

———. 1996. "The Eclectic Center of the New Institutionalism." *Social Science History* 19:467.

Fineman, Martha. 1983. "Implementing Equality: Ideology, Contradiction, and Social Change." *Wisconsin Law Review* 1983:789–886.

Fish, Stanley. 1980. *Is There a Text in This Class? The Authority of Interpretive Communities.* Cambridge: Harvard University Press.

———. 1982. "Working on the Chain Gang: Interpretation in Law and Literature." *Texas Law Review* 60:551–95.

———. 1995. *Professional Correctness: Literary Studies and Political Change.* Oxford: Clarendon Press.

Forbath, William E. 1991. *Law and the Shaping of the American Labor Movement.* Cambridge: Harvard University Press.

Foucault, Michel. 1970. *The Order of Things: An Archaeology of the Human Sciences.* New York: Random House.

———. 1992. *The Archaeology of Knowledge.* Trans. A. M. Sheridan Smith. New York: Pantheon Books.

Friedman, Barry. 1997. "The Turn to History." Book review of Laura Kalman, *The Strange Career of Legal Liberalism. New York University Law Review* 72:928–66.

Friedman, Barry. 1997. "Valuing Federalism." *Minnesota Law Review* 82:317–412.

———. 1998. "The History of the Countermajoritarian Difficulty, Part One: The Road to Judicial Supremacy." *New York University Law Review* 73:333–433.

———. 1998. "'Things Forgotten' in the Debate over Judicial Independence." *Georgia State University Law Review* 14:737–66.

Gillman, Howard. 1993. *The Constitution Besieged: The Rise and Demise of Lochner Era Police Powers Jurisprudence.* Durham, N.C.: Duke University Press.

———. 1999. "Reconnecting the Modern Supreme Court to the Historical Evolution of American Capitalism." In *The Supreme Court in American Politics: New Institutionalist Interpretations,* ed. Howard Gillman and Cornell Clayton. Lawrence: University Press of Kansas.

Gordon, Linda. 1995. "Putting Children First: Women, Maternalism, and Welfare in the Early Twentieth Century." In *U.S. History as Women's History: New Feminist Essays,* ed. Linda Kerber, Alice Kessler-Harris, and Kathryn Kish Sklar. Chapel Hill: University of North Carolina Press.

Green, Louisa Bertch. 1999. "The Liberal Tradition in American Politics: A Slow Boat to Democracy." In *The Liberal Tradition in American Politics: Reassessing the Legacy of American Liberalism,* ed. David Ericson and Louisa Bertch Green. New York: Routledge.

Harley, Sharon. 1991. "When Your Work Is Not Who You Are: The Development of a Working-Class Consciousness among Afro-American Women." In *Gender, Class, Race, and Reform in the Progressive Era,* ed. Noralee Frankel and Nancy Dye. Lexington: University of Kentucky Press.

Hart, Vivian. 1994. *Bound by Our Constitution: Women, Workers, and the Minimum Wage.* Princeton, N.J.: Princeton University Press.

Hegel, Georg. 1967. *Philosophy of Right.* Trans. T. M. Knox. London: Oxford University Press.

Helly, Dorothy O., and Susan M. Reverby, eds. 1992. *Gendered Domains: Rethinking Public and Private in Women's History.* Ithaca, N.Y.: Cornell University Press.

Horton, Carol. 1999. "Liberal Equality and the Civic Subject: Identity and Citizenship in Reconstruction America." In *The Liberal Tradition in American Politics: Reassessing the Legacy of American Liberalism,* ed. David Ericson and Louisa Bertch Green. New York: Routledge.

Horwitz, Morton. 1993. "The Constitution of Change: Legal Fundamentality without Fundamentalism." *Harvard Law Review* 107:30–117.

Janiewski, Dolores. 1992. "Learning to Live 'Just Like White Folks': Gender, Ethnicity, and the State in the Inland Northwest." In *Gendered Domains: Rethinking Public and Private in Women's History,* ed. Dorothy O. Helly and Susan M. Reverby. Ithaca, N.Y.: Cornell University Press.

Kahn, Ronald. 1999. "Institutional Norms and the Historical Development of Supreme Court Politics: Changing 'Social Facts' and Doctrinal Development." In *The Supreme Court in American Politics: New Institutionalist Interpretations,* ed. Howard Gillman and Cornell Clayton. Lawrence: University Press of Kansas.

———. 1999. "Institutional Norms and Supreme Court Decision-Making: The

Rehnquist Court on Privacy and Religion." In *Supreme Court Decision-Making: New Institutionalist Approaches*, ed. Cornell Clayton and Howard Gillman. Chicago: University of Chicago Press.

———. 1999. "Liberalism, Political Culture, and the Rights of Subordinated Groups: Constitutional Theory and Practice at a Crossroads." In *The Liberal Tradition in American Politics: Reassessing the Legacy of American Liberalism*, ed. David Ericson and Louisa Bertch Green. New York: Routledge.

Kens, Paul. 1990. *Judicial Power and Reform Politics: The Anatomy of Lochner v. New York*. Lawrence: University of Kansas Press.

———. 1995. "*Lochner v. New York*: Rehabilitated and Revised, but Still Reviled." *Journal of Supreme Court History*, 31–46.

———. 1997. *Justice Stephen Field: Shaping Liberty from the Gold Rush to the Gilded Age*. Lawrence: University Press of Kansas.

Kenyatta, Muhammed. 1987. "From *Lochner* to *Roe*: Community Consciousness as Constitutional Context." *Legal Studies Forum* 11:29–40.

Kerber, Linda. 1988. "Separate Spheres, Female Worlds, Woman's Place: The Rhetoric of Women's History." *Journal of American History* 75:9–39.

Kessler-Harris, Alice. 1982. *Out to Work: A History of Wage-Earning Women in the United States*. Oxford: Oxford University Press.

———. 1985. "Organizing the Unorganizable: Three Jewish Women and Their Union." In *The Labor History Reader*, ed. David Leab. Urbana: University of Illinois Press.

———. 1991. "Law and a Living: The Gendered Content of 'Free Labor.'" In *Gender, Class, Race, and Reform in the Progressive Era*, ed. Noralee Frankel and Nancy Dye. Lexington: University of Kentucky Press.

———. 1992. "The Just Price, the Free Market, and the Value of Women." In *Gendered Domains: Rethinking Public and Private in Women's History*, ed. Dorothy O. Helly and Susan M. Reverby. Ithaca, N.Y.: Cornell University Press.

———. 1995. "The Paradox of Motherhood: Night Work Restrictions in the United States." In *Protecting Women: Labor Legislation in Europe, the United States, and Australia, 1880–1920*, ed. Ulla Wikander, Alice Kessler-Harris, and Jane Lewis. Urbana: University of Illinois Press.

Kloppenberg, James. 1995. "Institutionalism, Rational Choice, and Historical Analysis." *Polity* 28:125–28.

Ladd-Taylor, Molly. 1991. "Hull House Goes to Washington: Women and the Children's Bureau." In *Gender, Class, Race, and Reform in the Progressive Era*, ed. Noralee Frankel and Nancy Dye. Lexington: University of Kentucky Press.

———. 1992. "Federal Help for Mothers: The Rise and Fall of the Sheppard-Towner Act in the 1920s." In *Gendered Domains: Rethinking Public and Private in Women's History*, ed. Dorothy O. Helly and Susan M. Reverby. Ithaca, N.Y.: Cornell University Press.

Laslett, John H. M. 1990. "Scottish-Americans and the Beginnings of the Modern Class Struggle: Immigrant Coal Miners in Northern Illinois, 1865–1889." In *Labor Divided: Race and Ethnicity in United States Labor Struggles,*

1835–1960, ed. Robert Asher and Charles Stephenson. New York: State University of New York Press.

Leuchtenberg, William. 1995. *The Supreme Court Reborn: The Constitutional Revolution in the Age of Roosevelt*. New York: Oxford University Press.

Lipschultz, Sybil. 1996. "Hours and Wages: The Gendering of Labor Standards in America." *Journal of Women's History* 8:114–36.

Lou, Raymond. 1990. "Chinese American Agricultural Workers and the Anti-Chinese Movement in Los Angeles, 1870–1890." In *Labor Divided: Race and Ethnicity in United States Labor Struggles, 1835–1960*, ed. Robert Asher and Charles Stephenson. New York: State University of New York Press.

MacKinnon, Catharine. 1990. "Sex Equality under Law." *Yale Law Journal* 100:1281–1328.

Maltzman, Forrest, James F. Spriggs, and Paul Wahlbeck. 1999. "Strategy and Judicial Choice: New Institutionalist Approaches to Supreme Court Decision-Making." In *Supreme Court Decision-Making: New Institutionalist Approaches*, ed. Cornell Clayton and Howard Gillman. Chicago: University of Chicago Press.

Marx, Karl. 1978. "On the Jewish Question." In *The Marx-Engels Reader*, ed. Robert C. Tucker. 2d ed. New York: Norton.

May, Martha. 1985. "Bread before Roses: American Workingmen, Labor Unions, and the Family Wage." In *Women, Work, and Protest*, ed. Ruth Milkman. Boston: Routledge and Kegan Paul.

McCann, Michael. 1999. "How the Supreme Court Matters in American Politics: New Institutionalist Perspectives." In *The Supreme Court in American Politics: New Institutionalist Interpretations*, ed. Howard Gillman and Cornell Clayton. Lawrence: University Press of Kansas.

McCloskey, Robert. 1962. "Economic Due Process and the Supreme Court: An Exhumation and Reburial." *Supreme Court Review* 1962: 34–62.

McCurdy, Charles W. 1975. "Justice Field and the Jurisprudence of Government-Business Relations: Some Parameters of Laissez-Faire Constitutionalism, 1863–1897." *Journal of American History* 61:970–1005.

———. 1984. "The Roots of 'Liberty of Contract' Reconsidered: Major Premises in the Law of Employment, 1867–1937." *Yearbook of the Supreme Court Historical Society* 1984: 20–33.

Mink, Gwendolyn. 1985. *The Wages of Motherhood: Inequality in the Welfare State, 1917–1942*. Ithaca, N.Y.: Cornell University Press.

Montgomery, David. 1985. "Workers' Control of Machine Production in the Nineteenth Century." In *The Labor History Reader*, ed. David Leab. Urbana: University of Illinois Press.

Montgomery, Scott L. 1994. *Minds for the Making: The Role of Science in American Education, 1750–1990*. New York: Guilford Press.

Moglen, Eben. 1994. "Toward a New Deal Legal History." *Virginia Law Review* 80:263–75.

Murphy, Walter, James Fleming, and William Harris. 1992. *American Constitutional Interpretation*. 2d ed. Chicago: Foundation Press.

Nackenoff, Carol. 1999. "Gendered Citizenship: Alternative Narratives of Political Incorporation in the United States, 1875–1925." In *The Liberal Tradition in American Politics: Reassessing the Legacy of American Liberalism*, ed. David Ericson and Louisa Bertch Green. New York: Routledge.

Novkov, Julie. 1997. "Historicizing the Figure of the Child in Legal Discourse: Nodes of Conflict and the Battle over the Regulation of Child Labor." Paper presented at the Annual Meeting of the Law and Society Association, St. Louis, June.

Okin, Susan Moller. 1979. *Women in Western Political Thought*. Princeton, N.J.: Princeton University Press.

Olsen, Frances. 1983. "The Family and the Market: A Study of Ideology and Legal Reform." *Harvard Law Review* 96:1497–1578.

Orren, Karen. 1991. *Belated Feudalism: Labor, the Law, and Liberal Development in the United States*. Cambridge: Cambridge University Press.

———. 1992. "Metaphysics and Reality in Labor Adjudication." In *Labor Law in America*, ed. Christopher L. Tomlins and Andrew J. King. Baltimore: Johns Hopkins University Press.

———. 1995. "Ideas and Institutions." *Polity* 28:97–101.

Ortner, Sherry, Geoff Eley, and Nicholas Dirks. 1989. "Culture/Power/History: Series Prospectus." CSST Working Paper no. 23/CRSO Working Paper no. 386, Ann Arbor, Mich., March.

Pateman, Carole. 1989. *The Disorder of Women: Democracy, Feminism, and Political Theory*. Stanford: Stanford University Press.

Phillips, Michael. 1987. "Another Look at Economic Substantive Due Process." *Wisconsin Law Review* 1987:285–324.

———. 1998. "The Progressiveness of the *Lochner* Court." *Denver University Law Review* 75:453–505.

Post, Robert. 1998. "Defending the Lifeworld: Substantive Due Process in the Taft Court Era." *Boston University Law Review* 78:1489–1545.

Purcell, Edward A. 1994. "Rethinking Constitutional Change." *Virginia Law Review* 80:277–90.

Rhode, Deborah. 1989. *Justice and Gender: Sex Discrimination and the Law*. Cambridge: Harvard University Press.

Rosenberg, Gerald. 1991. *The Hollow Hope: Can Courts Bring About Social Change?* Chicago: University of Chicago.

Ross, Dorothy. 1991. *The Origins of American Social Science*. Cambridge: Cambridge University Press.

———. 1995. "The Many Lives of Institutionalism in American Social Science." *Polity* 28:117–23.

Rowe, Gary D. 1999. "Book Review: *Lochner* Revisionism Revisited." *Law and Social Inquiry* 24:221–52.

Schattschneider, E. E. 1960. *The Semisovereign People: A Realist's View of Democracy in America*. New York: Holt, Rinehart and Winston.

Scheiber, Harry N. 1997. "Book Review: Private Rights and Public Power: American Law, Capitalism, and the Republican Polity in Nineteenth-Century America." *Yale Law Review* 107:823–61.

Schieberger, Londa. 1992. "Maria Winkelmann at the Berlin Academy: The Clash between Craft Traditions and Professional Science." In *Gendered Domains: Rethinking Public and Private in Women's History*, ed. Dorothy O. Helly and Susan M. Reverby. Ithaca, N.Y.: Cornell University Press.

Schneider, Dorothee. 1990. "The German Brewery Workers of New York City in the Late Nineteenth Century." *Labor Divided: Race and Ethnicity in United States Labor Struggles, 1835–1960*, ed. Robert Asher and Charles Stephenson. New York: State University of New York Press.

Semonche, John. 1978. *Charting the Future: The Supreme Court Responds to a Changing Society, 1890–1920.* Westport, Conn.: Greenwood Press.

Shapiro, Ann-Louise. 1992. "Disordered Bodies/Disorderly Acts: Medical Discourse and the Female Criminal in Nineteenth Century Paris." In *Gendered Domains: Rethinking Public and Private in Women's History*, ed. Dorothy O. Helly and Susan M. Reverby. Ithaca, N.Y.: Cornell University Press.

Sheppard, A. T. 1988. "Private Passion, Public Outrage: Thoughts on *Bowers v. Hardwick*." *Rutgers Law Review* 40:521–66.

Sicherman, Barbara. 1991. "Working It Out: Gender, Profession, and Reform in the Career of Alice Hamilton." In *Gender, Class, Race, and Reform in the Progressive Era*, ed. Noralee Frankel and Nancy Dye. Lexington: University of Kentucky Press.

Siegan, Bernard. 1985. "Rehabilitating Lochner." *San Diego Law Review* 22: 452–97.

Sklansky, Jeff. 2000. "Corporate Property and Social Psychology: Thomas M. Cooley, Charles H. Cooley, and the Ideological Origins of the Social Self." *Radical History Review* 76:90–114.

Skocpol, Theda. 1995. *Protecting Soldiers and Mothers: The Political Origins of Social Policy in the United States.* Cambridge: Belknap Press of Harvard University Press.

———. 1995. "Why I Am an Historical Institutionalist." *Polity* 28:103–6.

Skowronek, Stephen. 1982. *Building a New American State: The Expansion of National Administrative Capacities, 1877–1920.* New York: Cambridge University Press.

———. 1995. "Order and Change." *Polity* 28:91–96.

Smith, Rogers. 1997. "Still Blowing in the Wind: The American Quest for a Democratic, Scientific Political Science." *Daedalus* 126:253.

Stanley, Amy Dru. 1998. *From Bondage to Contract: Wage Labor, Marriage, and the Market in the Age of Slave Emancipation.* Cambridge: Cambridge University Press.

Stoddard, T. B. 1987. "*Bowers v. Hardwick:* Precedent by Personal Predilection." *University of Chicago Law Review* 54:648–56.

Suchman, Mark, and Lauren Edelman. 1996. "Legal Rational Myths: The New Institutionalism and the Law and Society Tradition." *Law and Social Inquiry* 21:903.

Sunstein, Cass. 1987. "Lochner's Legacy." *Columbia Law Review* 87:873–919.

Takaki, Ronald. 1990. "Ethnicity and Class in Hawaii: The Plantation Labor

Experience, 1835–1920." *Labor Divided: Race and Ethnicity in United States Labor Struggles, 1835–1960,* ed. Robert Asher and Charles Stephenson. New York: State University of New York Press.

Tomlins, Christopher L. 1992. "Law and Power in the Employment Relationship." In *Labor Law in America,* ed. Christopher L. Tomlins and Andrew J. King. Baltimore: Johns Hopkins University Press.

Turkel, Gerald. 1992. *Dividing Public and Private: Law, Politics, and Social Theory.* Westport, Conn.: Praeger.

Tyrrell, Ian. 1991. *Woman's World/Woman's Empire: The Woman's Christian Temperance Union in International Perspective, 1800–1930.* Chapel Hill: University of North Carolina Press.

Urofsky, Melvin. 1983. "Myth and Reality: The Supreme Court and Protective Legislation in the Progressive Era." In *Yearbook of the Supreme Court Historical Society 1983:* 53–72.

VanderVelde, Lea. 1992. "Hidden Dimensions in Labor Law History: Gender Variations on the Theme of Free Labor." In *Labor Law in America,* ed. Christopher L. Tomlins and Andrew J. King. Baltimore: Johns Hopkins University Press.

Weir, Margaret, Ann Shola Orloff, and Theda Skocpol. 1988. "Introduction: Understanding American Social Policies." In *The Politics of Social Policy in the United States.* Princeton, N.J.: Princeton University Press.

Wikander, Ulla, Alice Kessler-Harris, and Jane Lewis, eds. 1995. *Protecting Women: Labor Legislation in Europe, the United States, and Australia, 1880–1920.* Urbana: University of Illinois Press.

Wood, Stephen. 1968. *Constitutional Politics in the Progressive Era: Child Labor and the Law.* Chicago: University of Chicago Press.

Worthman, Paul B. 1985. "Black Workers and Labor Unions in Birmingham, Alabama, 1897–1904." In *The Labor History Reader,* ed. David Leab. Urbana: University of Illinois Press.

Zelizer, Viviana. 1985. *Pricing the Priceless Child: The Changing Social Value of Children.* New York: Basic Books.

Cases Cited

Cases are listed in chronological order, with federal cases first, followed by state cases, and finally those cases decided after *West Coast v. Parrish*.

FEDERAL CASES

SUPREME COURT

Butchers' Benevolent Association v. Crescent City Livestock Landing & Slaughter-house Co. [The Slaughter-House Cases], 83 U.S. 36 (1873).
Bradwell v. Illinois, 83 U.S. 130 (1873).
Minor v. Happersett, 88 U.S. 162 (1875).
Munn v. Illinois, 89 U.S. 113 (1876).
U.S. v. Martin, 94 U.S. 400 (1877).
Barbier v. Connolly, 113 U.S. 27 (1885).
Powell v. Pennsylvania, 127 U.S. 678 (1888).
In re Lockwood, 154 U.S. 116 (1894).
Hennington v. Georgia, 163 U.S. 299 (1896).
Allgeyer v. Louisiana, 165 U.S. 578 (1897).
Holden v. Hardy, 169 U.S. 366 (1898).
Petit v. Minnesota, 177 U.S. 164 (1899).
Texas & Pacific Ry. Co. v. Humble, 181 U.S. 57 (1901).
Cotting v. Kansas, 183 U.S. 79 (1901).
Connolly v. Union Sewer Pipe Co., 184 U.S. 540 (1902).
Atkin v. Kansas, 191 U.S. 207 (1904).
Cronin v. Adams, 192 U.S. 109 (1904).
Jacobson v. Massachusetts, 197 U.S. 11 (1905).
Lochner v. New York, 198 U.S. 45 (1905).
Ellis v. U.S., 206 U.S. 246 (1906).
Muller v. Oregon, 208 U.S. 416 (1908).
Adair v. U.S., 208 U.S. 161 (1908).
McLean v. Arkansas, 211 U.S. 539 (1909).
Chicago, B. & Quincy R.R. Co. v. McGuire, 219 U.S. 549 (1910).
Central Lumber Co. v. South Dakota, 226 U.S. 157 (1912).
Quong Wing v. Kirkendall, 223 U.S. 59 (1912).
Sturges & Burn v. Beauchamp, 231 U.S. 320 (1914).

Walker v. Chapman, 17 F. Supp. 308 (S.D. Ohio 1936).
Western Union Telegraph Co. v. Ind. Commission of Minn., 24 F. Supp. 370 (D. Minn. 1938).

STATE CASES

ALABAMA

Boone v. State, 170 Ala. 57 (1911).

ALASKA

U.S. & Northern Commercial Co., 6 Alaska 94 (1918).

ARKANSAS

State v. Crowe, 130 Ark. 272 (1917).
Terry Dairy Co. v. Nally, 146 Ark. 448 (1920).

ARIZONA

Dominion Hotel v. State, 161 P. 682 (Ariz. 1916).

CALIFORNIA

In re Maguire, 57 Cal. 604 (1881).
Schuler v. Savings & Loan Society, 64 Cal. 397 (1883).
Ex parte Kuback, 85 Cal. 274 (1890).
Ex parte Hayes, 98 Cal. 555 (1893).
Foster v. Police Commissioners, 102 Cal. 483 (1894).
Ex parte Jentzsch, 112 Cal. 468 (1896).
Ex parte Weber, 149 Cal. 392 (1906).
Ex parte Spencer, 149 Cal. 396 (1906).
People v. Conness, 150 Cal. 115 (1906).
In re Martin, 157 Cal. 51 (1909).
Ex parte Miller, 162 Cal. 687 (1912).

COLORADO

In re Morgan, 26 Colo. 415 (1899).
Adams v. Cronin, 29 Colo. 488 (1902).
Burcher v. People, 41 Colo. 495 (1907).

CONNECTICUT

O'Brien's Petition, 79 Conn. 46 (1906).

GEORGIA

Railroad Commission of Ga. v. Louisville & Nashville Ry. Co., 140 Ga. 817 (1913).
Chaires v. City of Atlanta, 164 Ga. 755 (1926).
City of Newnan v. Atlanta Laundries Inc., 174 Ga. 99 (1931).

ILLINOIS

Millett v. People, 117 Ill. 294 (1886).
Frorer v. People, 141 Ill. 171 (1892).
Ramsey v. People, 142 Ill. 380 (1892).
Braceville Coal Co. v. People, 147 Ill. 66 (1893).
Ritchie v. People, 155 Ill. 98 (1895).
Eden v. People, 43 N.E. 1108 (Ill. 1896)
Gillespie v. People, 188 Ill. 176 (1900).
Fiske v. People, 188 Ill. 206 (1900).
Booth v. People, 186 Ill. 43 (1900).
Bailey v. People, 190 Ill. 28 (1901).
Mathews v. People, 202 Ill. 389 (1903).
O'Brien v. People, 216 Ill. 354 (1905).
Ritchie & Co. v. Wayman, 244 Ill. 509 (1910).
People v. Elerding, 254 Ill. 579 (1912).
People v. Chicago, 256 Ill. 558 (1912).

INDIANA

Blair v. Kilpatrick, 40 Ind. 312 (1873).
Street v. Varney Elec. Supply Co., 160 Ind. 338 (1903).
Inland Steel Co. v. Yedinak, 172 Ind. 423 (1909).

IOWA

Hunter v. Colfax Consolidated Coal Co., 175 Iowa 245 (1916).

KANSAS

Haun v. State, 7 Kans. App. 130 (1898).
State v. Haun, 61 Kans. 146 (1899).
State v. Atkin, 64 Kans. 174 (1902).
Coffeyfield Vitrified Brick & Tile Co. v. Perry, 69 Kans. 297 (1904).
State v. Howat, 109 Kans. 376 (1921).
Wolff v. Court of Industrial Relations, 109 Kans. 629 (1921).
Wolff v. Court of Industrial Relations, 111 Kans. 501 (1922).
Topeka Laundry Co. v. Court of Industrial Relations, 119 Kans. 12 (1925).

KENTUCKY

City of Lexington v. Thompson, 113 Ky. 540 (1902).

LOUISIANA

State v. Rose, 125 La. 462 (1910).
State v. Barba, 132 La. 768 (1913).

MASSACHUSETTS

Commonwealth v. Hamilton Mfg. Co., 120 Mass. 383 (1876).
Commonwealth v. Perry, 155 Mass. 117 (1891).
Mutual Loan Co. v. Martell, 200 Mass. 482 (1909).
Commonwealth v. Riley, 97 N.E. 367 (Mass. 1912).
Commonwealth v. Boston & M.R.R., 110 N.E. 264 (Mass. 1915).
Holcombe v. Creamer, 231 Mass. 99 (1918).
Commonwealth v. Boston Transcript Co., 249 Mass. 477 (1924).

MICHIGAN

Attorney General v. Abbott, 121 Mich. 540 (1899).
Withey v. Bloem, 128 N.W. 913 (Mich. 1907).

MINNESOTA

State v. Petit, 74 Minn. 376 (1898).
Fitzgerald v. Int. Flax Twine Co., 104 Minn. 138 (1908).
Williams v. Evans, 139 Minn. 32 (1917).
G. O. Miller Telephone Co. v. Minimum Wage Comm., 145 Minn. 262 (1920).
Stevenson v. St. Clair, 161 Minn. 444 (1925).

MISSISSIPPI

State v. J. J. Newman Lumber Co., 102 Miss. 802 (1912).

MISSOURI

State v. Loomis, 115 Mo. 307 (1893).
State v. Julow, 129 Mo. 163 (1895).
State v. Cantwell, 179 Mo. 245 (1903).
State v. Milsicek, 225 Mo. 561 (1909).

MONTANA

Quong Wing v. Kirkendall, 39 Mont. 64 (1911).

NEBRASKA

Low v. Reis Printing Co., 41 Neb. 127 (1894).
Wenham v. State, 65 Neb. 394 (1902).

NEVADA

In re Boyce, 27 Nev. 299 (1904).

NEW JERSEY

City of Hoboken v. Goodman, 68 N.J. 217 (1902).
Bryant v. Skillman Hardware Co., 76 N.J. 45 (1908).

NEW YORK

Wynehamer v. People, 13 N.Y. 378 (1856).
In re Jacobs, 98 N.Y. 98 (1885).
People v. Marx, 99 N.Y. 377 (1885).
People v. Gillson, 109 N.Y. 389 (1888).
People v. Phyfe, 136 N.Y. 554 (1893).
People v. Rosenberg, 138 N.Y. 410 (1893).
People v. Ewer, 141 N.Y. 129 (1894).
Knisley v. Pratt, 148 N.Y. 372 (1896).
People v. Havnor, 149 N.Y. 195 (1896).
People v. Coler, 166 N.Y. 1 (1901).
People v. Orange County Road Constr. Co., 175 N.Y. 84 (1903).
People v. Lochner, 177 N.Y. 145 (1904).
Wright v. Hart, 182 N.Y. 330 (1905).
People v. Williams, 189 N.Y. 131 (1907).
People v. Taylor, 192 N.Y. 398 (1908).
People v. Metz, 193 N.Y. 148 (1908).
Ives v. Buffalo Ry. Co., 201 N.Y. 271 (1911).
People v. Kane, 139 N.Y.S. 350 (Kings Co. S. Ct. 1913).
People v. Warden, 215 N.Y. 701 (1915).
People v. Charles Schweinler Press, 214 N.Y. 395 (1915).
People v. Morehead, 282 N.Y.S. 576 (Kings Co. Sup. Ct. 1935).
People v. Morehead, 200 N.E. 799 (N.Y. 1936).

NORTH CAROLINA

Starnes v. Albion Mfg. Co., 147 N.C. 556 (1908).

NORTH DAKOTA

Minot Special School Dist. v. Olsness, 53 N. Dak. 683 (1926).

OHIO

Bergman v. Cleveland, 39 Ohio 651 (1884).
Palmer & Crawford v. Tingle, 55 Ohio 423 (1896).
State v. Gravett, 65 Ohio 289 (1901).
City of Cleveland v. Clements, 67 Ohio 197 (1902).
Ex parte Hawley, 85 Ohio 495 (1912).

OREGON

State v. Muller, 48 Ore. 252 (1906).
State v. Shorey, 48 Ore. 396 (1906).
Stettler v. O'Hara, 69 Ore. 519 (1914).
Simpson v. O'Hara, 70 Ore. 261 (1914).
State v. Bunting, 71 Ore. 259 (1914).

PENNSYLVANIA

Wheeler v. Philadelphia, 77 Penn. 338 (1875).
Godcharles & Co. v. Wigeman, 113 Penn. 431 (1886).
Baxter v. Maxwell, 115 Penn. 467 (1886).
Commonwealth v. Beatty, 15 Penn. Sup. Ct. 5 (Penn. Sup. Ct. 1900).
Commonwealth v. Fisher, 213 Penn. 48 (1905).

TENNESSEE

Breyer v. State, 102 Tenn. 103 (1899).

TEXAS

Poye v. Texas, 230 SW 161 (Tex. Crim. App. 1921).

UTAH

Holden v. Hardy, 14 Utah 71 (1894).

VERMONT

Atkins & Co. v. Town of Randolph, 31 Vt. 227 (1858).

WASHINGTON

Ah Lim v. Territory, 1 Wash. 156 (1890).
State v. Considine, 16 Wash. 358 (1897).
Seattle v. Smyth, 22 Wash. 327 (1900).
State v. Buchanan, 29 Wash. 602 (1902).
State v. Somerville, 67 Wash. 638 (1912).
Larsen v. Rice, 100 Wash. 642 (1918).
Spokane v. Younger, 113 Wash. 359 (1920).
Parrish v. West Coast Hotel, 55 P.2d 1083 (Wash. 1936).

WEST VIRGINIA

State v. Goodwill, 33 W. Va. 179 (1889).
State v. Peel Splint Coal Co., 36 W. Va. 802 (1892).

WISCONSIN

State v. Kreutzberg, 114 Wisc. 530 (1902).

WYOMING

State v. LeBarron, 162 P. 265 (Wyo. 1917).
State v. City of Sheridan, 25 Wyo. 347 (1917).

CASES DECIDED AFTER *WEST COAST HOTEL v. PARRISH*

FEDERAL CASES

National Labor Relations Board v. Jones & Laughlin Steel Corp., 301 U.S. 1 (1937).
Senn v. Tile Layers Union, 301 U.S. 468 (1937).
Carmichael v. Southern Coal Co., 301 U.S. 495 (1937).
Thornhill v. Alabama, 310 U.S. 88 (1940).
Olsen v. Nebraska, 313 U.S. 236 (1941).
U.S. v. Darby, 312 U.S. 100 (1941).
Ballard v. U.S., 329 U.S. 187 (1946).
Lincoln Federal Labor Union v. Northwestern Iron & Metal Co., 335 U.S. 525 (1949).
AFL v. American Sash & Door Co., 335 U.S. 538 (1949).
Day-Brite Lighting, Inc. v. Missouri, 342 U.S. 421 (1952).
Williamson v. Lee Optical Co., 348 U.S. 483 (1955).

STATE CASES

Ex parte Kazas, 70 P.2d 962 (Cal. 1937).
Akins' Case, 20 N.E.2d 453 (Mass. 1938).

State v. Safeway Stores, 76 P.2d 81 (Montana 1938).

Herrin v. Arnold, 82 P.2d 977 (Okla. 1938).

Oklahoma City v. Johnson, 82 P.2d (Okla. 1938).

Farris-Cantrell, Inc. v. State Industrial Commission, 82 P.2d 984 (Okla. 1938).

McGrew v. Industrial Commission, 85 P.2d 608 (Utah 1938).

McKay v. Retail Automobile Salesmen's Labor Union, 90 P.2d 113 (Cal. 1939).

Pearce v. Moffatt, 92 P.2d 146 (Idaho 1939).

In re Opinion of the Justices, 22 N.E.2d 49 (Mass. 1939).

Ex parte Herrin, 93 P.2d 21 (Okla. 1939).

Associated Industries v. Industrial Welfare Commission, 90 P.2d 899 (Okla. 1939).

Gasque, Inc. v. Nates, 2 S.E.2d 36 (S.C. 1939).

State v. Greeson, 124 S.W.2d 253 (Tenn. 1939).

Doncourt v. Danaher, 13 A.2d 868 (Conn. 1940).

General Motors Corp. v. Read, 293 N.W. 751 (Mich. 1940).

People v. Johnson, 109 P.2d 770 (Cal. 1941).

Smith Brothers Cleaners & Dyers v. People, 119 P.2d 623 (Colo. 1941).

Arkansas-Missouri Power Corp. v. City of Kennett, 156 S.W.2d 913 (Mo. 1941).

Arnold v. Board of Barber Examiners, 109 P.2d 779 (N.M. 1941).

Noble v. Davis, 161 S.W.2d 189 (Ark. 1942).

California Drive-In Restaurant Assn. v. Clark, 129 P.2d 169 (Cal. Superior Ct., LA County 1942).

McRae v. Robbins, 9 So.2d 284 (Fla. 1942).

Tepel v. Sima, 7 N.W.2d 532 (Minn. 1942).

Mary Lincoln Candies, Inc. v. Department of Labor, 45 N.E.2d 434 (N.Y. 1942).

California Drive-In Restaurant Association v. Clark, 140 P.2d 657 (Cal. 1943).

City of Cincinnati v. Correll, 49 N.E.2d 412 (Ohio 1943).

Jack Lincoln Shops v. State Dry Cleaning Board, 135 P.2d 334 (Okla. 1943).

Amodio v. Board of Commissioners, 43 A.2d 889 (N.J. 1945).

Strain v. Southerton, 62 N.E.2d 633 (Ohio Ct. of Appeals 1945).

Strain v. Southerton, 74 N.E.2d 69 (Ohio 1947).

American Federation of Labor v. American Sash & Door Co., 189 P.2d 914 (Ariz. 1948).

Anderson v. City of St. Paul, 32 N.W.2d 538 (Minn. 1948).

Lincoln Federal Labor Union v. Northwestern Iron & Metal Co., 31 N.W. 2d 477 (Neb. 1948).

Finney v. Hawkins, 54 S.E.2d 872 (Va. 1949).

Index